Peacebuilding Online

Rachel Nolte-Laird

Peacebuilding Online

Dialogue and Enabling Positive Peace

Rachel Nolte-Laird
National Centre for Peace & Conflict Studies
University of Otago
Dunedin, New Zealand

ISBN 978-981-16-6012-2   ISBN 978-981-16-6013-9 (eBook)
https://doi.org/10.1007/978-981-16-6013-9

© The Editor(s) (if applicable) and The Author(s), under exclusive license to Springer Nature Singapore Pte Ltd. 2022

This work is subject to copyright. All rights are solely and exclusively licensed by the Publisher, whether the whole or part of the material is concerned, specifically the rights of translation, reprinting, reuse of illustrations, recitation, broadcasting, reproduction on microfilms or in any other physical way, and transmission or information storage and retrieval, electronic adaptation, computer software, or by similar or dissimilar methodology now known or hereafter developed.

The use of general descriptive names, registered names, trademarks, service marks, etc. in this publication does not imply, even in the absence of a specific statement, that such names are exempt from the relevant protective laws and regulations and therefore free for general use.

The publisher, the authors and the editors are safe to assume that the advice and information in this book are believed to be true and accurate at the date of publication. Neither the publisher nor the authors or the editors give a warranty, expressed or implied, with respect to the material contained herein or for any errors or omissions that may have been made. The publisher remains neutral with regard to jurisdictional claims in published maps and institutional affiliations.

Cover illustration: @Orbon Alija/GettyImages

This Palgrave Macmillan imprint is published by the registered company Springer Nature Singapore Pte Ltd.
The registered company address is: 152 Beach Road, #21-01/04 Gateway East, Singapore 189721, Singapore

Preface

I first drafted the final pages of this book during the early days of the global COVID-19 pandemic, when many of us were experiencing "lockdown" situations, isolated and disjointed from normalcy. Since writing that first draft, there has arisen an international reckoning with racial injustices driven by the Black Lives Matter movement in the United States, a movement Ta-Nehisi Coates refers to as a "Great Fire" (Coates, 2020). In my own country of Canada, we are being (rightly) confronted with, and held to account for, our racist and genocidal policies and treatment of Indigenous peoples, such as the residential school system (Truth and Reconciliation Commission of Canada, 2015). I am aware of the potential resonance this work may have with the present experiences of many around the world. In this time where people are experiencing extreme isolation in the face of a common yet invisible "enemy," and when there are global demands for transformed perceptions of those historically viewed as *other*, it feels exceptionally timely to be discussing how we can utilize the connective properties of the internet to encounter each other in ways that create humanized relations.

The COVID-19 pandemic has surfaced issues of inequality and "uncovered social and political fractures within communities…disproportionately affecting marginalised groups" (Devakumar et al., 2020). I do not know what the world will look like when we eventually move past this global crisis; there will most likely be increases in inequality, with soaring unemployment rates, crippling medical debt, and business closures. The economic fallout is potentially catastrophic and will impact those already economically fragile, first and most profoundly. I would like to imagine that the response will be one of solidarity, full of emboldened acts of courageous love in order to address these issues; however, looking to the past shows us that, historically, "infectious diseases have been associated with othering" (Devakumar et al., 2020). With the knowledge that this global experience could entrench fear and deepen divides, it becomes imperative for those working towards positive peace to harness all the means available to us that will engender collective solidarity against systemic oppression—oppression, which intensifies the vulnerability of already marginalized groups.

We need to call upon all of our tools, online and offline, which bring opportunities for humanizing encounters, and use this moment as a catalyst for emergence from the previously "dense, enveloping reality or a tormenting blind alley" (Freire, 2000, p. 109)—to remind one another of our common humanity, while surfacing how systemic power imbalances will result in this experience uplifting some and oppressing countless more. If it is within our capacity, we must do what we can to weave together a more durable and more inclusive fabric of society. I believe that online connections—opportunities for dialogue and meaningful encounters—are an essential tool in this cause.

I hope that this book provides a thoughtful contribution to an unfolding understanding of what constitutes dialogue as theory and practice, how they can inter-relate and inform one another, and how we apply both theory and practice within online settings. And even more than all of that, I hope that this work can offer even the slightest glimpse into how we might use this present, historical moment in the pursuit of creating positive peace.

Dunedin, New Zealand   Rachel Nolte-Laird

References

Coates, T. (2020, August 24). Editor's letter. *Vanity Fair*. Retrieved from: https://www.vanityfair.com.
Devakumar, D., Shannon, G., Bhopal, S. S., & Abubakar, I. (2020). Racism and discrimination in COVID-19 responses. *The Lancet*, 395(10231), 1194. https://doi.org/10.1016/S0140-6736(20)30792-3.

Freire, P. (2000). *Pedagogy of the oppressed* (30th anniversary ed.) (M. B. Ramos, Trans). Continuum.

Truth and Reconciliation Commission of Canada. (2015). *Honouring the truth, reconciling for the future: Summary of the final report of the Truth and Reconciliation Commission of Canada.* Retrieved from: http://www.trc.ca/assets/pdf/Executive_Summary_English_Web.pdf.

Acknowledgements

I am grateful to many individuals for their support and encouragement in completing this book. First, to the 24 individuals who so graciously participated in my research, thank you for your insights and vulnerability, without which this book would not have been possible. To Dr. Katerina Standish (who first planted the idea of writing this book) and Dr. Heather Devere for your wisdom and insights. My colleagues at the National Centre for Peace and Conflict Studies, particularly Dr. Alejandra Del Pilar, for your faithful encouragement. The publication of this book was made possible by The University of Otago Postgraduate Publishing Bursary (Doctoral). Finally, to my family; Flannery, Dave, forthcoming W., Penny, and Larry. At the end of this particular journey, I am standing here in no small part because of your steadfast belief in me and willingness to up-end your own lives to make this dream possible.

Contents

1	**Introduction**	1
1.1	Background	2
1.2	Why Online?	4
1.3	Research Design	5
1.4	Reflexivity & Cogitatio	6
1.5	Book Structure	7
	References	9
2	**Positive Peace and Dialogue: A Theoretical Framework**	13
2.1	Positive Peace	13
2.2	Dialogue Theory	15
	Martin Buber	16
	Paulo Freire	18
2.3	Qualities of Dialogue	20
	Dialogic Moments and the Sphere of Between	20
	Presentness	21
	Awareness	22
	Authenticity	22
	Mutuality	22
2.4	Dialogue as Humanization	23
2.5	Dialogue as Transformation	24
	Conscientization	25
2.6	Critiques	27
	Positive Peace Theory	28

		Dialogue Theory	28
	2.7	Summary	31
	References		32
3	**Community-Based Dialogue and Online Peacebuilding Practice**		37
	3.1	*Dialogue in Peacebuilding Practice*	37
		Characteristics of Dialogue in Community Peacebuilding	40
		Outcomes of Dialogue in Community Peacebuilding	45
		Critiques & Limitations of Dialogue in Community Peacebuilding	46
	3.2	*Online Dialogue-Based Peacebuilding*	49
		Online Peacebuilding Models	50
		Critiques of Online Dialogue for Peacebuilding	54
	3.3	*Gaps*	58
	3.4	*Summary*	59
	References		59
4	**Bringing Into**		69
	4.1	*Introducing the Participants*	70
	4.2	*"Journey to Soliya"*	73
		"A Marriage Between Two Worlds"	73
		"Try Something New with Different People"	76
		"An Experience Issue"	77
		"Was Not Voluntary for Me"	80
		"Itsy Bitsy Teeny Weeny Little Constructive, Positive Thing"	80
	4.3	*"I Expected To…"*	81
		"The Muslims, the Americans, and Us"	81
		"Disagreement Is Natural"	82
	4.4	*"The Source of My Knowledge"*	85
		"Of Course, the Media"	85
		"Like a Taboo"	86
	4.5	*Cogitatio*	88
	4.6	*Summary*	89
	References		89

5 The Setting 91
5.1 *Connect Program and Characteristics of Dialogue in Community Peacebuilding* 93
    Encountering Other and Exploring Identity 93
    Safe Space 95
    Examination of 'Truth' 96
    Relational Movement 96
5.2 *Program Design: Influencing Factors* 97
    The Facilitator 97
    The Curriculum 100
5.3 *'The Water'* 102
    "We Thought the Group is Stuck" 102
    "An Expression of International Power Dynamics" 104
5.4 *Benefits* 110
    "There Are No Barriers of Borders, or Religion, or Anything." 111
    "You Can Make It a Very Inclusive Environment" 112
    "I Think That This Makes People Brave to Speak" 114
5.5 *Limitations* 115
    "Technology Tends to Fail Us" 115
    "We're in the Car!" 116
    "There Is a Kind of Spirit that You Miss" 117
5.6 *'The Setting' and Positive Peace* 119
5.7 *Cogitatio* 120
    'Insider' 120
    Power 122
5.8 *Summary* 123
References 124

6 The Encounter 127
6.1 *Individual in Encounter* 127
    Distinctiveness 128
    "Think About My Identity and My Values and Beliefs" 130
6.2 *The Sphere of Between* 133
    Presentness 134
    Awareness 136
    Authenticity 139
    Mutuality 141
6.3 *Cogitatio* 146
6.4 *Summary* 148
References 148

7	**Potentialities**	151
	7.1 "New and Beautiful Friends"	152
	"Not Friends in Reality."	156
	7.2 "To See Something Different"	157
	"I Never Thought of Myself as…"	157
	"These People Are Not Monsters."	160
	7.3 How's the Water?	165
	"The Circumstances and the Situation and the Differences."	166
	"I Won't Hold My Tongue."	169
	7.4 "I Don't Change Easily"	173
	7.5 Cogitatio	174
	7.6 Summary	175
	References	176
8	**The Conditions of Positive Peace**	177
	8.1 Positive Peace: The Conditions	179
	Condition: Friendship	179
	Findings: Friendships & Changed Perceptions	183
	Condition: Love	186
	Findings: Emergence & Intervention	189
	8.2 Critiques of the Findings	191
	Dialogue Without Emergence	191
	Emergence Without Intervention	192
	Friendships Without Emergence or Intervention	193
	Ideal Setting	194
	Variations in Potentialities	195
	8.3 Can Online Dialogue Enable Positive Peace?	195
	8.4 Summary	197
	References	198
9	**Conclusion**	203
	9.1 Contributions to Knowledge	205
	9.2 Recommendations & Future Directions	207
	Practice & Policy	207
	Future Research Directions	208
	References	209
Index		211

List of Figures

Fig. 1.1	Represents the narrative of the findings	8
Fig. 2.1	Visual representation of the "triangular syndrome of peace" (Galtung, 1990, p. 302)	15
Fig. 4.1	Location of Chapter 4 in overarching narrative & the content of each findings chapter	70
Fig. 5.1	Location of Chapter 5 in overarching findings narrative	92
Fig. 6.1	Location of Chapter 6 in overarching findings narrative	128
Fig. 7.1	Location of Chapter 7 in overarching findings narrative	152
Fig. 8.1	Representation of humanization in relation to friendship	181
Fig. 8.2	Actions related to the dimensions of positive peace, described by Hansen (2016)	187
Fig. 8.3	Relationship between conscientization and love as action with transformation	189

List of Tables

Table 4.1	Summary of research participants	72
Table 8.1	Tiers of positive peace, adapted from Galtung (2012, p. 58; 2015, p. 1)	178

CHAPTER 1

Introduction

This book explores the intersection of online dialogue and peacebuilding practices. This inquiry began forming in my mind in 2014 while working with a dialogue-based peacebuilding organization in the Middle East. Over that summer, the 2014 Gaza war occurred, and the organization had to abruptly cancel a summit they had been planning between youth participants from the West Bank and Israel. This group had been meeting regularly over several years, and each summit was significant for the program and the youth. This type of disruption, of course, is a regular occurrence for anyone working in peacebuilding in a situation of ongoing conflict or violence. I began to explore the opportunities, platforms, and models for meeting online. As I delved in, it was quickly apparent how minimal the resources or knowledge were in both practice and literature. Organizational priorities shifted, as they often do, and I moved off to other projects after a short time, but the question stayed with me. Years later, I returned to the subject through the qualitative inquiry presented within this book.

In a radio interview, just months before his passing, the Irish poet, author, and theologian John O'Donohue (2008) spoke of the obstacles to authentic human connection as he reflected:

> I mean when you think about language and you think about consciousness, it's just incredible to think that we can make any sounds that can reach over [and] across to each other at all. ...I think the beauty of being human

is that we are incredibly, intimately near each other, we know about each other, but yet we do not know or never can know what it's like inside another person. (para. 15)

His comments resonate when considering the experience of dialogic encounters with *other*. There are the inherent barriers to reaching "over [and] across to each other" (para. 15), often involving language, geographic distance, historical injustices, modern inequalities, and myriad other obstacles. And yet, in entering into dialogue, there becomes the opportunity to be "incredibly, intimately near" to the *other*. While we "never can know what it's like inside another person," dialogue enables individuals to reveal themselves to each other, and in doing so, encounter *other* in ways that facilitate humanization and transformation. This book explores the experience of dialogic encounters within online environments and the connection between those experiences and positive peace—presented here as *humanization* and *transformation*.

1.1 Background

Peace practices, particularly indigenous peace practices, have occurred in myriad forms throughout history. For example, in Aotearoa New Zealand, the Moriori people of Rēkohu recommitted each generation to a peace covenant, abandoning "warfare and killing" (Devere et al., 2017, p. 55). Close (2017) describes the Indigenous East Timorese peacebuilding practices of *tarabandu, nahe biti, juramentu, matak-malarin*, and *halerik* as "complex…systems [which] are continuous, non-linear and multidimensional…connect[ing] multiple generations, lineages and clans, land, customary houses, the future, and the ancestors" (p. 134). These are just two examples of unique Indigenous peace practices and cultures. While peace practices have a diverse and long tradition, the articulation of the present-day peacebuilding concept can be attributed to Galtung in 1976 (Paffenholz, 2013; Ryan, 2013). Although this modern concept of peacebuilding originated with Galtung in the 1970s, it did not become part of mainstream political discourse until the publication of *An Agenda for Peace* in 1992 by the UN Secretary-General (Boutros-Ghali, 1992). *An Agenda for Peace* set out an ethos for liberal peacebuilding, primarily focused on structural over individual and community changes.

Towards the end of the Cold War, there was a turn towards including social-psychological approaches within peacebuilding practices. In tandem with this move towards social-psychological methods was a transition to viewing peacebuilding as requiring both work at the top, elite levels, regarding policy and structural changes, as well as grassroots transformation to alter "social attitudes and perceptions at the societal levels" (Steinberg, 2013, p. 43). Paffenholz (2013) identifies the sustainable peacebuilding model as the impetus for this multi-level approach to peacebuilding:

> The discourse on sustainable peacebuilding dates back to the emergence of the conflict-resolution school…it was further developed and conceptualized by John Paul Lederach's conflict-transformation school (Lederach, 1997). Both schools aim at addressing the underlying causes of conflict and rebuilding the destroyed relationships between parties and society, thereby supporting sustainable reconciliation. (p. 349)

Nested within this focus on underlying causes of conflict, and the focus on grassroots, are people-to-people (P2P) initiatives. P2P initiatives focus on creating integrative bonds amongst individuals in situations of conflict. These programs may include cooperative activities "focused on the social or economic realm and/or centered on scientific or technical issues" (Gawerc, 2006, p. 446), while other programs generate opportunities to share culture and art. These people-to-people programs are primarily predicated on Gordon Allport's Contact Hypothesis. The Contact Hypothesis was developed in the field of psychology in 1954 and posited that, under specific conditions, contact between out-groups could reduce prejudice between members of distinct identity groups (Allport, 1954). From this foundation of the Contact Hypothesis evolved peacebuilding practices that assumed:

> the existence of a common foundation based on shared human values. Contact theory, dialogue, cross-cultural communications and interaction, as well as forgiveness, reconciliation, and even quasi-legal arguments (or at least legal discourse) are among the main dimensions used in this approach, from which mutual understanding and compromise are expected to flow. (Steinberg, 2013, pp. 36–37)

As signalled by Steinberg, dialogue models are one of the people-to-people initiatives developed from the intersection of grassroots peacebuilding and the Contact Hypothesis. While dialogue as a peacebuilding practice does not have a universal, agreed-upon model, this book explores dialogue as a sustained and intentional encounter amongst individuals at a community or grassroots level—these practices are presented in further detail in Chapter 3.

As peacebuilding has grown to incorporate a focus on dialogue as a grassroots initiative, it has also become increasingly committed to integrating technology into relevant practices (Kahl & Puig Larrauri, 2013). Despite this imperative to explore the application of technology within peacebuilding practice, little is found in the existing literature regarding dialogue models in online environments. While technology encompasses a wide swath of subject matter and fields of inquiry, this book is interested in the connective properties of the internet that allow for individuals to interact and connect with those who are *other* to them—specifically through online dialogue. As peacebuilding initiatives are frequently situated in conflict scenarios or in situations where face-to-face meetings are challenging, costly, and potentially dangerous, the internet offers an alternative platform for community dialogue practices to be held to mitigate these barriers.

1.2 Why Online?

Attention is often given to the use of the internet for divisive means, such as the proliferation of online bullying (Lumsden & Harmer, 2019; Sylwander, 2019), political and ideological polarization through social media (Bryson, 2020), and the use of online platforms to promote terrorism and violent extremism (Littler & Lee, 2020; Weimann, 2016). However, the same technology used for divisive means and to create echo chambers that amplify existing ideas of *other*, self-identity, and narratives can also contribute towards more pro-social ends of building new relationships, reshaping notions of *other*, and creating a path forward towards positive peace.

While dialogue in peacebuilding is well-established as a field of study and practice, it is also evident that face-to-face encounters can be fraught and challenging. As such, online dialogue is poised to become a valuable addition within peacebuilding practice. Additionally, there is broad consensus that technology and the connective tissue of the internet have not been thoroughly examined for the benefits and contributions it can offer to the field of peacebuilding (Amichai-Hamburger et al., 2015; White et al., 2015). This book addresses this evident gap by exploring how online environments can be utilized for dialogic peacebuilding practice. The existing literature indicates positive outcomes from online encounters between out-groups (White et al., 2018), and there is some research examining unstructured dialogue practices (Chaitin, 2012; Mor et al., 2016). In this book, I marry these two bodies of knowledge and examine if structured dialogic encounters online can produce outcomes at an individual level that enable the conditions for positive peace.

Lederach (2005) argues that peacebuilding is about the "quality of relational spaces, intersections, and interactions that affect a social process" (p. 100). Suppose the quality of space, intersection, and interactions for dialogue-based peacebuilding can be successfully implemented within an online environment. In that case, there is immense potential for both scope and scale to create the conditions for positive peace. The increasing accessibility of the internet and immersive technologies allow people to encounter each other in ways previously unimaginable. With the diversification of tools that connect and transform people and their relationships comes the increased opportunity for positive peace to be realized by broadening access to participation of individuals at the grassroots level. By providing more opportunity for transformative encounters, there can be movement beyond the suspension of violence in conflict and into a reality where people can become morally inclusive of those who were previously *other* (Opotow, 2012). The wellbeing and flourishing of broader society can become something, not in the abstract, but within the capacity of everyday people to envision and actively work towards.

1.3 Research Design

The research discussed within this book explores sustained dialogue—the intentional encounters between individuals that occur over a period of time—in online environments. Specifically, I examine the individual experience within a dialogic encounter, including reflections on how notions of identity and perceptions of *other* shift through the encounter and if those experiences relate to changes for the individual that support the possibility for positive peace. The central research question explored within the pages of this book is, "can engaging *other* through dialogic encounters within an online environment enable conditions for positive peace?".

I conducted this research utilizing online ethnography, a method that, similar to offline ethnographies, relies on observation—the researcher undertakes sustained engagement in the shared online space to capture in writing a deep and nuanced description of the online environment and interactions (Kozinets, 2010). Online ethnography allows immersion in the participant experience and the ability to capture the nuance of each online setting and encounter (Markham, 1998).

For this research, I partnered with Soliya, an organization specializing in facilitated virtual dialogues through their 'Connect' programs. Soliya seeks to combine technology, peacebuilding, and global education to "empower young people to establish more effective, cooperative, and compassionate relations within and between their societies" ("About Us," 2018). Soliya provided the opportunity to explore dialogue within a well-established program conducted by experienced practitioners and with consistent participation numbers in a defined setting over a sustained period. During the period in which I completed data collection, there were two streams of Connect programs, the flagship Connect Global, which ran for eight-weeks, and the Connect Express program, which was over a four-week period. I took on the facilitator role in the Spring 2019 Connect program to support observations during data collection. Acting as a facilitator allowed for deep immersion into the program, including familiarity with the setting, the platform, and program design, affording additional insights and perspectives that may otherwise have been unavailable as a pure observer.

In addition to facilitator-observations, this research also incorporated semi-structured interviews with participants. Twenty-four individuals were involved in this research project, 13 facilitators and 11 participants, from geographic locations across the Middle East, North Africa, Europe, and North America.

1.4   Reflexivity & Cogitatio

Within the qualitative tradition, there is the recognition that the researcher brings their own experiences and perspectives into their interpretation of the data. Ethnography moves beyond recognition of these influences and asks the researcher to be reflexive in their work to bring further depth and value to the project (Hammersly & Atkinson, 2007)— "in reflexive ethnography, the ethnographer becomes part of the inquiry" (Behar et al., 2011).

The reflexive researcher thoughtfully records their journey through the research process, including reflections, emotions, and realizations, and integrates those into the findings. They bring this reflexivity to illuminate their journey and process and demonstrate the factors that influenced the interpretation of the data, such as biases, identity, and ideology. In this way, the researcher is dialogically engaging with the research journey themselves—allowing insight of their own experience to inform the ongoing nature of the research and bringing complexity to the final analysis (Creswell & Poth, 2018).

Reflexivity is intimately connected to positionality, "which refers to the way we as researchers view our position in the world in relation to others, especially those who are involved in or may read our research" (Call-Cummings & Ross, 2019, p. 4). As the researcher, I incorporate my positionality, musings, and dialogic journey with the research process through passages in Chapters 4 through 7. These sections are indicated through the heading 'Cogitatio,' from the Latin term defined as "thinking, meditation, reflection" ("Cogitatio," n.d). These interludes weave my own reflections and narratives into the text. They offer transparency into my individual identity, who I am as a researcher, and how I show up in this work. The cogitatio passages draw from my journals, memos, and conversations throughout the research and analysis journey and knit in thoughts that surfaced during the writing process.

1.5 Book Structure

Following this introductory chapter, Chapter 2 constructs a theoretical framework that informs and 'holds' the research inquiry and discussion presented in this book. The chapter offers an understanding of positive peace as holistic and self-reinforcing across structural, direct, and cultural dimensions. The chapter intertwines the dialogue theories of Martin Buber and Paulo Freire, specifically exploring their work related to dialogic moments, the sphere of between, presentness, awareness, authenticity, and mutuality. Further examination is given to Freire's understanding of conscientization, specifically exploring power and its relationship to dialogue. The chapter constructs a theoretical framing for navigating the link between positive peace and dialogue as *humanization* and *transformation*.

Chapter 3 investigates the existing literature on two essential areas: dialogue in community-based peacebuilding and peacebuilding practices in online settings. This examination of the literature reveals gaps in knowledge related to implementing dialogue-based peacebuilding practices in online environments while addressing the critiques and limitations of those practices. The chapter first establishes an understanding of track-three, community-based dialogue, presenting five characteristics identified within the literature that typically embody an intentional and sustained dialogue model. Known outcomes, along with critiques of community-based dialogue practices, are also presented. The chapter then reviews peacebuilding practices in online environments, including online dialogue initiatives, peace-education models, the Contact Hypothesis online, and games-based models. This examination of existing literature surfaces the opportunity to bring new insight to future practices as peacebuilding moves increasingly into online spaces.

Chapters 4 through 7 contain the findings which emerged out of this online ethnographic inquiry. These chapters are organized according to the overarching narrative, which emerged from the findings. This narrative encompasses 'bringing into,' 'the encounter,' and 'what shifted,' as illustrated in Fig. 1.1.

Chapter 4 explores the element of 'bringing into'—including an introduction to the research participants, their motivations for joining, expectations of the experience, and pre-existing narratives and perceptions of each other. Chapter 5 describes the program setting, establishing a visualization of the environment and context in which the online dialogue unfolds. Chapter 6 moves into an exploration of the dialogue encounter itself, while Chapter 7, the final findings chapter, explores 'what shifted' for individuals out of their dialogic encounters.

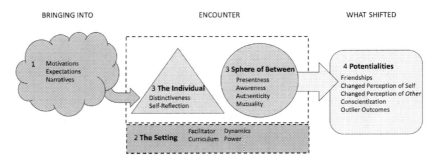

Fig. 1.1 Represents the narrative of the findings

Chapter 8 then presents a discussion of the overarching research question explored in this book: can engaging *other* through dialogic encounters within an online environment enable conditions for positive peace? Finally, Chapter 9 offers a summation of the entire book, along with the contributions to knowledge made by this research, including:

1. Unique and meaningful insight into the micro-level of dialogue encounters in an online context, specifically, identifying the sphere of between including the dialogue characteristics of presentness, awareness, authenticity, and mutuality.
2. The relationship between positive peace and online dialogue practice for peacebuilding. In particular, the identification of the conditions for positive peace presented as a humanized I-Thou relation and love as action as embodied by conscientization.

Chapter 9 closes with recommendations regarding future research and practice in this field.

This book provides valuable knowledge regarding the use of dialogue-based peacebuilding practice in online settings and the application of dialogue theory in online contexts. The research presented in these pages demonstrates that online dialogue can allow authentic and meaningful encounters to occur and that dialogue within online settings can enable the conditions for positive peace.

References

About Us. (2018). Retrieved from the Soliya website: https://www.soliya.net.

Allport, G. (1954). *The nature of prejudice*. Addison-Wesley.

Amichai-Hamburger, Y., Hasler, B. S., & Shani-Sherman, T. (2015). Structured and unstructured intergroup contact in the digital age. *Computers in Human Behavior, 52*, 515–522. https://doi.org/10.1016/j.chb.2015.02.022

Behar, R., Ellis, C., Bochner, A., Kincheloe, J. L., McLaren, P., Richardson, L., & Visweswaran, K. (2011). Reflexive ethnography. In N. K. Denzin & Y. S. Lincoln (Eds.), *The qualitative inquiry reader*. Sage.

Boutros-Ghali, B. (1992). *An agenda for peace: Preventive diplomacy, peace-making and peace-keeping*. United Nations.

Bryson, B. P. (2020). Polarizing the middle: Internet exposure and public opinion. *International Journal of Sociology and Social Policy, 40*(1/2), 99–113. https://doi.org/10.1108/IJSSP-09-2019-0181

Call-Cummings, M., & Ross, K. (2019). Re-positioning power and re-imagining reflexivity: Examining positionality and building validity through reconstructive horizon analysis. In K. K. Strunk & L. A. Locke (Eds.), *Research methods for social justice and equity in education* (pp. 3–13). Springer International Publishing. https://doi.org/10.1007/978-3-030-05900-2_1

Chaitin, J. (2012). Co-creating peace: Confronting psychosocial-economic injustices in the Israeli-Palestinian context. In B. Charbonneau & G. Parent (Eds.), *Peacebuilding, memory and reconciliation: Bridging top-down and bottom-up approaches* (pp. 146–162). Routledge.

Close, S. (2017). Indigenous East-Timorese practices of building and sustaining peace. In H. Devere, K. Te Maihāroa, & J. P. Synott (Eds.), *Peacebuilding and the rights of indigenous peoples: Experiences and strategies for the 21st century* (pp. 131–142). Springer International Publishing. doi: https://doi.org/10.1007/978-3-319-45011-7_11

Cogitatio. (n.d.). In *Latin dictionary*. Retrieved from the Latin Dictionary website: https://latin-dictionary.net/definition/10797/cogitatio-cogitationis

Creswell, J. W., & Poth, C. N. (2018). *Qualitative inquiry & research design: Choosing among five approaches* (4th ed.). Sage.

Devere, H., Te Maihāroa, K., Solomon, M., & Wharehoka, M. (2017). Regeneration of indigenous peace traditions in Aotearoa New Zealand. In H. Devere, K. Te Maihāroa, & J. P. Synott (Eds.), *Peacebuilding and the rights of indigenous peoples: Experiences and strategies for the 21st century* (pp. 53–63). Springer International Publishing. doi: https://doi.org/10.1007/978-3-319-45011-7_5

Gawerc, M. (2006). Peace-building: Theoretical and concrete perspectives. *Peace & Change, 31*(4), 435–478. https://doi.org/10.1111/j.1468-0130.2006.00387.x

Hammersley, M., & Atkinson, P. (2007). *Ethnography: Principles in practice* (1st ed.). Routledge.

Kahl, A., & Puig Larrauri, H. (2013). Technology for peacebuilding. *Stability: International Journal of Security and Development, 2*(3), 61, 1–15. doi: https://doi.org/10.5334/sta.cv

Kozinets, R. V. (2010). *Netnography: Doing ethnographic research online*. Sage.

Lederach, J. P. (1997). *Building peace: Sustainable reconciliation in divided societies*. United States Institute of Peace Press.

Lederach, J. P. (2005). *The moral imagination: The art and soul of building peace*. Oxford University Press.

Littler, M., & Lee, B. (2020). *Digital extremisms: Readings in violence, radicalisation and extremism in the online space* (1st ed.). Palgrave Macmillan.

Lumsden, K., & Harmer, E. (2019). *Online othering: Exploring digital violence and discrimination on the web* (1st ed.). Palgrave Macmillan.

Markham, A. N. (1998). *Life online: Researching real experience in virtual space*. Altamira Press.

Mor, Y., Ron, Y., & Maoz, I. (2016). "Likes" for peace: Can facebook promote dialogue in the Israeli-Palestinian conflict? *Media and Communication*, 4(1), 15–26. https://doi.org/10.17645/mac.v4i1.298

O'Donohue, J. (2008, February 28). The inner landscape of beauty [audio podcast]. In *On being with Krista Tippett*. Retrieved from https://onbeing.org/programs/john-odonohue-the-inner-landscape-of-beauty-aug2017/

Opotow, S. (2012). The scope of justice, intergroup conflict, and peace. In L. R. Tropp (Ed.), *The Oxford handbook of intergroup conflict* (pp. 72–86). Oxford University Press. doi: https://doi.org/10.1093/oxfordhb/9780199747672.013.0005

Paffenholz, T. (2013). Civil society. In R. Mac Ginty (Ed.), *Routledge handbook of peacebuilding* (pp. 347–359). Routledge.

Ryan, S. (2013). The evolution of peacebuilding. In R. Mac Ginty (Ed.), *Routledge handbook of peacebuilding* (pp. 25–35). Routledge.

Steinberg, G. M. (2013). The limits of peacebuilding theory. In R. Mac Ginty (Ed.), *Routledge handbook of peacebuilding* (pp. 36–53). Routledge.

Sylwander, K. R. (2019). Affective atmospheres of sexualized hate among youth online: A contribution to bullying and cyberbullying research on social atmosphere. *International Journal of Bullying Prevention*, 1(4), 269–284. https://doi.org/10.1007/s42380-019-00044-4

Weimann, G. (2016). Why do terrorists migrate to social media? In A. Aly, S. Macdonald, L. Jarvis, & T. Chen (Eds.), *Violent extremism online new perspectives on terrorism and the internet* (1st ed., pp. 45–64). Routledge. doi: https://doi.org/10.4324/9781315692029

White, F. A., Harvey, L. J., & Abu-Rayya, H. M. (2015). Improving intergroup relations in the internet age: A critical review. *Review of General Psychology*, 19(2), 129–139. https://doi.org/10.1037/gpr0000036

White, F. A., Turner, R. N., Verrelli, S., Harvey, L. J., & Hanna, J. R. (2018). Improving intergroup relations between Catholics and Protestants in Northern Ireland via E-contact. *European Journal of Social Psychology*. https://doi.org/10.1002/ejsp.2515

CHAPTER 2

Positive Peace and Dialogue: A Theoretical Framework

The locus of interest for me when exploring dialogue centers on the experiences of individuals within intentional and sustained online dialogic encounters, and how those encounters can enable the conditions for positive peace. To assist our exploration of these discrete experiences within this book, I present here a theoretical framework which facilitates insight into what occurs between and within individuals in dialogue. This scaffolding provides the framing, the container if you will, for everything else that unfolds within this book. There are two main theoretical points of interest; the first is a holistic, tripartite theory of positive peace. The second is dialogue theory, specifically the work of Martin Buber and Paulo Freire. Woven together, these two dialogue theorists generate a comprehension of dialogue as *humanization* and *transformation*, which become critical for the discussions presented later.

2.1 Positive Peace

The notion of positive peace was put forward by Galtung (1969) as a way of conceptualizing peace that moves beyond the cessation of direct violence, which he termed negative peace. Positive peace occurs when issues of structural and cultural violence are addressed and transformed (Galtung, 1969, 1996). As such, positive peace is relevant to any context or setting where issues of inequity or injustice are present. Galtung

© The Author(s), under exclusive license to Springer Nature Singapore Pte Ltd. 2022
R. Nolte-Laird, *Peacebuilding Online*,
https://doi.org/10.1007/978-981-16-6013-9_2

usefully breaks down the constructs of positive peace into three dimensions: direct, cultural, and structural (Galtung, 1990, 1996). These three dimensions indicate the holistic assembly of positive peace that must transcend any silos by being only relevant to one aspect of society. Galtung contrasts this tripartite construction of positive peace with his writing on the dimensions of violence by providing an understanding that the counterbalance to cultural peace is cultural violence, to direct peace is direct violence, and to structural peace is structural violence (Galtung, 1990).

Direct positive peace addresses the interpersonal; it is predicated on respectful and inclusive relationships that value diversity and seek the wellbeing of one another despite differences: "love is the epitome of this: a union of bodies, minds and spirits" (Galtung, 1996, p. 32). The contrast to direct positive peace is direct, interpersonal violence, where an individual, or individuals, commit an act of violence against another.

Cultural positive peace relates to the cultural constructs and institutions in a society such as "religion, law, and ideology; in language; in art and science; in schools, universities, and the media" (Galtung, 1996, p. 32). Cultural peace considers how notions or discourse around peace and violence permeate thought and conversation, how these ideas are reflected in art and the academy. As cultural peace contributes to the humanization and valuing of people, so cultural violence contributes to the dehumanization of *other* in such a way that violence, both structural and direct, become acceptable under certain conditions (Galtung, 1990).

Finally, structural positive peace is a reshaping of institutions to ensure universal dignity and liberties; it would "substitute freedom for repression and equity for exploitation, and then reinforce this with dialogue instead of penetration, integration instead of segmentation, solidarity instead of fragmentation, and participation instead of marginalization" (Galtung, 1996, p. 32). Structural violence, similar to cultural violence, is often invisible—it is the insidious, institutionalized means by which those who have been made to be marginalized are oppressed.

As seen in Fig. 2.1, Galtung (1990) provides a triangle as the visual construct of the three dimensions of positive peace, "in which cultural peace engenders structural peace, with symbiotic, equitable relations among diverse partners, and direct peace with acts of cooperation, friendliness and love. It could be a virtuous rather than vicious triangle, also self-reinforcing" (p. 302). In this way, peacebuilding must work towards establishing peace in all three areas to enable an authentic and holistic positive peace (Standish, 2014).

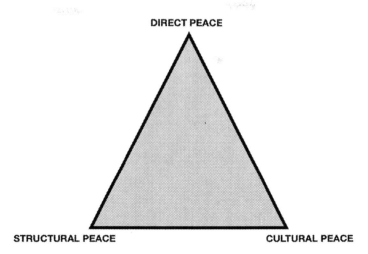

Fig. 2.1 Visual representation of the "triangular syndrome of peace" (Galtung, 1990, p. 302)

Predicated on this conceptualization of interconnectedness, this book envisions a relationship between the individual(s) in dialogue encounters and a holistic construction of positive peace across all three dimensions.

For positive peace to occur, there must be psychosocial restoration and reconciliation among individuals who are perceived as *other* (Gawerc, 2006). The work of theorists, such as Martin Buber and Paulo Freire, help construct a theoretical framework for understanding how dialogue enables this relational transformation to occur as *humanization* and the link to *transformation*.

2.2 Dialogue Theory

Within the realm of dialogue theory, there is an abundance of areas in which one might delve to form a conceptualization of what is meant by 'dialogue.' These areas include but are not limited to dialogue as the expression of humanization and relationship (my primary interest), dialogue as interpretation and understating of conversation and culture, dialogue for public discourse and ways of knowing, and textual or literary dialogue (Cissna & Anderson, 1994). As this research requires a theoretical lens through which to interpret the dialogic journey of individuals in encounter connected to transformation, I have elected not to use dialogue theorists who explore dialogue as meaning-making such as Mikhail Bakhtin, dialogue situated in public or group contexts such as David Bohm and Jürgen Habermas, or dialogue related to hermeneutics such as Hans-Georg Gadamer. Instead, I draw on two foundational dialogue theorists: Martin Buber and Paulo Freire who both lend to an understanding of dialogue as *humanization* and *transformation*.

Martin Buber

Widely held as one of the foremost dialogue theorists, Martin Buber was an early twentieth-century philosopher; born in 1878 in Austria he lived most of his life in Germany and Israel (Westoby, 2014). Buber was an influential Jewish leader in Germany, during Adolf Hitler's rise and time in power, and in Israel as a Zionist thinker (Friedman, 2004). Buber's seminal work was *Ich und Du* (*I and Thou*) published originally in 1923; many of his future works further explored the ideas developed in *I and Thou*.

Buber situates an understanding of human existence through two ontological movements: the I-It and the I-Thou. Later in his writings, these two movements extend to the notion of *setting at a distance* and *relating* (Czubaroff, 2000; Friedman, 2004). Buber (1970) identifies these two movements as basic words that, through expression, bring into existence relations with nature, humankind, and the spiritual realm. It is through these movements that the clarity of oneself comes into existence:

> Basic words do not state something that might exist outside them; by being spoken they establish a mode of existence
> Basic words are spoken with one's being
> When one says You, the I of the word pair I-You is said, too
> When one says It, the I of the word pair I-It is said, too
> The basic word I-You can only be spoken with one's whole being
> The basic word I-It can never be spoken with one's whole being. (Buber, 1970, pp. 53–54)

Buber offers an understanding that, for each person to be wholly *human*, they must engage with the full humanity of others (I-Thou). In the absence of that type of relation, when we hold people as *other* and set them at a distance, we are limiting the fullness of our own humanity.

I-It

The I-It relation understands the world through experience, through measured observations, and through utilization (Buber, 1970; Friedman, 2004). Aspects of nature and the inanimate world are It. Those who are outside the boundaries of one's understanding of themselves, the I, are also It—essentially an object. As one studies and examines *other*, but does not relate, the *other* as It further becomes merely a facet of the world around I. The I-It relation by necessity is monological, as one cannot be in dialogue with something that is not Thou (Johannesen, 2000). The I-It relation serves one's own ambitions, goals, and aims (Kim & Kim, 2008). When one cultivates an I-It relation, that relation becomes "characterized in varying degrees by self-centeredness, deception, pretense, display, artifice, using, profit, unapproachableness, seduction, domination, exploitation, and manipulation" (Johannesen, 2000, p. 153). The further one delves into the I-It relation, the more difficult it becomes to transition to I-Thou, as Buber (1970) explains: "the improvement of the ability to experience and use generally involves a decrease in man's power to relate" (p. 92). The I-It relation is essential; the natural and created world in which we live requires I-It. However, for Buber, the fullness of life is found in the I-Thou. Buber expresses this equilibrium as such: "in all the seriousness of truth, listen: without It a human being cannot live. But whoever lives only with that is not human" (Buber, 1970, p. 85).

I-Thou

In contrast to the I-It, it is the I-Thou relation that sees and encounters the fullness of the other person; one does not generalize or categorize them as *other* if they have met them as Thou. Thou are fully embodied, whole beings; it is through the I-Thou that the "world of relation" occurs (Buber, 1970, p. 56). Dialogue is the expression of I-Thou relation, it is in the present, and without ambition or intended outcome, "no purpose intervenes between I and You, no greed and no anticipation" (Buber, 1970, p. 63). It is in this pure relation that we become human, and in turn, humanize *other*.

Paulo Freire

Paulo Freire was a Brazilian educator and theorist whose ideas, as with Buber, developed out of his lived experiences (Macedo, 2000). Freire was born to middle-class parents who fell into poverty during his childhood. Freire's experiences with deep hunger and scarcity during that time engendered lifelong solidarity with the poor and marginalized of society. In adulthood, he spent time in exile from Brazil, during which he published his seminal book *Pedagogy of the Oppressed* (Freire, 2000).

The Oppressor and the oppressed

For Freire (2000), "dialogue is the encounter between men, mediated by the world, to name the world" (p. 88). Freire's positioning of dialogue—the naming of the world—is situated in the tension between the oppressor and the oppressed. He recognized throughout his work that structures of oppression cross-over simplistic classifications of identity groups or inequalities. He saw that "the object of oppression is cut across by such factors as race, class, gender, culture, language, and ethnicity. Thus, he would reject any theoretical analysis that would collapse the multiplicity of factors into a monolithic entity, including class" (Macedo, 2000, p. 15). Freire's conception of the overlapping structures of oppression is further understood when a theory of intersectionality is applied. Intersectionality provides an avenue of identifying and articulating how aspects of one's social identity are linked to systemic oppression. As Tapper (2013) explains, "each of us has several social identities—identities based in relation to ethnicity, gender, sexual orientation, socioeconomic class, and so on. In addition, each of us has an individual identity…shaped in relation to our manifold social identities" (p. 422). These social identities relate to how each person experiences systems of power and oppression. When a person holds multiple social identities that are subject to systemic oppression, that person's experience of power differs from that of other individuals who may embody fewer of those same intersecting identities. Crenshaw (1995) provides an example:

> women of color are situated within at least two subordinated groups that frequently pursue conflicting political agendas. The need to split one's political energies between two sometimes-opposing groups is a dimension of intersectional disempowerment which men of color and white women seldom confront. (p. 360)

A theoretical analysis utilizing Freire proposes that society is embedded with systems that benefit the oppressor and subjugate the oppressed while acknowledging that who occupies the role of oppressor and oppressed can shift and change in varying contexts (Riddle, 2017). Each one of us participates, either with intention or without, in the systems and structures of power we inhabit (Tapper, 2013).

For the oppressor, there is a temptation to engage with *other* through what Freire (2000) identifies as a "false generosity" (p. 44). Interactions, which on the surface, appear to support the empowerment and edification of those who are oppressed but yet in imposing the will or opinions of the oppressor are inauthentic and complicit in that oppression.

Martin Luther King Jr. spoke to this connection between inauthenticity and positive peace in his famous 1963 Letter from Birmingham Jail:

> I must confess that over the last few years I have been gravely disappointed with the white moderate. I have almost reached the regrettable conclusion that the Negro's great stumbling block in the stride toward freedom is not the White Citizens Counciller or the Ku Klux Klanner but the white moderate who is more devoted to 'order' than to justice; who prefers a negative peace which is the absence of tension to a positive peace which is the presence of justice; who constantly says, 'I agree with you in the goal you seek, but I can't agree with your methods of direct action'; who paternalistically feels that he can set the timetable for another man's freedom; who lives by the myth of time; and who constantly advises the Negro to wait until a 'more convenient season.' Shallow understanding from people of good will is more frustrating than absolute misunderstanding from people of ill will. Lukewarm acceptance is much more bewildering than outright rejection. (King, 1993, p. 842)

In his letter, King addresses the heart of Freire's (2000) theory of oppression, that those who present themselves as allies but offer a "false generosity" (p. 44) towards the oppressed are more of a threat than the obvious oppressor, as they obscure the path towards authentic systemic transformation by maintaining the status quo. For authentic dialogue to occur between individuals, there must be a sincere "*communion* (italics in original)" (Freire, 2000, p. 61), and abandoning of the heritages that privilege the oppressor. The significance of the dialogic act and its transformational power originate from the empowerment of the oppressed in finding and speaking their voice.

2.3 Qualities of Dialogue

Several dialogue qualities are essential to the theoretical framing presented in this chapter, including dialogic moments, the sphere of between, and the four defining attributes of Buber's theory of dialogue.

Dialogic Moments and the Sphere of Between

While this book examines dialogue in the specific context of intentional, structured, and sustained dialogue program, it can also occur—and some argue that it most often transpires—in ordinary moments and spaces of life if we are open and present (Kim & Kim, 2008). Buber identifies this idea as 'dialogic moments' (Buber, 1967, p. 692) when there is a mutuality of the encounter of the fullness of the *other* (Cissna & Anderson, 1998). Dialogic moments are often fleeting, a flash of authentic I-Thou relation. As such, even within structured dialogue programs, dialogic moments are usually brief and interspersed throughout the experience. However, everyday routines of life can act as barriers to dialogic encounters with *other*, as people typically seek out those who reinforce pre-existing perceptions and notions of the world. Intentional dialogue programs offer the physical context to allow for encounters with *other* that may not otherwise occur. By engaging the concept of dialogic moments, an understanding emerges that dialogue is not limited to specific strategies or tactics, but rather is internal mindfulness and positioning that allows for the openness of encounter (Johannesen, 2000). This openness in encounter distinguishes dialogue as both practice and theory from other forms of intentional interactions across differences, such as debate. Bryn (2015) discusses debate in contrast to dialogue, explaining that debate "strengthens defense and positioning while dialogue creates movement" (p. 373). This illustration from Bryn signals the importance of dialogue as a movement towards openness and self-reflection, whereas in a debate there is an inherent defensiveness and lack of openness to changing positions or modifying perspectives.

Buber understands dialogue as occurring not within the individual or in the broader context in which those encountering each other are situated, but instead as a third space which he terms "the sphere of between" (Buber, 1947, p. 241). Buber (1947) articulates his understanding of this sphere as the following:

The view which establishes the concept of "between" is to be acquired by no longer localizing the relation between human beings, as is customary, either within individual souls or in a general world which embraces and determines them, but in actual fact between them. "Between" is not an auxiliary construction, but the real place and bearer of what happens between men; it has received no specific attention because, in distinction from the individual soul and its context, it does not exhibit a smooth continuity. (p. 241)

There are several key attributes of the dialogic encounter found in Buber's work, which aid in identifying and characterizing these dialogic moments. Scholars have articulated the qualities of Buber's notion of dialogue in many ways. I have found it most useful to summarize with the following four attributes: presentness, awareness, authenticity, and mutuality.

Presentness

Presentness captures the impression that full attention must be given to the dialogic moment and experience—one gives their focus and attention to the *other*, listens, and reflects within the totality of the moment. In being present, one opens and shares without self-seeking motive, to communicate with transparency to the *other* in a spirit of reciprocity.[1] Presentness recognizes that dialogue is not happenstance; it requires intentionality to create the space for it to occur. However, even with intentionality, there is no guarantee of dialogue transpiring (Anderson et al., 2004). McNamee and Shotter (2004) frames it this way:

> entering into dialogue so as to invite the unexpected requires preparation. It requires us to give up on our desire to explain the present by pointing to the past. It requires us to replace our abstract positions with our lived stories—the richly textured, relational scenarios we engage in with others. It requires us to listen for, to provide the space for, and to invite difference—for ourselves and for our dialogic partners. (p. 104)

---

[1] The essence of presentness is reflected in work by scholars presenting characteristics of Buber's conception of dialogue through further terminologies such as 'openheartedness,' 'communion,' and 'intensity' (Atkinson, 2013; Friedman, 2004; Johannesen, 2000; White, 2008)

Awareness

The characteristic of awareness enables one to be open to the *other* and to the possibility of what might emerge in the space of dialogue (Cissna & Anderson, 1998). This conception can be understood as a holding of self while encountering *other*. Dialogue exists in the tension between one's understanding and that of the *other*; to be in dialogue, one must acquaint themselves with the discomfort of hearing the voice of *other* without seeking to dominate or impose their view (Wood, 2004). Ideas or perspectives that are in opposition to their own do not threaten participants in dialogue; they can hold open without agenda (Ganesh & Zoller, 2012). In an I-Thou relation, there is no imposition of self, but an ability to hold one's understandings and experiences while endeavouring to know the expressions and articulations of the *other*. The concept of awareness has also been articulated as 'inclusion,' as Johannesen (2000) expresses:

> we attempt to 'see the other,' to 'experience the other side,' to 'imagine the real,' the reality of the other's viewpoint for that person. Without giving up our own convictions or views, without yielding our own ground or sense of self. (p. 153)

Authenticity

Authenticity is essential to the enabling of dialogue; there must be sincerity in what is being communicated without obscuring oneself or presenting a facade.[2] Authenticity supposes a truthful representation—where participants are not required to share everything but indicates that what is being shared is honest and no one is holding back.

Mutuality

The quality of mutuality is widely identified as a central feature of Buber's understanding of dialogue (Kim & Kim, 2008).[3] Mutuality enables one

---

[2] Authenticity is also described as a 'lack of pretense,' 'frankness,' 'honesty,' 'directness,' 'a lack of manipulation,' 'unreservedness,' and an 'uninhibited expression' (Atkinson, 2013; Cissna & Anderson, 1998; Czubaroff, 2000; Friedman, 2004; Johannesen, 2000; White 2008).

[3] Scholars have echoed this concept of mutuality with terms such as 'confirmation' and 'reciprocity' (Johannesen, 2000; Kim & Kim, 2008).

to see the *other* as their whole self, appreciating their distinctive personhood and attending with respect to all they bring into the encounter, even if they hold opposing positions (Cissna & Anderson, 1998). Hammond et al. (2003) defines it as such:

> Mutuality emphasizes an awareness of the uniqueness of others. It encourages authenticity but requires neither the renunciation of roles nor the disclosure of all personal thoughts. It presumes a respect for others that includes confirmation and the willingness not to impose one's beliefs or standards, but does not presume power parity. (p. 141)

In mutuality, the situating of one's voice in their own historical, social, and cultural narratives meets the *other's* situated voice, and within those differences, creates a harmony in the conversation as it unfolds (Baxter, 2004). There is an extreme openness within mutuality, a shared extending of oneself towards the *other* that allows trust. It is in the mutuality of dialogue that the I-Thou becomes authentic (Friedman, 2004).

2.4 Dialogue as Humanization

For both Buber and Freire, dialogue is the full expression of the human experience (Atkinson, 2013; Johannesen, 2000). Dialogue requires the entirety of who we are—and it is through the engagement of our whole being that our humanity emerges.

As dialogue is the embrace of the fullness of the *other*, the I-It is transformed into the I-Thou, thus humanizing what was once It. When one engages *other* as It, the *other* is seen as an object and is not encountered in their full personhood, thereby barring a mutuality in the dialogic meeting (Friedman, 2004). Within the space between I and Thou our own selves are more fully realized and formed (Johannesen, 2000), as Buber (1947) explored; "being, lived in dialogue, receives even in extreme dereliction a harsh and strengthening sense of reciprocity; being, lived in monologue, will not, even in the tenderest intimacy, grope out over the outlines of the self" (p. 24). It is through relation with *other* that the outlines of one's self come into focus—without I-Thou, the fullness of human expression cannot be realized. Friedman (2004) expresses the humanization of dialogue as such: "Man can only enter relation with the whole being; yet it is through the relation, through the speaking of Thou, that concentration and fusion into the whole being takes place. 'As I become I, I say Thou'" (p. 67).

While Buber identifies the I-Thou encounter as *humanization*, for Freire (2000), "to exist, humanly, is to *name* the world, to change it. ... Human beings are not built in silence, but in word, in work, in action-reflection" (p. 88). It is the speaking together, the co-naming of the world, which becomes the humanizing act. For Freire, it is only in dialogue of mutuality that we fully encounter our own humanity and the humanity of *other*. Inherent within Freire's (2000) understanding of *humanization* is that the encounter between people must be predicated on the empowerment and authentic voice of the oppressed:

> dialogue cannot occur between those who want to name the world and those who do not wish this naming—between those who deny others the right to speak their word and those whose right to speak has been denied them. (p. 88)

This act of creation is itself the transformational nature of dialogue, and it is the collective naming of the world that makes us most human (Cissna & Anderson, 1998).

2.5 Dialogue as Transformation

Once we understand the above facets of dialogue, as expressed by Buber and Freire, we can appreciate how dialogue becomes transformational. It can be personally transformational as the opening up to another in a way that humanizes and produces an internal alteration. As Westoby (2014) says, "if someone genuinely turns towards the *other*, opens themselves to the flow of conversation and difference, then there will be a disruption to their perspective and experience of the world" (p. 79). The act of "turning towards" (Buber, 1947, p. 22) enables this transformative encounter; it is movement towards openness and possibility (Czubaroff, 2000). Buber also understands dialogue as influencing structural transformations: "a just and free society is dependent on the ability to say Thou. Where Thou is said, just institutions will exist" (Gordon, 2004, p. 112).

Freire adds to this understanding, theorizing that for dialogue to be authentic, it must catalyze into social and structural transformation. Freire (2000) articulates this through an understanding of praxis: "authentic liberation… is a praxis: the action and reflection of men and women upon their world in order to transform it" (p. 79). As people encounter *other*, they begin to see and identify their own context; through this identification, the creative act of renaming takes shape. In this renaming, the oppressor and the oppressed act in fellowship towards transforming the contexts they have identified (Westoby, 2014).

As dialogue creates the space for co-creation of new understandings, it should also be viewed as inherently creative. From that creativity comes the emergence of previously unseen paths towards a more equitable and inclusive whole—towards positive peace (Hammond et al., 2003). Even if participants in a dialogic encounter seem to hold opposing views, it is the holding open to *other* that enables a subtle building of exchange that allows for new conceptions to surface (Wood, 2004). This creativity is fuel for the transformative nature of dialogue.

A way of interpreting the creative action in Freire's praxis is articulated by Lederach (2005) as the "moral imagination." This innovative spark moves transformation from the interpersonal and into systemic change. The moral imagination is predicated on relationships; for Lederach (2005), "the center of building sustainable justice and peace is the quality and nature of people's relationships. A key to constructive social change lies in that which makes social fabric, relationships, and relational spaces" (p. 76). It is once we understand the web of interconnected relationships in which we live, and how those interconnections are both influenced by us and influence us, that we can move into creatively reimagining our broader societal structure.

Conscientization

As dialogue occurs, so must critical thinking and reflection to situate the encounter within the social and historical context. In doing so, those engaged in dialogue can identify the systemic structures of oppression that require action towards transformation (Freire, 2000). Freire defines this concept within dialogue as conscientization (2000). Conscientization occurs as one reflects and names the invisible constructs of oppression and, through the illumination that comes from recognition and naming, moves to address those factors (Bebbington et al., 2007; Freire, 2000; Lederach, 2005). Freire (2000) articulates the journey this way:

> Reflection upon situationality is reflection about the very condition of existence: critical thinking by means of which people discover each other

to be "in a situation." Only as the situation ceases to present itself as a dense, enveloping reality or a tormenting blind alley, and they can come to perceive it as an objective-problematic situation—only then can commitment exist. Humankind *emerge* from their *submersion* and acquire the ability to *intervene* in reality as it is unveiled. *Intervention* in reality—historical awareness itself—thus represents a step forward from *emergence*, and results from the *conscientização* of the situation. *Conscientização* is the deepening of the attitude of awareness characteristic of all emergence. (p. 109) (italics in original)

In this passage, Freire evokes the language of *emergence* and *intervention* as the articulation and action against oppression. Conscientization embodies both these elements, and there is a dynamic of fluidity as they reinforce and unfold back on one another.

The American author David Foster Wallace provides a useful analogy for the concept of *emergence* in a commencement address he made at Kenyon College:

There are these two young fish swimming along, and they happen to meet an older fish swimming the other way, who nods at them and says, "Morning, boys. How's the water?" And the two young fish swim on for a bit, and then eventually one of them looks over at the other and goes, "What the hell is water?" (Wallace, 2006)

In essence, *emergence* occurs as one has an encounter that causes them to identify and name the previously unseen setting in which they live. As they name their context, the water, they are then able to move more effectively into identifying the factors that pollute or contaminate that water—systemic injustice.

Power dynamics and structural violence

With this understanding of conscientization, dialogue must be specifically attuned to, and inclusive of, understandings of power and oppression (Ganesh & Zoller, 2012). Recognition of power dynamics acknowledges that "power is a description of a relation, not a 'thing' which people 'have.'... [and that in] everyday encounters, individuals are both reproducing and challenging, or changing, systematic relations" (Nelson & Wright, 1995, p. 8). In pursuing opportunities for dialogic transformation, recognition must be given to how systemic inequalities and positions of privilege create dominance in social interactions (Tapper, 2013).

We have all been socialized in our understandings and interactions with the world in ways that inform how we present and relate to the contexts we find ourselves in and people who surround us (Cho et al., 2013; Tapper, 2013). While those who are systemically privileged or, put another way,—those who have not been taught to silence their own voice—may have great intentionality in being dialogically open to *other*, they will face challenges when attempting to reflectively engage dialogically without moving toward monologue (Hammond et al., 2003). Further, those at the margins will likely not be invited into dialogic encounters, nor would they inherently see a place for themselves in those encounters (Burkitt, 1999). This exclusion creates a significant barrier to dialogic spaces and moments to emerge (Deetz & Simpson, 2004; Hammond et al., 2003).

Human interactions are imbued with the invisible social discourses of each societal and cultural setting. When engaging dialogically with people who are *other*, there will be inherent issues of power and privilege; artificial conceptions of equality ignore these issues and therefore are ineffective at surfacing the concerns critical for transformational dialogic encounters (Nolte-Laird, 2021; Simpson, 2008). As Deetz and Simpson (2004) point out, "calls for 'coming together' and 'finding common ground' de facto reproduce the status quo because the ground that is common between participants is that of the dominant culture" (p. 145). If a dialogic pursuit is based on notions of 'finding common ground,' it is likely to be driven by conceptions of civility that tend to privilege the oppressor.

As I have highlighted here, considerations of power and inequality must be considered in framing a theory of dialogue, especially in connection to positive peace. When the power imbalances contained in the social, historical, and cultural contexts in which dialogic encounters occur are made visible, there can then be the possibility for a transformation of those conditions of dominance. When we are attuned to those considerations in dialogue, the concealed tools for oppression are brought to light, and imaginative solutions are co-created (Bebbington et al., 2007).

2.6 Critiques

In employing the theories presented in this chapter, I also want to allow space for exploring some of the valid critiques leveled against them. There are several relevant critiques which I will address in this section, including binary classifications within positive peace theory as well as both Buber and Freire's work, issues with gender in the work of Freire, and Freire's theory as idealistic.

Positive Peace Theory

Employing the terminology of 'negative' and 'positive' peace can create an unfortunate perception of two conditions in opposition to one another. This dualistic notion is misleading, as the concepts of negative and positive peace are on a continuum and are intertwined. From this perspective, Galtung's choice of terms have been criticized for creating the illusion of a hidden value judgment as it can convey that 'negative' equates deficient while 'positive' is the only valuable option or pursuit (Hansen, 2016). Additionally, it is important to note that the concept of positive peace holds normative aspirations (Boulding, 1977), and that, "with its passionate embrace of vigorous egalitarianism and distrust of hierarchy and dominance, is clearly not an apolitical concept" (Sharp, 2018, p. 9). Finally, critics have taken issue with the vague definition of positive peace, arguing that the term lacks specificity and leans too heavily on identifying what it is not rather than what it is (Boulding, 1977; Sharp, 2018).

I believe that this absence of specificity can also be treated as an asset, as it holds open the possibilities for context-appropriate and locally led innovation and social action rather than being prescriptive about what must occur.

Dialogue Theory

Critical examinations of both Freire and Buber often focus on the binary aspects of how they present their theories. For Buber, this critique arises from an interpretation of his work that he identifies only two ways of relating: the I-Thou and the I-It (Metcalfe & Game, 2012). However, Metcalfe and Game (2012) provide a compelling response to this critique that, "in Buber's dia-logic, there is simultaneous presence of difference-and-sameness" (p. 358). That is to say, that the relation between I-It and I-Thou is not dualistic but rather "forms that unfold into each other" (p. 356). I find this reading helpful as a rejection of an 'either-or' scenario; instead, it presents an embrace of the complexity involved in moving from an I-It to an I-Thou relation within the dialogic encounter.

A primary criticism of Freire's work is his tendency, especially in his earlier works such as *Pedagogy of the Oppressed*, to create a binary of oppressed categorization without recognition of the various facets that intersect and contribute to oppression, such as ethnicity, gender, ableness, sexual orientation, class, and religion (Freire & Macedo, 1993; Glass, 2001; McLaren & da Silva, 1993). I have previously addressed the importance of understanding intersectional identities, privilege, and oppression in both the work and theoretical framing of dialogue; however, I wish to address these issues as a critique of Freire explicitly. Scholars and critics have highlighted the binary aspects of Freire's work and commented that he often employed a universal understanding of the oppressor and the oppressed based on notions of class (Ellsworth, 1989; Taylor, 1993). That is to say, a reading of Freire's early work creates the perspective that all poor are oppressed, and all wealthy are oppressors. This homogenous classification negates the complexity of inequality and prejudice that crosses beyond the boundaries of economics and creates a clear-cut form of oppression when the world is not experienced in such a dualistic way (Giroux, 1993; Schugurensky, 2014). An analysis of class as the defining marker of oppressed or oppressor ignores that people can be both; a wealthy person of colour can also experience oppression due to systemic racism, while a man living in poverty can simultaneously act as an oppressor to his wife within a patriarchal system. As Glass (2001) articulates;

> the theory does not adequately recognize that race, class, and gender oppressions are geared to specific concrete conditions that can be contradictory, such that simultaneous positions of oppression and dominance can be occupied by particular individuals (for example, someone privileged by racial and class location but oppressed by the gender order, as with a White middle-class woman). (p. 21)

By employing universal classifications of the oppressor and oppressed, the complexities of real-life can appear oversimplified within Freire's conception of the world, and specifically in his understanding of dialogue and critical pedagogy (Freire & Macedo, 1993; Schugurensky, 2014).

An extension to the critique of the binary classification of oppressor and oppressed has aimed explicitly at Freire's omission of gender considerations and the experiences of women. Early critiques on this topic focus on Freire's use of language—that he used male pronouns and descriptors as the universal for humankind. Freire was responsive to these criticisms and ensured that future work and translations used language that was inclusive of women (Freire & Macedo, 1993; Weiler, 1996). However, as Weiler (1996) points out, Freire often conflated the criticisms of sexist language with the separate, valid, critiques of his understanding of gender and its role in relation to issues of oppression and power when "he subsumes gender within class" (p. 396). When Freire did respond to these critiques of his work, he maintained a tendency towards the generalization of all women or feminists:

> rather than examine and understand the levels of women's oppression - the different forms of oppression and privilege of black and white women, for example, or the differences between working class and bourgeois women, or the different positionings and interests of lesbian, bisexual, and heterosexual women. (Weiler, 1996, p. 369)

Due to this patriarchal understanding of 'the oppressed,' Freire "constructs a phallocentric paradigm of liberations - wherein freedom and the experience of patriarchal manhood are always linked as though they are one and the same" (hooks, 1993, p. 148). This limited view of systemic oppression thereby restricts how the oppressed find their voice, as a simplistic classification can lead to naïve solutions that are ignorant of complexities that genuinely exist in lived experiences.

These are valuable critiques, and ones that, to his credit, Freire himself addressed. Freire remained open and changed by the criticisms of his work, seeking to continue learning through dialogic encounters. He revisited much of his previous work throughout his career, looking to reflect a growing understanding of the intersectional nature of oppression (Freire, 1993; Schugurensky, 2014).

In engaging with these critiques, I am encouraged by bell hooks' thoughtful response as someone deeply inspired by Freire's work, and yet as a critical feminist thinker, painfully aware of its shortcomings. In her essay, *bell hooks speaking about Paulo Freire - the man, his work*, hooks (1993) presents a compelling argument that "critical interrogation is not the same as dismissal" (p. 148). That part of engaging critically with any work is to take the opportunity to "learn from the insights" (p.148) and grow from the flaws. This same view is one shared by Freire as he acknowledged that his insights, twenty years after writing *Pedagogy of the Oppressed,* were much more profound and more vibrant than they were at the time of its writing (Freire & Macedo, 1993). This is the task at hand—to take the richness of what Freire offers and engage critically with the theory, pairing it with current understandings and insights related to oppression to ensure the work is appropriately situated in the current context.

Further criticisms center on the idealistic nature of Freire's theory, which many critics believe goes too far in establishing a utopian concept of dialogue (Schugurensky, 2014). The sentiments expressed by Anderson et al. (2004), that "we are wise to be skeptical about dialogue, but unwise to be dismissive" (p. 16), resonate for me in response to this criticism. I would argue that both Freire and Buber were intimately aware of the complexities of the world and the shortcomings of humankind through their lived experiences. These are not thinkers who are ignorant of human pain and suffering, and yet they hold to a view of dialogue as *humanization* and *transformation* that is inherently hopeful. They hold faith in the powerful encounter between those who are *other* to move into new ways of knowing ourselves, the world, and the people around us. This view connects with the inherently hopeful notion of positive peace, which is, in part, why I have chosen to draw on these theorists in this book. I believe the theoretical lens through which to seek insight regarding dialogic encounters must be both profoundly cognizant of issues of oppression, power, and inequality, while also maintaining a hopeful view towards how we can experience *humanization* and *transformation* in connection to positive peace.

2.7 Summary

This chapter constructed a theoretical framework for this book, beginning with an understanding of positive peace as holistic and self-reinforcing, and across structural, direct, and cultural dimensions. The works of the dialogue theorists, Buber and Freire, were then presented, including an overview of the characteristics and qualities of dialogue: dialogic moments, the sphere of between, presentness, awareness, authenticity, and mutuality. Buber and Freire's theories were woven together to illustrate how, in an authentic dialogical meeting of *other*, the It becomes Thou, and within that humanizing encounter, the opportunity arises to identify and name the world. This third space of encounter, the sphere of between, allows for the rise of the moral imagination, the identification of new possibilities that move into transforming action aimed towards the norms and practices that shape the cultural and structural status quo. In dialogue encounters, individuals recognize and name issues of systemic oppression through *emergence* and reject the structures that privilege one group over another. The dialogic space of *humanization* and *transformation* theoretically link to positive peace as individuals take acts of *intervention* towards creating a more equitable, just, and inclusive society. Further consideration was also given to critiques of both dialogue and positive peace theory.

REFERENCES

Anderson, R., Baxter, L. A., & Cissna, K. N. (2004). Texts and contexts of dialogue. In R. Anderson, L. A. Baxter, & K. N. Cissna (Eds.), *Dialogue: Theorizing difference in communication studies* (pp. 1–17). Sage.

Atkinson, M. (2013). Intergroup dialogue: A theoretical positioning. *Journal of Dialogue Studies, 1*(1), 63–80.

Baxter, L. A. (2004). Dialogues of relating. In R. Anderson, L. A. Baxter, & K. N. Cissna (Eds.), *Dialogue: Theorizing difference in communication studies* (pp. 107–124). Sage.

Bebbington, J., Brown, J., Frame, B., & Thomson, I. (2007). Theorizing engagement: The potential of a critical dialogic approach. *Accounting, Auditing & Accountability Journal, 20*(3), 356–381. https://doi.org/10.1108/09513570710748544

Boulding, K. E. (1977). Twelve friendly quarrels with Johan Galtung. *Journal of Peace Research, 14*(1), 75–86. https://doi.org/10.1177/002234337701400105

Bryn, S. (2015). Can dialogue make a difference?: The experience of the Nansen dialogue network. In S. P. Ramet, A Simkus & O. Listhaug (Eds.), *Civic and uncivic values in Kosovo* (pp. 365–394). Central European University Press. Retrieved from http://www.jstor.org/stable/10.7829/j.ctt13wzttq.21

Buber, M. (1947). *Between man and man* (R. G. Smith, Trans.). Routledge.

Buber, M. (1967). Replies to my critics. In P. A. Schilpp & M. S. Friedman (Eds.), *The philosophy of Martin Buber* (pp. 689–744). Open Court.

Buber, M. (1970). *I and Thou* (W. Kaufmann, Trans.). Scribner.

Burkitt, I. (1999). Relational Moves and Generative Dances. In S. McNamee & K. J. Gergen (Eds.), *Relational responsibility resources for sustainable dialogue* (pp. 71–80). Sage.

Cho, S., Crenshaw, K. W., & McCall, L. (2013). Toward a field of intersectionality studies: Theory, applications, and praxis. *Signs: Journal of Women in Culture and Society, 38*(4), 785–810. https://doi.org/10.1086/669608

Cissna, K. N., & Anderson, R. (1994). Communication and the ground of dialogue. In R. Anderson, K. N. Cissna, & R. Arnett (Eds.), *The reach of dialogue: Confirmation, voice, and community* (pp. 9–30). Hampton Press.

Cissna, K. N., & Anderson, R. (1998). Theorizing about dialogic moments: The Buber-Rogers position and postmodern themes. *Communication Theory, 8*(1), 63–104.

Crenshaw, K. W. (1995). The intersection of race and gender. In K. W. Crenshaw, N. Gotanda, G. Peller, & K. Thomas (Eds.), *Critical race theory: The key writings that formed the movement*. New Press.

Czubaroff, J. (2000). Dialogical rhetoric: An application of Martin Buber's philosophy of dialogue. *Quarterly Journal of Speech, 86*(2), 168–189. https://doi.org/10.1080/00335630009384288

Deetz, S., & Simpson, J. (2004). Critical organizational dialogue. In R. Anderson, L. A. Baxter, & K. N. Cissna (Eds.), *Dialogue: Theorizing difference in communication studies* (pp. 141–158). Sage.

Ellsworth, E. (1989). Why doesn't this feel empowering? Working through the repressive myths of critical pedagogy. *Harvard Educational Review, 59*(3), 297.

Freire, P. (1993). Foreword. In P. McLaren & P. Leonard (Eds.) and D. Macedo (Trans.), *Paulo Freire: A critical encounter* (pp. ix–xii). Routledge.

Freire, P. (2000). *Pedagogy of the oppressed* (30th anniversary ed., M. B. Ramos, Trans.). Continuum.

Freire, P., & Macedo, D. (1993). A dialogue with Paulo Freire. In P. McLaren & P. Leonard (Eds.), *Paulo Freire: A critical encounter* (pp. 169–176). Routledge.

Friedman, M. S. (2004). *Martin Buber: The life of dialogue*. Routledge.

Galtung, J. (1969). Violence, peace, and peace research. *Journal of Peace Research, 6*(3), 167–191. https://doi.org/10.1177/002234336900600301

Galtung, J. (1990). Cultural violence. *Journal of Peace Research, 27*(3), 291–305. Retrieved from http://www.jstor.org/stable/423472

Galtung, J. (1996). *Peace by peaceful means: Peace and conflict, development and civilization*. Sage. https://doi.org/10.4135/9781446221631

Ganesh, S., & Zoller, H. M. (2012). Dialogue, activism, and democratic social change. *Communication Theory, 22*(1), 66–91. https://doi.org/10.1111/j.1468-2885.2011.01396.x

Gawerc, M. (2006). Peace-building: Theoretical and concrete perspectives. *Peace & Change, 31*(4), 435–478. https://doi.org/10.1111/j.1468-0130.2006.00387.x

Giroux, H. A. (1993). A dialogue with Paulo Freire. In P. McLaren & P. Leonard (Eds.), *Paulo Freire: A critical encounter* (pp. 177–188). Routledge.

Glass, R. D. (2001). On Paulo Freire's philosophy of praxis and the foundations of liberation education. *Educational Researcher*, *30*(2), 15–25. Retrieved from https://www.jstor.org/stable/3594336

Gordon, N. (2004). Ethics and the place of the other. In P. Atterton, M. Calarco, & M. S. Friedman (Eds.), *Levinas & Buber : Dialogue and Difference* (pp. 98–115). Duquesne University Press.

Hammond, S. C., Anderson, R., & Cissna, K. N. (2003). The problematics of dialogue and power. *Annals of the International Communication Association*, *27*(1), 125–157. https://doi.org/10.1080/23808985.2003.11679024

Hansen, T. (2016). Holistic peace. *Peace Review*, *28*(2), 212–219. https://doi.org/10.1080/10402659.2016.1166758

hooks, b. (1993). bell hooks speaking about Paulo Freire—The man, his work. In P. McLaren & P. Leonard (Eds.), *Paulo Freire: A critical encounter* (pp. 146–154). Routledge.

Johannesen, R. L. (2000). Nel Noddings's uses of Martin Buber's philosophy of dialogue. *Southern Communication Journal*, *65*(2–3), 151–160. https://doi.org/10.1080/10417940009373164

Kim, J., & Kim, E. J. (2008). Theorizing dialogic deliberation: Everyday political talk as communicative action and dialogue. *Communication Theory*, *18*(1), 51–70. https://doi.org/10.1111/j.1468-2885.2007.00313.x

King, M. L. (1993). Letter from Birmingham jail. *U.C. Davis Law Review*, *26*, 835–1045.

Lederach, J. P. (2005). *The Moral Imagination: The art and soul of building peace*. Oxford University Press.

Macedo, D. (2000). Introduction. In P. Freire (Ed.), *Pedagogy of the oppressed* (30th anniversary, pp. 11–27). Continuum.

McLaren, P., & da Silva, T. T. (1993). Decentering pedagogy: Critical literacy, resistance and the politics of memory. In P. McLaren & P. Leonard (Eds.), *Paulo Freire: A critical encounter* (pp. 47–89). Routledge.

McNamee, S., & Shotter, J. (2004). Dialogue, creativity, and change. In R. Anderson, L. A. Baxter, & K. N. Cissna (Eds.), *Dialogue: Theorizing difference in communication studies* (pp. 91–104). Sage Publications.

Metcalfe, A., & Game, A. (2012). 'In the beginning is relation': Martin Buber's alternative to binary oppositions. *Sophia*, *51*(3), 351–363. https://doi.org/10.1007/s11841-011-0278-9

Nelson, N., & Wright, S. (1995). *Power and participatory development: Theory and practice*. Intermediate Technology Publications.

Nolte-Laird, R. (2021). Contact programs and the pursuit of positive peace: Reframing perceptions of equality. In K. Standish, H. Devere, A. E. Suazo, & R. Rafferty (Eds.), *The Palgrave handbook of positive peace* (pp. 1–18). Springer Singapore. https://doi.org/10.1007/978-981-15-3877-3_55-1

Riddle, K. C. (2017). Structural Violence, intersectionality, and justpeace: Evaluating women's peacebuilding agency in Manipur. India. *Hypatia, 32*(3), 574–592. https://doi.org/10.1111/hypa.12340

Schugurensky, D. (2014). The reception and influence of Freire's work. In *Paulo Freire* (1st ed.). Bloomsbury.

Sharp, D. N. (2018). Positive peace, paradox, and contested liberalisms. (Pre-Publication). Retrieved from https://ssrn.com/abstract=3161742

Simpson, J. L. (2008). The color-blind double bind: Whiteness and the (im)possibility of dialogue. *Communication Theory, 18*(1), 139–159. https://doi.org/10.1111/j.1468-2885.2007.00317.x

Standish, K. (2014). Cultural nonviolence: The other side of Galtung. *Global Journal of Peace Research and Praxis, 1*(1), 46–54.

Tapper, A. J. H. (2013). A pedagogy of social justice education: Social identity theory, intersectionality, and empowerment. *Conflict Resolution Quarterly, 30*(4), 411–445. https://doi.org/10.1002/crq.21072

Taylor, P. V. (1993). *The texts of Paulo Freire*. Open University Press.

Wallace, D. F. (2006). Kenyon commencement speech. In D. Eggers (Ed.), *The Best American Nonrequired Reading 2006* (pp. 355–364). Houghton Mifflin Print.

Weiler, K. (1996). Myths of Paulo Freire. *Educational Theory, 46*(3), 353–371. https://doi.org/10.1111/j.1741-5446.1996.00353.x

Westoby, P. (2014). Theorising dialogue for community development practice—An exploration of crucial thinkers. *Journal of Dialogue Studies, 2*(1), 69–85.

White, W. J. (2008). The interlocutor's dilemma: The place of strategy in dialogic theory. *Communication Theory, 18*(1), 5–26. https://doi.org/10.1111/j.1468-2885.2007.00311.x

Wood, J. T. (2004). Foreword: Entering into dialogue. In R. Anderson, L. A. Baxter, & K. N. Cissna (Eds.), *Dialogue: Theorizing difference in communication studies* (pp. xv–xxii). Sage.

CHAPTER 3

Community-Based Dialogue and Online Peacebuilding Practice

The following chapter presents an overview of the existing literature and knowledge relating to the primary question posed in this book: can engaging *other* through dialogic encounters within an online environment enable conditions for positive peace? As such, the chapter encompasses two significant bodies of knowledge. The first section will examine dialogue as practice in community-based peacebuilding, including the outcomes and critiques of those practices. The second section of this chapter will explore existing literature related to online dialogue-based peacebuilding practices, along with other online peacebuilding models. By examining these two areas of literature, I present a clear understanding of the pre-existing body of knowledge, the current gaps in knowledge, and illustrate this research's opportunity and relevance.

3.1 Dialogue in Peacebuilding Practice

Peacebuilding practice is diverse and multi-faceted, with many different theoretical lenses from which to build an understanding and methodology. I draw from Gawerc's (2006) definition of peacebuilding, that "the intention of peace-building is to create a structure of peace that is based on justice, equity, and cooperation (i.e., positive peace), thereby addressing the underlying causes of violent conflict so that they become less likely in the future" (p. 439). As such, peacebuilding occurs in many different contexts, not exclusively within conflict or post-conflict settings. Rather, peacebuilding initiatives are appropriate wherever latent issues of conflict, division, inequity, or injustice are present. With this definition in mind, this chapter discusses a wide range of initiatives and models that are considered dialogue and occur in different environments—from the United States-based higher education to widespread conflict contexts. For the purposes of this book, I identify dialogue as a peacebuilding methodology within a visioning of holistic peacebuilding. In other words, peacebuilding that is multi-disciplinary, and occurs across all spheres of society—and dialogue as a method that can be applied in different contexts.

As conflict and violence can manifest across all spaces of society—from institutional to individual interactions—so peacebuilding work must respond in kind, by applying strategies thoughtfully based on context and audience across all spheres of community and population (Charbonneau & Parent, 2012; Kahl & Puig Larrauri, 2013; Maoz, 2000). Within both literature and practice, it is commonly understood that peacebuilding work occurs across three tracks or levels (Gawerc, 2006). There is the top-level, or track-one, work typically involving a national leadership and policy focus. The middle-level, or track-two, focuses predominately on regional leadership, or culturally influential individuals such as scholars and religious leaders. Finally, there are track-three, or local, grassroots initiatives, sometimes called 'people to people' (P2P) initiatives (Gawerc, 2006). These local initiatives, such as grassroots dialogue, are often designed to complement other tracks to create a community context that will embrace political peace processes or outcomes (Dessel & Ali, 2012). Dialogue as terminology is often applied to many diverse approaches and methodologies, including track-one and track-two peacebuilding work such as negotiations and mediation (Ropers, 2004). My research inquiry is interested in sustained dialogue at an individual level within a track-three or local context—the intentional encounters between individuals that occur over time, which allow for the transformation of relationships.

There are various theories and models from which encounter-based initiatives, specifically dialogue models, originate from. However, the two most prominent of these theories, Contact Hypothesis and Social Identity Theory, are worth exploring further.

Contact hypothesis.

As discussed in Chapter 1, many present-day P2P initiatives, including dialogue practices, evolved out of Gordon Allport's Contact Hypothesis (Steinberg, 2013). Contact Hypothesis was developed in the field of psychology by Allport in 1954 and provides a well-regarded framework for reducing intergroup prejudice amongst separate identity groups.[1] The foundational hypothesis is that, when certain conditions are met, contact between out-groups can be a positive experience, resulting in prejudice reduction, improved perception of the *other*, and more positive intergroup relationships (Pettigrew & Tropp, 2011). Contact Hypothesis is unique from structured dialogue practices as its core features include equality in status amongst group members, supporting collaboration and a shared purpose, the pursuit of meaningful objectives, and having the support of the community context in which they occur (Allport, 1954). While some of these traits, such as equality, overlap with dialogue practice, they are distinct from the characteristics of dialogue peacebuilding practice outlined in this chapter. It is important to note that contact can remain effective even if all of these conditions are not present (Hasler & Amichai-Hamburger, 2013), thus not all literature discussed in this chapter fulfills all four conditions.

Social identity theory.

While many dialogue approaches find their origins in the Contact Hypothesis, others have developed from Social Identity Theory (SIT). SIT initially developed in the 1970s and suggests that individuals view themselves and others in relation to their membership and non-membership within social groups (Tajfel & Turner, 1986). Usage of SIT within dialogue practices offers a means through which group members can explore power dynamics originating from their social identities more broadly, and not restrict dialogic interactions to a limited examination of individual differences (Ross, 2017; Tapper, 2013).

---

[1] For more on Contact Hypothesis and Peacebuilding, see: Amichai-Hamburger et al., (2015), Austin (2006), Hasler and Amichai-Hamburger (2013), Maoz et al., (2002), McKenna et al., (2009), and Pettigrew & Tropp, 2011.

Prominent models.

One present-day example of a sustained and structured dialogue approach is termed Intergroup Dialogue (IGD) (Dessel & Ali, 2012; Nagda & Maxwell, 2011). IGD emerged out of bias and prejudice reduction initiatives (Gurin et al., 2013), and is designed to occur in face-to-face settings, addressing social identity issues between groups with "a history of tension between them" (Frantell et al., 2019, p. 655). As with other dialogue models, IGD occurs in various contexts and is not necessarily tied to peacebuilding practice. Another prominent model within peace and conflict studies is Hal Saunders's sustained dialogue, which comprises five stages: deciding to engage, mapping relationships and naming problems, probing problems and relationships, scenario building, and acting together (Saunders, 2011). While IGD occurs in various settings, Saunders' sustained dialogue "applies where societies have experienced deep-rooted human conflict and torn relationships" (Kelleher & Ryan, 2012, p. 67). These approaches act as two tools amongst many that can contribute to establishing both negative and positive peace.[2]

There is a rich body of knowledge to draw on when exploring how dialogue has been used within community-based peacebuilding practice.[3] In the following section, I present key characteristics that are significant in conceptualizing dialogue practice and then examine the outcomes and critiques of this approach to peacebuilding.

Characteristics of Dialogue in Community Peacebuilding

Within peacebuilding dialogue practices, many different processes and frameworks have been effective in creating the appropriate conditions for interaction and producing positive outcomes in individual participants (Dessel & Ali, 2012; Ropers, 2004). In the absence of a universally agreed definition and structure, I have identified the following characteristics of dialogic encounters from the relevant research and theoretical

---

[2] While Sustained and IGD are specific models in the field of peace and conflict, this chapter seeks to synthesize an array of models and theories, including but not limited to these. Therefore, while elements of IGD and Saunders's sustained dialogue are incorporated within this chapter, I am not exclusively drawing from these two definitions.

[3] For more on dialogue in community-based peacebuilding see: Dessel and Rogge (2008), Gawerc (2006), Maoz et al., (2002) Phipps (2014), and Ron and Maoz (2013b).

literature that falls within the scope of this research inquiry: encountering *other*, establishing a safe space that addresses issues of inequality amongst participants, attending to issues of identity both within in-group and out-group contexts, the examination of truth and narratives, and creating relationships with *other* that enable a movement towards change or action. While these characteristics are explored separately in this chapter, they are intrinsically linked, and they can contribute or detract from each other. Further, it should be noted that these characteristics are not universal to all dialogue practices.

Encountering other.

A common understanding of community dialogue in the literature is that it involves encountering of the *other* (Chaitin, 2012; Mor et al., 2016). This encountering can be interpreted as both a physical manifestation as well as the act of revealing one's true self to the *other* and allowing the *other* to reveal themselves to you (Bryn, 2015). Part of this act of encountering is the transparency that occurs in participants revealing themselves—their identity, their truths, and their narratives—in seeking to be heard and seen by the *other* to forge a path towards peace by transforming perceptions (Ellis & Maoz, 2012; Lederach, 1997). However, the work does not end at being seen by the *other*, as Lederach (1997) articulates, "it is one thing to *know*; it is yet a very different social phenomenon to *acknowledge*. Acknowledgement through hearing one another's stories validates experience and feelings and represents the first step towards restoration of the person and the relationship" (p. 26).

The significance of engaging in this process of being *seen* should not be underestimated or viewed in simplistic terms. In many cases, participants come from situations with direct experience of the conflict—they, or those close to them, have experienced trauma perceived to have been caused by those they now sit beside. The fear, mistrust, and hostility are deeply rooted, and it can be challenging to move beyond these influences in a face-to-face setting (Lederach, 1997). Additionally, it is difficult to simultaneously acknowledge the validity of experiences and identity of the *other* while also holding to your own narratives and identity when those two things appear to be in direct opposition (Burkhardt-Vetter, 2018). Participants must establish within themselves an ability to listen deeply to one another, to seek fully to understand and reflect back to themselves and their identity group their newly acquired knowledge. Saunders identifies this ability to listen to one another as the definition of dialogue itself:

> dialogue is a particular way of communicating in which the parties listen to each other carefully enough to be changed by what they hear. Dialogue may be more about listening, hearing, and internalizing than it is about talking. Because one person has truly heard another's pain or inner hopes, the hearer will respond at a deeper level than before. (Saunders, 2011, p. 265)

There is deep attention required to being present, to actively listening and putting to the side one's own need to impose one's view or contradictory narrative, to establish the trust that is possible when each participant feels truly heard (Dessel & Rogge, 2008; Senesh, 2012). As this trust begins to develop, it can contribute to the establishment of a safe or sacred space for participants.

Establishing brave space.

As dialogic work can create psychological vulnerability, facilitators and organizers cannot take lightly the attentiveness required to ensure participants feel secure enough in the environment to both reveal and question aspects of their own identities and narratives. The encountering of *other* in a supportive environment can allow participants to cross over the visible and invisible boundaries that commonly prevent them from engaging together to establish trust and understanding on the path to co-creating a future of sustainable peace (Lederach, 1997). Therefore, a critical element of dialogue practice is to establish a physical and psychological environment that enables participants to engage with themselves and others. The dialogue process will often surface fundamental views or ideas related to their individual and collective identities that can be painful to encounter (Phipps, 2014). This emergence of deeply held beliefs can be a difficult and often emotional process requiring both a sense of safety along with thoughtful facilitation and guidance. As such, the role of the facilitator is vital to ensuring a safe and trusting environment. Typically, dialogue initiatives are co-facilitated by trained representatives of the groups engaging in the dialogue (Nagda & Maxwell, 2011).

A common barrier to the establishment of a safe environment is inherent power imbalances or issues of inequality amongst participants

(Maoz et al., 2002). Considerations of gender, socio-economic status indicators, and language, are all relevant factors that may relate to power dynamics within the dialogue encounter. Thoughtfulness must be given to the creation of a space that takes into account these considerations so that marginalized members of the group can feel both empowered and safe to share their perspectives (Nagda & Gurin, 2007).

However, the notion of the word 'safe' has been challenged when considering these aspects of intersectional power dynamics. As Arao and Clemens (2013) articulate, "the language of safety may actually encourage entrenchment in privilege...[and] contributes to the replication of dominance and subordination, rather than a dismantling thereof" (pp. 140–141). They identify that safety infers the removal of risk for the group members with higher power status, therefore equating safety with comfort. However, as this section has articulated, dialogue must interrogate constructs of privilege and power—thereby causing discomfort for the higher power group members. Arao and Clemens (2013) suggest the language of 'brave spaces' in place of 'safe space.'

Exploring identity.

Participants in a dialogic encounter often examine and challenge their own identity and the narratives that have contributed to the construction of that identity (Maoz et al., 2002). Issues of identity can be central to informing preconceptions and narratives of *other* as distinct from one's own identity or social group (Dessel & Ali, 2012). Therefore, it is important that within a structured process there is the ability for members of a single identity group, or 'in-group,' to grapple together with their narratives and understanding before engaging with the *other* or the 'out-group' (Senesh, 2012). This exploration into identity often happens during the initial stages of a dialogue program, with opportunities to explore and debrief throughout the experience.

Often, within conflict scenarios, identity becomes intrinsically linked to belonging to one side or group (Chaitin, 2012). A collective, or 'master,' narrative related to the conflict can become a facet within one's identity construction (Hammack, 2008). Engaging with the *other* through dialogue not only confronts deeply held beliefs, but it also can result in dismantling and reworking of one's own identity (Ross, 2014). Without 'belonging' to a side to help rebuild that identity, consideration must be given to how individuals move forward with restoring a sense of self.

Confronting these essential elements of identity can, at times, hinder the work towards peace more than outright violence (Bar-Tal, 2007). The security of a set identity can be comforting, aid in coping with the stress of living in conflict and provide continuity in situations of physical insecurity (Bar-Tal, 2007; Lederach, 1997). For vulnerable or marginalized groups, a collective narrative provides reassurance of group solidarity and "ontological security" (Hammack, 2008, p. 225). Thus, the feeling of 'belonging' is not a simple thing to give up.

Examination of 'truth.'

Experiences in dialogue programs can causes participants to reflect and analyze their own cultural, societal, and often familial narratives (Dessel & Rogge, 2008). The act of listening with seeking to understand the *other* can cause participants to confront how one's understanding of *truth* can be counter to what others know of that *truth*. Ungerleider (2012) believes that this recognition of myriad perceptions and beliefs related to the same truth "is a precondition for realizing that a common history can be seen through very different ideological lenses" (p. 395). Bryn (2015) describes this multiplicity of *truth* as "the radical dimension of dialogue work; it alters perceptions of reality by making alternative truths and alternative explanations visible" (p. 376). This is a critical aspect of the dialogic encounter, to hold both the known and the unfamiliar narratives and accept the dissonance that exists between them. The goal is not a uniform or sanitized collective truth, but rather an ability to recognize the diversity and validity of both experiences (Bar-Tal & Hammack, 2012). This examination of truth has also been termed *dialogic remembering,* where the objective is "not to create a unitary master narrative, but rather a compatible understanding of history defined by mutual acknowledgement and referentiality" (Burkhardt-Vetter, 2018, pp. 242–243). In learning to be comfortable with complexity around issues of *truth*, narratives, and identity, participants can start to reframe how they behave and the decisions they make related to *other.*

Relational movement.

The characteristics explored above that create the context for dialogic encounters are significant; however, ultimately, dialogue must produce tangible outcomes to be a relevant practice within the field of peacebuilding. I define such tangible outcomes as *relational movement*—action that springs from the relational formation with *other*. As participants engage together and grapple with their narratives and identities, the boundaries around *self* can widen to become more inclusive of what was once *other* (Chaitin, 2012; Maoz et al., 2002). This phenomenon might also be viewed through the lens of moral inclusion, those who were *other* were once perceived as outside one's moral responsibility, but now there is an obligation to attend to their suffering and to address systemic issues that affect them (Abramovich, 2005; Maoz, 2000; Opotow, 2012). Gergen et al. (2001) have identified this as when dialogue becomes transformational, such that it allows for the "collaborative construction of new realities" (p. 697) or "what Lederach (2005) has termed the 'moral imagination,' a shared imaginary of a peaceful future, which is fundamental in moving societies frozen in conflict towards meaningful reconciliation" (as cited in Burkhardt-Vetter, 2018, p. 239). Collective visioning is inclusive of the unique stories, identities, needs, and desires of all individuals who make up the diversity of society. To support the development of positive peace, the shared vision must be especially attentive to issues of inequity and systemic inequality for those who have been oppressed or marginalized (Ross, 2015). This imagining of a collective future enables *relational movement*, as participants must reflect their agency and their capacity to take action towards the creation of that vision of a shared future (Ellis & Maoz, 2012; Saunders, 2011).

Outcomes of Dialogue in Community Peacebuilding

Dialogue can have a long-term outcome on participants in how they perceive the *other*, engage in their world, and understand their own identities, in ways that create conditions for positive peace within their broader community and society.[4] It is claimed that participants of dialogic encounters become "true agent[s] of peace" (Lefranc, 2012, p. 34), representatives who extend their influence and voice out into their

---

[4] For more on dialogue outcomes see Bryn (2015), Burkhardt-Vetter (2018), Dessel and Ali (2012), Hoover (2011), Kelleher and Ryan (2012), Maoz et al., (2002), Mor et al., (2016), Ron and Maoz (2013b), and Ross and Lazarus (2015), Ungerleider (2012), and Zartman (2008).

spheres of influence, creating a dispersion into the broader community, culture, and society (Dessel & Ali, 2012; Ron & Maoz, 2013b). Dialogue can cause participants to reflect on themselves, their community, and their institutions in ways that create more active participants in the broader democratic fabric as they develop critical thinking skills, feel more comfortable giving voice to their views and experiences, envision an inclusive and peaceful future, and practice taking social action (Ross, 2017; Tapper, 2013). In their literature review on research relating to intergroup dialogues, Dessel and Rogge (2008) found that "in community settings outcomes of dialogues have implications for individual, interpersonal, and systemic change" (p. 225). These outcomes included "initiating joint action on shared issues of concern...[and] many who participated in these dialogues evidenced an increase in civic engagement" (p. 226). Further, resilient relationships at a community level provide a protective factor against the possibility of renewed violence or conflict, as those who were once *other* are now viewed through a more inclusive understanding of the collective (Senesh, 2012).

Ultimately, if peacebuilding strategies are not inclusive of initiatives that allow for reconciliation and transformed relationships between individuals, peace agreements will not be the hoped-for mechanism for sustainable peace. The conditions amongst people must shift to allow for a shared vision of the future to reduce the likelihood of renewed violence or conflict (Charbonneau & Parent, 2012). Dialogue as a grassroots endeavour can create the conditions for this possibility of stability by fortifying the social resilience and infrastructure amongst individuals at a community level. However, the work of dialogue should move beyond attaining the absence of violence or negative peace and look at the *relational movement* necessary for enabling the possibility for positive peace. Dialogue initiatives do not always produce the transformation required to allow for positive peace, and it is essential to weigh the benefits of dialogue practice against its criticisms and provide thoughtful means of addressing those shortcomings.

Critiques & Limitations of Dialogue in Community Peacebuilding

Dialogue as a tool for peacebuilding is not without its valid critiques and risks, such as failure to adequately address power dynamics, normalization of the status quo, negative contact outcomes, and variations in outcomes.

Further consideration is given to each of these criticisms in the following sections.

Power dynamics.

Power is a critical consideration within face-to-face encounters that intend to contribute to peace (Gawerc, 2006; Senesh, 2012)—even in seeking to establish a neutral environment for meetings, power imbalances are present. Attention must be given to understanding the complex notion of equality related to the multi-faceted nature of identity for each individual. While it is simpler to view intergroup encounters through ethnic or religious divisions alone, doing so undermines potential positive outcomes by disregarding the intricacies, such as gender identity, age, ableness, and sexual orientation, that make each participant unique (Tapper, 2013). These, amongst many other nuanced contributors to individual identities, are compounded in visible and invisible ways that add complexity to establishing a safe environment and empowering individual agency (Riddle, 2017). If these multiple facets of social identity are not addressed within the dialogue process, issues of systemic inequality can inadvertently be reinforced even when attempts have been made to create a safe or neutral environment (Tapper, 2013). These arguments directly challenge the notion of equality—if it is attainable, or should be sought, in dialogue settings when accounting for social identity and systemic inequality (Nolte-Laird, 2021).

Normalization.

Dialogue practices risk normalizing the status quo of pre-existing power imbalances, by creating relationships between individuals without a mechanism to take action in a way that addresses ongoing issues of inequality, violence, or oppression (Graf et al., 2014; Maoz, 2011). Some, such as Phipps (2014), have argued that the meaning of 'dialogue' as a term is diluted when painful, and potentially volatile, topics are ignored:

> If uncomfortable, political, sensitive issues are not part of Intercultural Dialogue, and the only scope for dialogue is discussion of ways in which people might be perceiving each other to be culturally different, then it is not possible for dialogue to achieve any change. (pp. 111–112)

When intergroup encounters focus on commonalities or shared experiences and ignore the underlying issues of the conflict, specifically power inequalities, the outcomes may be positive attitude and perception changes, but the opportunity for transformational action is potentially squandered (Saguy et al., 2009). As explored previously, efforts at dialogue must be focused on transforming relationships and creating action that enables the conditions for positive peace by ensuring issues of inequality and oppression are addressed clearly and thoughtfully.

Negative contact.

In conflict and post-conflict scenarios, where stereotypes and negative perceptions of *other* are already intensified, a salient risk is that these views become reinforced and further entrenched if the intergroup experience is negative (Pettigrew & Tropp, 2011). While intergroup contact initiatives commonly produce positive results, outcomes of a negative experience permeate deeper than the positive effects (Graf et al., 2014; Meleady & Forder, 2018). A negative experience can result from the degree of superficiality found in the contact setting. If participants do not deal with the underlying conflict issues or dimensions of power, they may feel that at best, the experience was a waste of time and, at worst, that it solidified their existing notions of *other*.

In situations of ongoing conflict or structural inequality, participants' views can remain static, or in some cases become more strongly entrenched within their in-group identity and stereotypes of *other* (Pilecki & Hammack, 2014; Ross, 2014). These outcomes are related to the power differentials between group members, as "dialogic encounters between groups in a situation of structural inequality and domination may solidify essentialist discourses of culture and identity" (Helman, 2002, p. 327). Additionally, negative contact often results from scenarios where individuals in the dialogue felt coerced, did not consent to the encounter, or felt unsafe (Pettigrew et al., 2011).

The concern of negative contact is intrinsically linked with the critiques presented above of normalization and power imbalances. If issues of inequality and oppression are ignored, it enhances the likelihood that the marginalized group will feel further diminished by the experience and exacerbate divisiveness between the groups. Individuals who have a negative encounter are more likely to deny systemic issues of oppression related to marginalized groups and less likely to willingly encounter the out-group again, jeopardizing future work towards a transformed society reflective of positive peace (Meleady & Forder, 2018; Tapper, 2013).

Variations in outcomes.

It is important to note that dialogue encounters are not universally successful. In many cases, the long-term outcomes, or sustainability of change in attitudes and behaviours, are unknown (Tapper, 2013). At times, studies focus exclusively on the outcomes in the dominant or privileged identity group (Ron & Maoz, 2013a, 2013b).

Dialogue practice can produce outcomes that enable positive peace through the transformation of individuals in how they perceive themselves and *other*. Peacebuilding outcomes must encompass transformed relationships and address the systemic obstacles that privilege one group above another to allow the conditions for positive peace (Atkinson, 2013; Nagda et al., 2012). The critiques presented here are relevant to dialogue in face-to-face practice and are also essential to consider when weighing the opportunities for structured dialogic encounters in online environments.

3.2 Online Dialogue-Based Peacebuilding

It is generally agreed within the field of peacebuilding that there should be an embrace of technological advancements that serve the aims and goals of peacebuilding, and the integration of those innovations into practice.[5] The ubiquitous nature of internet-based technologies uniquely positions it to enable the engagement of individuals in grassroots peacebuilding. The widespread accessibility of the internet provides a means of empowerment to engage in issues that are relevant to everyday lives and provides a platform for citizen activism, knowledge sharing, and collaboration. This grassroots capacity allows access for voices into broader conversations where before those voices may have been inaccessible or silenced.

Online technology affords many conveniences and brings value to dialogue-based peacebuilding practices such as efficiency, affordability, and the ability for initiatives to be located within geographically diverse

---

[5] For more on technology integration into peacebuilding see: Best (2013), Peace Direct (2020), Hattotuwa (2004), Kahl and Puig Larrauri (2013), Manojlovic (2018), Miklian and Hoelscher (2017), Roy and Kundu (2017) Schumann et al., (2017), Tellidis and Kappler (2016), White et al. (2015b).

communities. Situations of ongoing violent conflict are especially fraught with challenges such as remote or segregated geography, language, permits and visas, blockades, and threats of violence, which create barriers to face-to-face meetings and would especially benefit from technology to maintain dialogic engagement when in-person encounters are nearly impossible (Amichai-Hamburger et al., 2015; Ellis & Maoz, 2007; Lev-On & Lissitsa, 2015). Studies across many fields demonstrate that online or virtual spaces provide an opportunity for people to create relationships that transcend their physical boundaries (Hasler & Amichai-Hamburger, 2013; McKenna et al., 2002).

Online Peacebuilding Models

While, as examined earlier in this chapter, there is a vast body of literature to support an understanding of the nature and impacts of dialogue as a peacebuilding practice, the topic of online dialogue in peacebuilding is relatively under-researched. In this section, I look at the existing knowledge related to online-based peacebuilding practices, including dialogue approaches, educational models, contact hypothesis online, and game theory, to provide a conception of online dialogue and its potential contribution to peacebuilding practice.

Dialogue models.

The majority of literature related to online dialogue-based peacebuilding practices is predicated on an unstructured dialogue approach—encounters based on either a model of practice or dialogue theory, without a guiding framework or facilitation structure.[6] These examples illustrate that, at a community level, the internet is being utilized as a means for connecting individuals and groups of people with those who are *other* to them especially in those circumstances where face-to-face meetings are fraught with political challenges and risks to physical security (Baraaz, 2015). There is an implicit belief within these models that, by encountering *other*, the perspectives and understanding of each individual will evolve (Amichai-Hamburger et al., 2015), and feelings of trust and understanding will

---

[6] Examples include Peace Factory (Amichai-Hamburger et al., (2015), Sechrist (2014), and Todd (2017), Tweeting Arabs (Mor et al., 2016), YaLa Young Leaders ("YaLa," 2016) and Other Voice (Baraaz, 2015; Chaitin, 2012; Roberts, 2009; Witte & Booth, 2014).

take root (Chaitin, 2012). This collection of literature, although minimal, suggests that friendships can be created and sustained through dialogic encounters online and that, to some extent, these encounters can catalyze into grassroots movement or activism. However, there is also evidence that within unstructured encounters, participants can fall into debate or argument rather than constructive dialogue—these interactions based on debate risk individuals further entrenching their pre-existing narratives of *other* (White, Harvey, & Abu-Rayya, 2015b).

Existing research related to structured and sustained dialogue models in online settings is very thin. Some models of virtual exchange, such as the Soliya Connect (which provides the setting for the research study discussed in this book) and the Sharing Perspectives Foundation programs (Peace Direct, 2020), provide examples of a sustained, structured dialogue program for peacebuilding purposes, while overlapping with research in the field of education and learning. The Soliya program provides an example of an online exchange platform based on dialogic principles (Kampf & Cuhadar, 2015). Drawing from a peacebuilding framework (Helm, 2018), Soliya Connect aims to "empower young adults from different societies to establish more cooperative and compassionate relations between their societies" (Kahl & Puig Larrauri, 2013, p. 10). In discussing Soliya from an American viewpoint, Klein et al. (2018) describe the program as a:

> track III diplomatic dialogue [focused on] exploring the relationship between 'the West' and 'the Muslim World.; ...In a contemporary American context, rampant with acute Islamophobia and where communities are socialized to dehumanize 'the other,' the Soliya insertion/immersion effort provides opportunities for students to build peer relationships across the Muslim majority world and beyond. (pp. 272–273)

Existing research related to the Soliya program includes Helm's, 2018 book, *Emerging Identities in Virtual Exchange,* which explores the topic of "identity as it emerges in interaction in a specific virtual exchange context" (p. 26). Further research includes Ross's, 2012 study exploring norms as a linkage between process and outcomes in dialogue programs. Ross's study provides insight into how "implicit and explicit" norms shape the dialogue encounters in Soliya. These norms are fluid and can shift dependent on "changes in the structure of a dialogue intervention or in its framing" (Ross, 2012, p. 215), while Helm offers means for "exploring identities as they emerge in online interactions" (p. 28). More generally, there is some literature related to language learning and attitudes towards language practices within both the Soliya context and the broader context of virtual exchange (Helm & Acconcia, 2019; O'Dowd, 2011), as well as research linking Soliya, and virtual exchange, to the study of global citizenship within the field of positive psychology (Roberts et al., 2013).[7]

Education-based online peacebuilding.

The above literature related to Soliya as a virtual exchange program is inter-related to the field of online education, and specifically online peace education. Within peacebuilding literature, there are several examples relevant to this research inquiry.[8] The outcomes of these studies and initiatives illustrate the reduction of prejudice amongst out-groups and the ability for friendships to develop between identity group members—although the friendships did not appear to be sustained post-program (Hoter et al., 2012). There was also increased awareness of the other culture and customs (Kampf, 2011), and increased comfort with diversity and difference (White et al., 2015b). Specific to the virtual nature of the interactions, participants reported feeling more confident, secure, and genuine in their interactions (Kampf, 2011), as well as "a greater sense of equality, and a greater ability to be more open and express their feelings in a constructive manner, as opposed to if they had just been asked to work together in a [face-to-face] context" (White et al., 2015b, p. 133).

Contact hypothesis online, computer-mediated communication, and e-contact.

As discussed earlier in this chapter, the study of Contact Hypothesis is robust and has demonstrated that contact can positively influence perceptions of *other* and reduce prejudice. Research on the employment of the

---

[7] Further examples of online dialogue programs include: wedialog.net (Selvanathan et al., 2019), Platform4Dialogue (Peace Direct, 2020), and 'Feeling Close from a Distance,' which offered a hybrid model of both online and face-to-face encounters (Yablon, 2007).

[8] Examples of online peace education include: Trust Building in Online Collaborative Environments (TOCE) (see: Ahmad & Hoter, 2019; Amichai-Hamburger et al., 2015; Hoter et al., 2012; Kampf, 2011; White et al., 2015b), Dissolving Boundaries (Amichai-Hamburger et al., 2015; Austin, 2006; Rickard, Grace, Austin, & Smyth, 2014; White et al., 2015b), Peace Gong in India (Roy & Kundu, 2017), and YaLa Academy("YaLa," 2016).

Contact Hypothesis in online environments is a growing field of inquiry—as dialogue practices often find their origins in the Contact Hypothesis, this offers a valuable area of exploration. Contact Hypothesis online has also been termed Computer-Mediated Communication (CMC) and e-Contact. Research conducted in this field helps understand how contact through the internet can impact perceptions and biases of *other* (White et al., 2015a).[9] Implementing Contact Hypothesis online has several positive outcomes, such as increasing knowledge of *other* (Kampf, 2011), establishing friendly interactions, and changing participants' perceptions of *other* in positive directions (Yablon & Katz, 2001). In their review of the literature in this field, Hasler and Amichai-Hamburger (2013) found that "when given enough time, online contact was equally suitable to promote cross-group friendships, and often resulted in more intimate relationships over time than [face-to-face] contact" (p. 225).

Further to these outcomes, a great deal of the literature related to Contact Hypothesis online argues that the anxiety participants often feel when encountering the *other* in a face-to-face environment can result in an unwillingness or inability of participants to reveal themselves and that the internet is a viable means of mitigating that anxiety. When participants engage online, they can exert control over several key psychological factors to mitigate the anxiety they might otherwise experience in person, such as "anonymity, control over the physical exposure, control over the interaction...universal and constant availability and accessibility of the Internet, [and] equality" (Amichai-Hamburger et al., 2015, p. 517). Research in this field also found that participants are more inclined to self-disclosure online because of the higher level of anonymity and protection against judgment from others available to them (McKenna et al., 2009). Additionally, McKenna et al. (2002) found that women formed deeper and more intimate relationships over the internet than their male counterparts, indicating online encounters aimed at women may have a more significant impact. Online interactions present a unique opportunity for addressing the issues of inequality presented in the earlier critiques of face-to-face dialogue practice. By removing the visual indicators of social

---

[9] For examples of Contact Hypothesis Online see: Amichai-Hamburger (2012), Amichai-Hamburger et al., (2015), Ellis and Maoz (2007), Kampf (2011), McKenna et al., (2009), Mollov and Schwartz (2010), White et al. (2015b, 2018), and Yablon and Katz (2001).

status or privilege, participants can engage with each other from a place of greater equality (Hasler & Amichai-Hamburger, 2013).

Games-based online peacebuilding.

The final relevant grouping of literature I will discuss is the growing field of games within online peacebuilding.[10] Most commonly, these games are used as an educational tool, to provide context, insight, and information to players about the conflict and the other side. Studies on these games confirm that participants leave with increased knowledge and in cases where third parties to the conflict were playing, they left with a more balanced view of the conflict (Cuhadar & Kampf, 2014; Kampf & Stolero, 2018). Several games are designed so that players must collaborate towards the shared goal of successful completion of the game; this cooperation allows players to interact with members of the out-group positively when they otherwise would not have such an opportunity (Kampf, 2011, 2014).

The collection of above literature related to online dialogue, online education for peace, Contact Hypothesis, and games for peace serve to demonstrate the potential of the internet as a means for peacebuilding practice. However, existing research also leaves many gaps for further investigation, which will be outlined later in this chapter.

Critiques of Online Dialogue for Peacebuilding

While the accessibility of the internet offers an enticing promise from a logistical perspective, questions remain regarding the effectiveness of virtual encounters, particularly in comparison to face-to-face programs. Critiques of the concept of online dialogue for peacebuilding include assertions of the need to meet face-to-face to be effective. Additionally,

---

[10] Examples of games in online peacebuilding include: PeaceMaker (Cuhadar & Kampf, 2014; Kampf, 2011; Kampf, 2014), Games for Peace (Amichai-Hamburger et al., 2015; Manojlovic, 2018), Peace App (Manojlovic, 2018; United Nations Alliance of Civilizations, 2014), Global Conflicts (Kampf & Cuhadar, 2015; Kampf & Stolero, 2018), and Sambaza Peace Game (Kahl & Puig Larrauri, 2013).

there are concerns about issues of accessibility, participant safety, language barriers, and the superficiality of the relationships formed.

Face-to-face.

Much of the literature on this topic either explicitly or implicitly states that dialogue must be a face-to-face encounter to be effective (Lefranc, 2012; Senesh, 2012). There is a valid argument that an element of physical movement is a prerequisite for authentic dialogue (Bryn, 2015). There is a belief that the physical act of "moving people from their side of the divide to a space that they temporarily share with the 'other'" (Feller & Ryan, 2012, p. 357) provides the impetus for future physical movement within the broader society, such as "shared community-building efforts, social interests, cultural production, and learning" (p. 357). The concept of physical movement is often embodied in dialogue-based programs, such as camps or summits, that take participants out of their community and transposes them into a more 'neutral' environment.

However, there are also critiques levelled at the practice of removing participants from their home communities and supplanting them in a new place for the duration of an encounter program (Ross, 2014). In these scenarios of removed locations, the changes that may occur within individuals are not always sustained when participants return to their homes, families, and communities and are confronted with narratives that are now at odds with how they perceive and understand *other*. This dissonance can be challenging to navigate, and thus the impact of the dialogue experience dilutes over time (Gawerc, 2006; Ross, 2014). Engaging online could allow participants to integrate their dialogic experiences into their day-to-day realities directly. Grappling with the cognitive dissonance immediately may allow for greater sustainability of outcomes in participants as their changing views of self, and *other* integrate an awareness of daily realities and pressures.

While physical movement can be a powerful component of in-person dialogue, it cannot always be realized with physical obstacles such as occupation, ongoing violence, and financial restraints. Even in post-conflict scenarios, there remain challenges in bringing out-groups together, such as continuing societal segregation (Žeželj et al., 2017). In speaking of *action,* Weiman (2008) says, "dialogue is not real unless it involves intense action: a generosity of spirit, open communication, and the formation of relationships. ... Trust is the desired outcome that indicates dialogue done well" (pp. 88–89). The description of action provided by Weiman evokes the notion of internal versus physical action. Although physical movement may have allowed the context for the internal action to take place, ultimately, dialogue is an internal movement towards *other*. It may be that the same cognitive movement that occurs in face-to-face dialogic encounters can be realized in the absence of the physical. Therefore, the question becomes, if it is physically unrealistic to engage with *other*, is there another means by which that encounter can occur?

Accessibility.

There are several accessibility limitations to using internet technology for dialogic encounters such as infrastructure, the digital divide, literacy, and language (Peace Direct, 2020). Internet accessibility is increasing, but access remains far from universal, with a 59% global penetration rate (Clement, 2020). In addition to infrastructure barriers to access, further concerns are contributing to the digital divide, such as economics, gender, age, and education (Ghobadi & Ghobadi, 2015; Royal, 2005). Socio-economic concerns limit access, as physical technology such as laptops and desktop computers can be expensive to purchase and costly to repair (Johnson, 2010). An argument has been made in the literature to focus on mobile technology platforms for peace and development initiatives, as these are far more ubiquitous and affordable on a global scale. Further access considerations include the role of gender in specific contexts (Johnson, 2010; Royal, 2005), the age of participants (Johnson, 2010), along with physical and cognitive ableness that can enact restrictions on usage (Dobransky & Hargittai, 2006; Warschauer & Newhart, 2016). Finally, reading and digital literacy are additional considerations for access. Attention must be given to these, amongst other concerns, in applying an online framework to dialogue encounters to identify limitations for scope, mitigate challenges, and increase inclusivity.

Safety & misunderstandings.

As with any form of contact program, there are safety considerations to account for, especially in situations of ongoing conflict and violence. There can easily be a perception that by coming together with the *other*, you are betraying your identity group. This perception of betrayal puts participants at risk of attack from other members of their group if not carefully mitigated. For example, in the case of the Good Neighbors project, participants raised concerns that by engaging with *other* in an online public forum such as blogs, they might be targeted for violence (McKenna et al., 2009). This fear of violence or reprisals extends to the threat of cyber-surveillance or cyber-violence from the state or national security apparatus (Peace Direct, 2020). In text-based encounters, there is also the risk that content will be misinterpreted (Bound, 2010; Kampf, 2011). In situations of ongoing violent conflict, misunderstandings can create dangerous implications for physical safety. The advantage of online spaces is that they can be created in such a way as to allow for privacy so that participants are not easily put at risk of being exposed. Thoughtfulness must be given to the design of the program with deep consideration and attention to participant's needs and concerns, given each unique context to ensure safety.

Language.

Intergroup encounters, in both face-to-face and online settings, should be concerned with language restrictions as a barrier to positive outcomes. In a face-to-face environment, participants whose first languages are different often rely on an interpreter or participate in a language that is not their first and may even be the dominant language of the majority participants, further emphasizing structural power imbalances. Language concerns also apply in online environments as participants may not speak the same language with fluency and therefore feel at a disadvantage in representing themselves accurately (Bali, 2014). These language barriers may impose restrictions on the potential demographics of participants for online dialogue, as it is critical that each individual feels they can accurately represent themselves, their thoughts, and their reflections. While some researchers have pointed to simultaneous text translation tools as an option for addressing language challenges, translation technology is not yet advanced enough to provide the nuance required for transformational dialogue experiences.

Superficiality of relationships.

A consideration within the literature also provides the caution that online encounters or forums can generate a shallow level of engagement from participants (Salter et al., 2017). This superficiality could impact the effectiveness of online dialogue for peacebuilding if participants are not able to truly engage with *other* and build relationships that transform into action. In online environments, participants can determine how much of themselves they reveal, as previously explored, this can be useful as a means of mitigating power dynamics and anxiety. However, on the contrasting side, it can also pose an obstacle to fully encounter *other* in a meaningful way.

As the examination of face-to-face dialogue practices revealed, there are always risks associated with bringing together people across differences and divides. These encounters risk a further entrenchment existing identities and perception of *other*—that they will not fully engage to be *seen* and to *see* the *other*. Just as careful thought must be given to this risk in face-to-face settings, it is also an essential consideration in the study of online encounters.

3.3 Gaps

While the collection of literature reviewed in this chapter provides an initial understanding of models of peacebuilding in online environments, with specific focus wherever possible on dialogic practices, there remain significant unknowns in this field. The most critical gap, addressed by this book, is the lack of research on sustained and structured dialogue practices in an online setting. More specifically, there is an opportunity to conduct research in online settings of dialogue that include the characteristics of: encountering other, creating safe space, exploring identity and truth, and *relational movement*. Further research is also needed to understand how online encounters translate into action, and the longevity of impact within participants, throughout their communities, and broader society. Additional gaps explored within this research include the participant experience and journey through dialogic encounters—how their identity, perceptions, and narratives shift through the experience (Maoz et al., 2002), and the linkages between these online encounters and the enablement of the conditions for positive peace.

3.4 Summary

This chapter presented synthesized existing literature related to two key areas. The first was an examination of dialogue as track-three, community-based peacebuilding practice, including the identified characteristics of these models, encountering *other*, safe space, exploring issues of identity, an examination of narratives, and *relational movement*. Further consideration was given to the known outcomes of community dialogue peacebuilding initiatives, as well as several critiques of those practices.

The second half of this chapter discussed the existing body of knowledge related to online peacebuilding practices. First, a case was made as to why online settings should be explored and utilized for dialogue-based peace practices. Then, specific focus was given to online dialogue initiatives, peace-education models, the Contact Hypothesis online, and finally, games-based models. This section of the chapter closed with a consideration of potential critiques against using online environments for dialogue peacebuilding practice.

Together, the topics covered in this chapter illustrate the gap in knowledge related to dialogue-based peacebuilding practices online, and their links to positive peace outcomes.

References

Abramovich, D. (2005). Overcoming the cultural barriers of conflict: Dialogue between Israelis and Palestinians, Jews and Muslims. *Journal of Intercultural Studies, 26*(4), 293–313. https://doi.org/10.1080/07256860500270189

Ahmad, M. Y. A., & Hoter, E. (2019). Online collaboration between Israeli Palestinian Arab and Jewish students: Fear and anxiety (Report). *International Journal of Multicultural Education, 21*(1), 62. https://doi.org/10.18251/IJME.V21I1.1726

Allport, G. (1954). *The nature of prejudice*. Addison-Wesley.

Amichai-Hamburger, Y. (2012). Reducing intergroup conflict in the digital age. In H. Giles (Ed.), *The handbook of intergroup communication* (pp. 181–193). Routledge.

Amichai-Hamburger, Y., Hasler, B. S., & Shani-Sherman, T. (2015). Structured and unstructured intergroup contact in the digital age. *Computers in Human Behavior, 52*, 515–522. https://doi.org/10.1016/j.chb.2015.02.022

Arao, B., & Clemens, K. (2013). From safe spaces to brave spaces. In L. M. Landreman (Ed.), *The art of effective facilitation: Reflections from social justice educators* (pp. 135–150). Stylus.

Atkinson, M. (2013). Intergroup dialogue: A theoretical positioning. *Journal of Dialogue Studies, 1*(1), 63–80.

Austin, R. (2006). The role of ICT in bridge-building and social inclusion: Theory, policy and practice issues. *European Journal of Teacher Education, 29*(2), 145–161. https://doi.org/10.1080/02619760600617284

Bali, M. (2014). Why doesn't this feel empowering? The challenges of web-based intercultural dialogue. *Teaching in Higher Education, 19*(2), 208–215. https://doi.org/10.1080/13562517.2014.867620

Bar-Tal, D. (2007). Sociopsychological foundations of intractable conflicts. *American Behavioral Scientist, 50*(11), 1430–1453. https://doi.org/10.1177/0002764207302462

Bar-Tal, D., & Hammack, P. L. (2012). Conflict, delegitimization, and violence. In L. R. Tropp (Ed.), *The Oxford handbook of intergroup conflict* (pp. 29–52). Oxford University Press. https://doi.org/10.1093/oxfordhb/9780199747672.013.0003

Baraaz, T. (2015, July 17). Lone voices. *Jerusalem Post*.

Best, M. L. (2013, April). Peacebuilding in a networked world. *Communications of the ACM, 56*(4), 30–32. https://doi.org/10.1145/2436256.2436265

Bound, H. (2010). Developing quality online dialogue: Dialogical inquiry. *International Journal of Teaching and Learning in Higher Education, 22*(2), 107–119.

Bryn, S. (2015). Can dialogue make a difference?: The experience of the Nansen dialogue network. In S. P. Ramet, A Simkus, & O. Listhaug (Eds.), *Civic and uncivic values in Kosovo* (pp. 365–394). Central European University Press. http://www.jstor.org/stable/10.7829/j.ctt13wzttq.21

Burkhardt-Vetter, O. (2018). Reconciliation in the making: Overcoming competitive victimhood through inter-group Dialogue in Palestine/Israel. In V. Druliolle & R. Brett (Eds.), *The politics of victimhood in post-conflict societies: Comparative and analytical perspectives* (pp. 237–263). Springer International Publishing. https://doi.org/10.1007/978-3-319-70202-5_10

Chaitin, J. (2012). Co-creating peace: Confronting psychosocial-economic injustices in the Israeli-Palestinian context. In B. Charbonneau & G. Parent (Eds.), *Peacebuilding, memory and reconciliation: Bridging top-down and bottom-up approaches* (pp. 146–162). Routledge.

Charbonneau, B., & Parent, G. (2012). *Peacebuilding, memory and reconciliation: Bridging top-down and bottom-up approaches*. Routledge.

Clement, J. (2020, April 24). *Worldwide digital populations as of April 2020*. Statista. https://www.statista.com/statistics/617136/digital-population-worldwide/

Cuhadar, E., & Kampf, R. (2014). Learning about conflict and negotiations through computer simulations: The case of PeaceMaker. *International Studies Perspectives, 15*(4), 509–524. https://doi.org/10.1111/insp.12076

Dessel, A., & Ali, N. (2012). The minds of peace and intergroup dialogue: Two complementary approaches to peace. *Israel Affairs, 18*(1), 123–139. https://doi.org/10.1080/13537121.2012.634276

Dessel, A., & Rogge, M. E. (2008). Evaluation of intergroup dialogue: A review of the empirical literature. *Conflict Resolution Quarterly, 26*(2), 199–238. https://doi.org/10.1002/crq.230

Dobransky, K., & Hargittai, E. (2006). The disability divide in internet access and use. *Information, Communication & Society, 9*(3), 313–334. https://doi.org/10.1080/13691180600751298

Ellis, D. G., & Maoz, I. (2007). Online argument between Israeli Jews and Palestinians. *Human Communication Research, 33*(3), 291–309. https://doi.org/10.1111/j.1468-2958.2007.00300.x

Ellis, D. G., & Maoz, I. (2012). Communication and reconciling intergroup conflict. In H. Giles (Ed.), *The handbook of intergroup communication* (pp. 153–166). Routledge.

Feller, A. E., & Ryan, K. K. (2012). Definition, necessity, and Nansen: Efficacy of dialogue in peacebuilding. *Conflict Resolution Quarterly, 29*(4), 351–380. https://doi.org/10.1002/crq.21049

Frantell, K. A., Miles, J. R., & Ruwe, A. M. (2019). Intergroup dialogue: A review of recent empirical research and its implications for research and practice. *Small Group Research, 50*(5), 654–695. https://doi.org/10.1177/1046496419835923

Gawerc, M. (2006). Peacebuilding: Theoretical and concrete perspectives. *Peace & Change, 31*(4), 435–478. https://doi.org/10.1111/j.1468-0130.2006.00387.x

Gergen, K. J., McNamee, S., & Barrett, F. J. (2001). Toward transformative dialogue. *International Journal of Public Administration, 24*(7–8), 679–707. https://doi.org/10.1081/PAD-100104770

Ghobadi, S., & Ghobadi, Z. (2015). How access gaps interact and shape digital divide: A cognitive investigation. *Behaviour & Information Technology, 34*(4), 330–340. https://doi.org/10.1080/0144929X.2013.833650

Graf, S., Paolini, S., & Rubin, M. (2014). Negative intergroup contact is more influential, but positive intergroup contact is more common: Assessing contact prominence and contact prevalence in five Central European countries. *European Journal of Social Psychology, 44*(6), 536–547. https://doi.org/10.1002/ejsp.2052

Gurin, P., Nagda, B. (Ratnesh) A., & Zúñiga, X. (2013). *Dialogue across difference: Practice, theory, and research on intergroup dialogue*. Russell Safe Foundation.

Hammack, P. L. (2008). Narrative and the cultural psychology of identity. *Personality and Social Psychology Review, 12*(3), 222–247. https://doi.org/10.1177/1088868308316892

Hasler, B. S., & Amichai-Hamburger, Y. (2013). Online intergroup contact. In Y. Amichai-Hamburger (Ed.), *The social net: Understanding our online behavior* (2nd ed., pp. 220–252). Oxford University Press.

Hattotuwa, S. (2004). Untying the Gordian knot: ICT for conflict transformation and peacebuilding. *Dialogue, 2*(2), 39–68.

Helm, F. (2018). *Emerging identities in virtual exchange.* researchpublishing.net.

Helm, F., & Acconcia, G. (2019). Interculturality and language in Erasmus+ Virtual Exchange. *European Journal of Language Policy, 11*(2), 211–233. Liverpool University Press. https://doi.org/10.3828/ejlp.2019.13

Helman, S. (2002). Monologic results of dialogue: Jewish-Palestinian encounter groups as sites of essentialization. *Identities, 9*(3), 327–354. https://doi.org/10.1080/10702890213971

Hoover, J. D. (2011). Dialogue: Our past, our present, our future. *Journal of Intercultural Communication Research, 40*(3), 203–218. https://doi.org/10.1080/17475759.2011.617771

Hoter, E., Shonfeld, M., & Ganayem, A. N. (2012). TEC center: Linking technology, education and cultural diversity. *I-Manager's Journal of Educational Technology, 9*(1), 15–22. https://search.proquest.com/docview/1473901542/abstract/3ED6FD97DD1A4672PQ/1

Johnson, V. (2010). Women and the internet. *Indian Journal of Gender Studies, 17*(1), 151–163. https://doi.org/10.1177/097152150901700107

Kahl, A., & Puig Larrauri, H. (2013). Technology for peacebuilding. *Stability: International Journal of Security and Development, 2*(3), 61, 1–15. https://doi.org/10.5334/sta.cv

Kampf, R. (2011). Internet, conflict and dialogue: The Israeli case. *Israel Affairs, 17*(3), 384–400. https://doi.org/10.1080/13537121.2011.584666

Kampf, R. (2014). Are two better than one? Playing singly, playing in dyads in a computerized simulation of the Israeli-Palestinian conflict. *Computers in Human Behavior, 32*, 9–14. https://doi.org/10.1016/j.chb.2013.11.005

Kampf, R., & Cuhadar, E. (2015). Do computer games enhance learning about conflicts? A cross-national inquiry into proximate and distant scenarios in Global Conflicts. *Computers in Human Behavior, 52*, 541–549. https://doi.org/10.1016/j.chb.2014.08.008

Kampf, R., & Stolero, N. (2018). Learning about the Israeli-Palestinian conflict through computerized simulations: The case of global conflicts. *Social Science Computer Review, 36*(1), 125–134. https://doi.org/10.1177/0894439316683641

Kelleher, A., & Ryan, K. (2012). Successful local peacebuilding in Macedonia: Sustained dialogue in practice. *Peace Research, 44*(1), 63–94. http://www.jstor.org/stable/23607918

Klein, M., Finnegan, A., & Nelson-Palmeyer, J. (2018). Circle of praxis pedagogy for peace studies. *Peace Review: A Journal of Social Justice*, *30*, 270–278. https://doi.org/10.1080/10402659.2018.1495802

Lederach, J. P. (1997). *Building peace: Sustainable reconciliation in divided societies*. United States Institute of Peace Press.

Lefranc, S. (2012). A critique of "bottom-up" peacebuilding: Do peaceful individuals make peaceful societies? In B. Charbonneau & G. Parent (Eds.), *Peacebuilding, memory and reconciliation: Bridging top-down and bottom-up approaches* (pp. 34–52). Routledge.

Lev-On, A., & Lissitsa, S. (2015). Studying the coevolution of social distance, offline- and online contacts. *Computers in Human Behavior*, *48*, 448–456. https://doi.org/10.1016/j.chb.2015.02.009

Manojlovic, B. (2018). The role of innovation in education for sustainable peace. In *Education for Sustainable Peace and Conflict Resilient Communities* (pp. 109–129). Palgrave Macmillan. https://doi.org/10.1007/978-3-319-57171-3_5

Maoz, I. (2000). An experiment in peace: Reconciliation-aimed workshops of Jewish-Israeli and Palestinian youth. *Journal of Peace Research*, *37*(6), 721–736. http://www.jstor.org/stable/424756

Maoz, I. (2011). Does contact work in protracted asymmetrical conflict? Appraising 20 years of reconciliation-aimed encounters between Israeli Jews and Palestinians. *Journal of Peace Research*, *48*(1), 115–125. https://doi.org/10.1177/0022343310389506

Maoz, I., Steinberg, S., Bar-On, D., & Fakhereldeen, M. (2002). The dialogue between the "Self" and the "Other": A process analysis of Palestinian-Jewish encounters in Israel. *Human Relations*, *55*(8), 931–962. https://doi.org/10.1177/0018726702055008178

McKenna, K. Y. A., Green, A. S., & Gleason, M. E. J. (2002). Relationship formation on the internet: What's the big attraction? *Journal of Social Issues*, *58*(1), 9–31. https://doi.org/10.1111/1540-4560.00246

McKenna, K. Y. A., Samuel-Azran, T., & Sutton-Balaban, N. (2009). Virtual meetings in the Middle East: Implementing the contact hypothesis on the internet. *The Israel Journal of Conflict Resolution*, *1*(1), 63–86.

Meleady, R., & Forder, L. (2018). When contact goes wrong: Negative intergroup contact promotes generalized out-group avoidance. *Group Processes & Intergroup Relations*, *00*, 1–20. https://doi.org/10.1177/1368430218761568

Miklian, J., & Hoelscher, K. (2017). A new research approach for peace innovation. *Innovation and Development*, 1–19https://doi.org/10.1080/2157930X.2017.1349580

Mollov, M. B., & Schwartz, D. G. (2010). Towards an integrated strategy for intercultural dialog: Computer-mediated communication and face to face.

Journal of Intercultural Communication Research, 39(3), 207–224. https://doi.org/10.1080/17475759.2010.534905

Mor, Y., Ron, Y., & Maoz, I. (2016). "Likes" for peace: Can facebook promote dialogue in the Israeli-Palestinian conflict? *Media and Communication, 4*(1), 15–26. https://doi.org/10.17645/mac.v4i1.298

Nagda, B. R. A., & Gurin, P. (2007). Intergroup dialogue: A critical-dialogic approach to learning about difference, inequality, and social justice. *New Directions for Teaching and Learning, 2007*(111), 35–45. https://doi.org/10.1002/tl.284

Nagda, B. (Ratnesh) A., & Maxwell, K. E. (2011). Deepening the layers of understanding and connection: A critical-dialogic approach to facilitating intergroup dialogues. In K. E. Maxwell, B. (Ratnesh) A. Nagda, & M. C. Thompson (Eds.), *Facilitating intergroup dialogues: Bridging differences, Catalyzing Change* (pp. 1–22). Stylus Publishing LLC.

Nagda, B. R. A., Yeakley, A., Gurin, P., & Sorensen, N. (2012). Intergroup dialogue: A critical-dialogic model for conflict engagement. In L. R. Tropp (Ed.), *The Oxford handbook of intergroup conflict* (pp. 210–228). Oxford University Press. https://doi.org/10.1093/oxfordhb/9780199747672.013.0007

Nolte-Laird, R. (2021). Contact programs and the pursuit of positive peace: Reframing perceptions of equality. In K. Standish, H. Devere, A. E. Suazo, & R. Rafferty (Eds.), *The Palgrave handbook of positive peace* (pp. 1–18). Springer Singapore. https://doi.org/10.1007/978-981-15-3877-3_55-1

O'Dowd, R. (2011). Online foreign language interaction: Moving from the periphery to the core of foreign language education? *Language Teaching, 44*(3), 368–380. Cambridge Core.https://doi.org/10.1017/S0261444810000194

Opotow, S. (2012). The scope of justice, intergroup conflict, and peace. In L. R. Tropp (Ed.), *The Oxford handbook of intergroup conflict* (pp. 72–86). Oxford University Press. https://doi.org/10.1093/oxfordhb/9780199747672.013.0005

Peace Direct. (2020). *Digital pathways for peace: Insights and lessons from a global online consultation.* https://www.peacedirect.org/wp-content/uploads/2020/08/PD-LVP-Tech-Report.pdf

Pettigrew, T. F., & Tropp, L. R. (2011). *When groups meet: The dynamics of intergroup contact.* Psychology Press.

Pettigrew, T. F., Tropp, L. R., Wagner, U., & Christ, O. (2011). Recent advances in intergroup contact theory. *International Journal of Intercultural Relations, 35*(3), 271–280. https://doi.org/10.1016/j.ijintrel.2011.03.001

Phipps, A. (2014). 'They are bombing now': 'Intercultural Dialogue' in times of conflict. *Language and Intercultural Communication, 14*(1), 108–124. https://doi.org/10.1080/14708477.2013.866127

Pilecki, A., & Hammack, P. (2014). Negotiating the past, imagining the future: Israeli and Palestinian narratives in intergroup dialog. *International Journal of Intercultural Relations, 43*, 100–113.

Rickard, A., Grace, A., Austin, R., & Smyth, J. (2014). Assessing impact of ICT intercultural work. *International Journal of Information and Communication Technology Education, 10*(3), 1–18. https://doi.org/10.4018/ijicte.2014070101

Riddle, K. C. (2017). Structural violence, intersectionality, and justpeace: Evaluating women's peacebuilding agency in Manipur India. *Hypatia, 32*(3), 574–592. https://doi.org/10.1111/hypa.12340

Roberts, D. C., Welch, L., & Al-Khanji, K. (2013). Preparing global citizens. *Journal of College and Character, 14*(1), 85–92. https://doi.org/10.1515/jcc-2013-0012

Roberts, J. (2009, January 13). 500 citizens of Sderot contradict the Israeli government. *Palestine Chronicle*.

Ron, Y., & Maoz, I. (2013). Dangerous stories: Encountering narratives of the other in the Israeli-Palestinian conflict. *Peace and Conflict: Journal of Peace Psychology, 19*(3), 281–294. https://doi.org/10.1037/a0033686

Ron, Y., & Maoz, I. (2013). Peacemaking through dialogue? Effects of intergroup dialogue on perceptions regarding the resolution of the Israeli-Palestinian conflict. *Dynamics of Asymmetric Conflict, 6*(1–3), 75–89. https://doi.org/10.1080/17467586.2013.861918

Ropers, N. (2004). From resolution to transformation: The role of dialogue projects. In A. Austin, M. Fischer, & N. Ropers (Eds.), *Transforming ethnopolitical conflict. The Berghof handbook* (pp. 255–269). VS Verlag. https://doi.org/10.1007/978-3-663-05642-3_13

Ross, K. (2012). Linking process to outcome: Implicit norms in a cross-cultural dialogue program. *Peace and Conflict Studies, 19*(2), 193–218.

Ross, K. (2014). Narratives of belonging (and not): Inter-group contact in Israel and the formation of ethno-national identity claims. *International Journal of Intercultural Relations, 42*, 38–52. https://doi.org/10.1016/j.ijintrel.2014.07.002

Ross, K. (2015). Quality as critique: Promoting critical reflection among youth in structured encounter programs. *Journal of Peace Education, 12*(2), 117–137. https://doi.org/10.1080/17400201.2014.979400

Ross, K. (2017). *Youth encounter programs in Israel: Pedagogy, identity, and social change*. Syracuse University Press.

Ross, K., & Lazarus, N. (2015). Tracing the long-term impacts of a generation of Israeli-Palestinian youth encounters. *International Journal of Conflict Engagement, 3*(2), 116–135.

Roy, S., & Kundu, D. V. (2017). Promoting youth participation for peace and intercultural dialogue through new media and digital literacy. *Research Expo International Multidisciplinary Research Journal*, *VII*(VII), 48–55.

Royal, C. (2005). A meta-analysis of journal articles intersecting issues of internet and gender. *Journal of Technical Writing and Communication*, *35*(4), 403–429. https://doi.org/10.2190/3RBM-XKEQ-TRAF-E8GN

Saguy, T., Tausch, N., Dovidio, J. F., & Pratto, F. (2009). The irony of harmony: Intergroup contact can produce false expectations for equality. *Psychological Science*, *20*(1), 114. https://doi.org/10.1111/j.1467-9280.2008.02261.x

Salter, S., Douglas, T., & Kember, D. (2017). Comparing face-to-face and asynchronous online communication as mechanisms for critical reflective dialogue. *Educational Action Research*, *25*(5), 790–805. https://doi.org/10.1080/09650792.2016.1245626

Saunders, H. H. (2011). *Sustained dialogue in conflicts: Transformation and change*. Palgrave Macmillan.

Schumann, S., Klein, O., Douglas, K., & Hewstone, M. (2017). When is computer-mediated intergroup contact most promising? Examining the effect of out-group members' anonymity on prejudice. *Computers in Human Behavior*, *77*, 198–210. https://doi.org/10.1016/j.chb.2017.08.006

Sechrist, C. (2014, March). Finding inspiration in Israel. *HOW*, 154+. http://link.galegroup.com/apps/doc/A359733551/PPFA?u=otago&sid=PPFA&xid=aa4257f0

Selvanathan, H. P., Leidner, B., Petrović, N., Prelić, N., Ivanek, I., Krugel, J., & Bjekić, J. (2019). Wedialog.net: A quantitative field test of the effects of online intergroup dialogue in promoting justice- versus harmony-oriented outcomes in Bosnia and Serbia. *Peace and Conflict: Journal of Peace Psychology*, *25*(4), 287–299. https://doi.org/10.1037/pac0000395

Senesh, D. (2012). Restorative moments: From First Nations people in Canada to conflicts in an Israeli-Palestinian dialogue group. In B. Charbonneau & G. Parent (Eds.), *Peacebuilding, memory and reconciliation: Bridging top-down and bottom-up approaches* (pp. 163–175). Routledge.

Steinberg, G. M. (2013). The limits of peacebuilding theory. In R. Mac Ginty (Ed.), *Routledge handbook of peacebuilding* (pp. 36–53). Routledge.

Tajfel, H., & Turner, J. C. (1986). The social identity theory of intergroup behavior. *Political Psychology*.

Tapper, A. J. H. (2013). A pedagogy of social justice education: Social identity theory, intersectionality, and empowerment. *Conflict Resolution Quarterly*, *30*(4), 411–445. https://doi.org/10.1002/crq.21072

Tellidis, I., & Kappler, S. (2016). Information and communication technologies in peacebuilding: Implications, opportunities and challenges. *Cooperation and Conflict*, *51*(1), 75–93. https://doi.org/10.1177/0010836715603752

Todd, D. (2017, February 10). Peace Factory brings its message to UBC; Social media network fosters dialogue over thorny Israel-Middle East conflict. *The Vancouver Sun.*, p. A.11. http://vancouversun.com/news/local-news/peace-factory-brings-middle-east-campaign-to-vancouver

United Nations Alliance of Civilizations. (2014, December). PEACEapp winners announced! http://www.unaoc.org/peaceapp-blog/peaceapp-winnersannounced/

Ungerleider, J. (2012). Structured youth dialogue to empower peacebuilding and leadership. *Conflict Resolution Quarterly, 29*(4), 381–402. https://doi.org/10.1002/crq.21046

Warschauer, M., & Newhart, V. (2016). Broadening our concepts of universal access. *Universal Access in the Information Society, 15*(2), 183–188. https://doi.org/10.1007/s10209-015-0417-0

Weiman, R. (2008). The power of hope. *Journal of Ecumenical Studies, 43*(2), 87–97.

White, F. A., Abu-Rayya, H. M., Bliuc, A.-M., & Faulkner, N. (2015). Emotion expression and intergroup bias reduction between Muslims and Christians: Long-term Internet contact. *Computers in Human Behavior, 53*, 435–442.

White, F. A., Harvey, L. J., & Abu-Rayya, H. M. (2015). Improving intergroup relations in the internet age: A critical review. *Review of General Psychology, 19*(2), 129–139. https://doi.org/10.1037/gpr0000036

White, F. A., Turner, R. N., Verrelli, S., Harvey, L. J., & Hanna, J. R. (2018). Improving intergroup relations between Catholics and Protestants in Northern Ireland via E-contact. *European Journal of Social Psychology.* https://doi.org/10.1002/ejsp.2515

Witte, G., & Booth, W. (2014, July 12). Unlikely friendship blossoms across front lines in Israel and Gaza. *The Washington Post.*

Yablon, Y. B. (2007). Feeling close from a distance: Peace encounters via internet technology. *New Directions for Youth Development, 2007*(116), 99–107. https://doi.org/10.1002/yd.237

Yablon, Y. B., & Katz, Y. J. (2001). Internet-based group relations: A high school peace education project in Israel. *Educational Media International, 38*(2–3), 175–182. https://doi.org/10.1080/09523980110043591

YaLa new media & citizen journalism leaders to receive 2016 IIE Victor J. Goldberg prize for peace in the Middle East. (2016, June 2). *Targeted News Service.*

Zartman, J. (2008). Negotiation, exclusion and durable peace: Dialogue and peacebuilding in Tajikistan. *International Negotiation, 13*(1), 55–72. https://doi.org/10.1163/138234008X297931

Žeželj, I. L., Ioannou, M., Franc, R., Psaltis, C., & Martinovic, B. (2017). The role of inter-ethnic online friendships in prejudice reduction in post-conflict societies: Evidence from Serbia, Croatia and Cyprus. *Computers in Human Behavior, 76*, 3.

CHAPTER 4

Bringing Into

The following four chapters present and discuss the findings that emerged out of the qualitative research study presented in this book. The findings are presented within an overarching narrative encompassing: what the participant brought into the encounter, what happened in the encounter, and what shifted as a result. A visual illustration of the conceptualization of this narrative is shown in Fig. 4.1. In alignment with this overarching storyline, the following chapters will each present a portion of the narrative. This current chapter will encompass the element of 'bringing into,' providing an introduction to the research participants, including their motivations for engaging in the dialogue program, their expectations of the experience, and their pre-existing narratives.

This chapter intends to introduce you, the reader, to the distinct group of individuals who comprised the participant group in this research project. The fullness of this research project would not have been possible without their involvement. Their willingness to engage in open and thoughtful conversations took vulnerability. I consider their participation to be a true act of generosity. I provided each participant the option of being named in the research or being provided a pseudonym. As a result, some of the participant names have been changed to preserve the anonymity of the participant.

While there are essentially two distinct groups of research participants as defined by their role in the Soliya program, those of facilitators and

© The Author(s), under exclusive license to Springer Nature Singapore Pte Ltd. 2022
R. Nolte-Laird, *Peacebuilding Online*,
https://doi.org/10.1007/978-981-16-6013-9_4

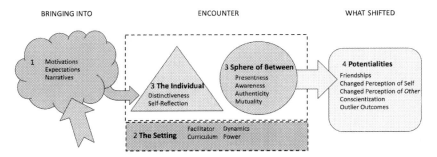

Fig. 4.1 Location of Chapter 4 in overarching narrative & the content of each findings chapter

those of participants, I will attempt to avoid strict binary distinctions between the two roles as it relates to their participation in the research. For both groups of people, regardless of role, the involvement within a space of dialogic encounter positioned each individual for the possibility of personal impact. As such, even though facilitators have a different viewpoint of the dialogue encounter, I wanted to ensure all possible findings were reflected in these pages, and that valuable reflections were not missed. However, at times a division will be necessary. So, with that in mind, I will introduce these groups of people separately and then seek to interweave them in my descriptions where possible.

4.1 Introducing the Participants

The research group comprised 24 individuals, 13 people engaged as facilitators and 11 who were participants in the Soliya programs. In describing those within the participant role cohort of this research, it would be easy to make a one-dimensional statement, such as 'they are all students' and it would be factually accurate. However, such an oversimplification would be a disservice to you, as the reader, and also to the participants and me as the researcher as it would ignore the nuanced identity of each individual, identities which inform how each person shows up in the dialogue space. While they are all students, they come to this experience with very different ways of seeing, navigating, and understanding the world. Their academic interests are vast and ranging, from engineering to translation, to business, to literature, to law. How they show up in each conversation is unique. I witnessed how some positioned themselves with a great deal of confidence and vulnerability, with a lack of self-consciousness to what they shared, as if they were not worried about taking up space. Others had a higher degree of timidity—perhaps due to language or other constraints on expression—they were more reserved and took greater prodding to be forthcoming in their comments. Still, others were more technical in their reflections, as if the conversation in and of itself was an academic exercise, which in some ways perhaps it was, for both of us. I sensed, although they never explicitly stated, that there were different motivations in accepting my invitation into this research. For some, it seemed this was simply a chance to share what had been, for them, a meaningful experience. For others, my research seemed to offer the opportunity to practice English language skills further—an opportunity which is not one quickly passed by for those who are seeking to work or live in the English-speaking world. Others shared explicitly that this was the chance to connect with a foreign national—and who knows what opportunities can come from that connection? I acknowledge that all these motivations—whether explicit or implicit—had a significant bearing on each conversation and what unfolded in the space between us.

The invitation to join the research was open, I was looking at the unique, individual, experience in the dialogic space and was not particularly concerned with generating participants from distinct geographic locations. However, I hoped some diversity in nationality and gender identities would organically occur.[1] In the end, the participant cohort drew individuals from North Africa and Europe, the majority of whom were in their early twenties. As mentioned earlier, all were University students or recent graduates. Just as the participant role comprised an array of unique individuals, there was also rich diversity in those I spoke to from the facilitator role. The range of age disclosed by the facilitators is more extensive than that of the participant group, from 19 years old and up. The facilitator cohort comes with a great diversity in professional background, and many of them have been Soliya participants at

---

[1] The demographic information included in the following sections was self-disclosed by the participants in our conversations. I did not intentionally collect personal information such as age, gender, religion, or nationality; however, if this information was self-disclosed by the participant it may be included. I also asked each interviewee to indicate which pronouns they preferred me to use when referring to them. As a result, there is a mix of she/her, he/him, and they/them pronoun use dependent on the interviewee's preference.

Table 4.1 Summary of research participants

Name (as used in book)	Geographical Location	Role in Soliya
Asma	Tunisia	Participant
Nidhal	Tunisia	Participant
Sarra	Tunisia	Participant
Oldez	Tunisia	Participant
Mostafa	Egypt	Participant
Duha	Egypt	Participant
Souhail	Morocco	Participant
Layla	Syria/living in Turkey	Participant (taking Facilitator Training)
Jacob	Eastern Europe	Participant
Anna	Italy	Participant
Karoline	Italy	Participant
Rianne	Netherlands	Facilitator
Amanda	United States	Facilitator
Nicolas	Canada	Facilitator
Arij	Tunisia	Facilitator
Beatrix	Hungary/living in Netherlands	Facilitator
Betül	Turkey	Facilitator
Burcu	Turkey	Facilitator
Oya	Turkey	Facilitator
Hassan	Egypt	Facilitator
Mai	Egypt	Facilitator
Joanna	Greece	Facilitator
Marjus	Italy	Facilitator
Mohamed	Libya	Facilitator

some stage. A few facilitators are currently students themselves or, in one case, a recent graduate. And, like many post-graduate students, many of these facilitators are balancing studies with work in their field. Others are further along in their chosen careers, be it engineering, teaching, working for a university, or non-profit. Further participant details are located in Table 4.1.

4.2 "Journey to Soliya"

As one might expect, there were a variety of motivations behind why each participant or facilitator became involved with Soliya. At the forefront of the motivators was a sense that backgrounds and life experiences had led them here or informed their desire to engage in a program like Connect.[2]

"A Marriage Between Two Worlds"

Of the facilitators, several have found this work as an organic evolution of their career development, interests, training, and expertise. For example, Amanda[3] comments:

> My journey to Soliya was really a match between my background in conflict resolution and mediation ... Specifically, dealing with areas of civil rights. So, I would work a lot with cases in regard to discrimination in the later part of my conflict resolution and mediation career. And I came across an informational piece in regard to online facilitation, which, I had a lot of experience in facilitation in a non-virtual environment. I wanted to be able to learn how to do this specific type of facilitation for this program, especially because of the changes in the global dialogue between the greater Western societies and Muslim societies, it was a great attraction to me, especially where I saw the influence in the civil rights cases that we were receiving in regards to discrimination and I thought there has to be a better way to deal with this from a people-to-people connection. So that's what really piqued my interest, so it was kind of like a marriage between two worlds, the work that I was doing on a daily basis at the local level to take that to a different context, to global discussions. (Amanda, Facilitator)

In Amanda's recollection of the career journey that brought her to Soliya, you can hear the undercurrents of her values—motivators that reveal an

---

[2] As discussed in Chapter 1, during the time I conducted this research, there were two streams of Connect programs; the flagship Connect Global (8 weeks) and Connect Express (4 weeks).

[3] Participant names are a combination of real names and pseudonyms.

excitement for this work and a desire to learn and develop skills that support that passion. This notion of significance or deep interest that draws people to online dialogue facilitation surfaced with others when speaking of their background. For example, Marjus was interested in the program because his parents were immigrants. For him, coming from an immigrant family established a lifelong interest in intercultural dialogue, and he saw this program as a prospect to develop skills around that topic:

> Actually, I have a passion about intercultural dialogue that started years ago, and as I told you I also have an immigrant background from my parents, so that means I was also interested about this topic since I was a child... Here I can see that I can practice it, and I can increase my expertise on the topic as well, it can benefit me, it can also benefit others. (Marjus, Facilitator)

Layla also reflected on how her life experiences sparked a curiosity to join the program. She saw Connect as an opportunity to explore how others, especially those from Europe, felt about issues related to refugees and meet people who could provide insight on the perspectives of those in the receiving countries towards refugees and immigrants:

> I was really interested also in the idea of integration of refugees and there are a number of Syrians in Germany, and in Europe in general. So, I felt that I want to have more hands-on experience, like the near experience of this problem—not a problem but this challenge, and how they see it in both ways... The locals, the Europeans, and the refugees from other parts of the world, Syrians, Iraqis, Africans...Pakistanis, we hear about Afghanis who also migrate, or trying to immigrate to Europe. So, I mean, it was the main interest in the subject and a way to get near and have more sense of the challenge. (Layla, Participant)

Layla's interest in these viewpoints on refugees stemmed from her familial experiences, as her sister lives in Germany after feeling forced to leave Syria:

> What is really interesting also is that my sister and brother are in Germany, and they are kind of refugees, not

legally as refugees but they have this limited protection residency…but they felt (*pause*) my sister, she herself felt like a refugee because she was forced to go out. She had her decision to marry and go there after her husband, but she made that decision on the basis that she was politically active before, and she wasn't really feeling safe in the country… So, she felt she can have that safety outside the country. (Layla, Participant)

Layla's motivation to understand the views of her fellow group members, who come from countries in Europe that might be receiving immigrants or refugees, informed what she brought forward into those conversations. Layla commented in our conversation that she would draw, at points throughout the Connect program, on her sister's experience to bring this topic forward in the group setting.

In addition to background motivators, several facilitators spoke to their experiences as a participant in the program acting as a catalyst for becoming a facilitator. Nicolas reflects on the personal growth he experienced through participation, using the language of "breakthrough moments" to evoke radical shifts in his perspectives. This experience meant so much to him that he prioritizes the commitment of taking on the facilitator role even amidst a demanding personal schedule:

I would say it was my own experience as a participant, my own personal breakthrough moments leading me to become a more open, more mature individual. I saw so much value in the growth throughout only eight weeks. And I found it important, I told myself that if I can have that same impact on other people that would be marvelous so (*pause*) I am someone who naturally looks for new opportunities to jump in, even if my schedule gets crowded sometimes. I saw it as a whole new project to embark on with a goal that was meaningful. (Nicolas, Facilitator)

Similarly, for Hassan, facilitating became about creating space for others to experience a significant encounter just as he did when he was a participant:

I think I had different motivations when I came, I was not thinking about being a facilitator, but I liked what we did. Maybe I had an experience from before, but what we had in Soliya was very different, so it just got me interested in being a part of this great work, you know?... I just wished that I could help as many people as possible to have the same experience. That's why I decided to join the facilitation training and then become a facilitator. (Hassan, Facilitator)

For many facilitators, taking on this role was a distinct decision on their part, one that culminated from various factors leading them to this point in their careers. In this way, the narrative related to "the journey" to Soliya was different dependent on the role of each individual; for most participants the decision to join felt less significant or meaningful in the overall scheme of their lives in contrast to facilitators.

"Try Something New with Different People"

While some motivators for participation emanated from their pasts—factors that, in a sense, led them to this role—others drew their motivation from what they wanted from their future. They shared a sense of curiosity and opening up to new opportunities through this experience. Many saw Soliya as an occasion to meet people from other places. For several, this was a rare opportunity to be exposed to different cultures and backgrounds. For example, Duha shared that their community in Egypt does not contain a vast amount of diversity, so they saw Soliya as a chance they had not had before to meet people from varied backgrounds:

Well actually I don't live in a multi-cultural community, all the people surrounding me are Egyptian, so I wanted to try to have a conversation or be connected to people from other countries because maybe in the future I will travel to another country, so it wouldn't be a new thing for me. (Duha, Participant)

Similarly, Oldez (Participant) found this to be a rare opportunity to meet people from other countries and explore new topics: "the important thing that I found exciting was to meet people around the world and to talk about things that we usually don't have the occasion to talk about it." Several people mentioned that meeting new people and exploring different cultures has always been an area of interest for them, but that they have not had much exposure or opportunity to delve into this interest area.

For a few, they were simply looking for something to occupy their time and the program aligned with their interests:

> Okay, I said that I had nothing to do apart from studies, so I was thinking of doing something just to fill my time. And, a friend of mine suggested Soliya … I like it because we have these people come here from different backgrounds; we speak about different topics from different perspectives, and I like that. (Souhail, Participant)

For those, such as Souhail, who were looking to fill their time, the program provided an avenue to engage in something interesting while treating it almost as a hobby, an area for personal growth. For others, such as Mohamed, the motivation to participate became about pushing themselves outside of their comfort zone while engaging with people across difference:

> I started to be more curious about facilitating and different perspectives from different people around the world… So yeah, as a shy person, I consider myself. I find it difficult to get into online dialogue, which is another thing why I joined Soliya; I wanted to get out of my comfort zone and try something new with different people. (Mohamed, Facilitator)

Several facilitators commented in similar terms to Mohamed, that they had not considered themselves as someone who could act as a facilitator; however, they pushed themselves to try something new in this role.

"An Experience Issue"

While the motivations explored above of feeling led to this work and meeting new people illuminate abstract underpinning for facilitators to be involved in the Soliya programs, the reasons for most people joining as participants are more practical. For many participants, the program provided an opportunity to practice their English skills. As Anna (Participant) explains, "my English teacher decided to tell us about this project and that it could be a great idea for us to practice our English and get to learn more about other cultures and other people." Many participants spoke of the importance and value of having high-level fluency in speaking and understanding English, and that any chance they have to work on their skills is one that they will readily take. Duha (Participant) shared that they "really wanted to chat with people in English, so I can enhance my English language." Similarly, Nidhal (Participant) commented that "in my country we speak Arabic, so English is not really something that we can practice daily."

For facilitators, this opportunity to practice using English was also a motivating factor in signing up. As Arij explains, there is limited opportunity in Tunisia for practicing English, so she looks for every opportunity that is available to her. She would have liked to have pursued a career teaching English but received advice to follow a different path instead and keep English as a hobby:

> Well, for me, it was practicing English because growing up, I loved English, and I really wanted to practice it, but I had no way to practice it being from Tunisia because our second language is French. So, when I graduated from high school, I had very high marks, and I wanted to be an English teacher, and then my parents said, "how come? You are a brilliant student, maybe you do engineering and keep English as a side gig or whatever." So whenever I find an opportunity to talk to people in English I would grab it, so I was visiting the American corner here in Tunisia and we were having discussion and conversation, and I heard of Soliya from there, and then I tracked it on Facebook and decided to go for it. (Arij, Facilitator)

With practicing English comes a more intimate knowledge of the language—how to navigate and express yourself in it:

> I also thought it could be useful for me to have my language practice, kind of practice because I have never lived abroad. And you know, okay, I can speak grammatically correct, but you know daily language is something different, so I need to hear it to accumulate that basic level of daily language let me say. So, you

know, I mean grammatically speaking, sometimes you just
show your ear like this, but also there is this option
[on-screen Betül is touching one ear by reaching over
her head and then again reaching for the ear from below]
(*laughter*). So, you cannot discover it before hearing it,
so yeah, it works well until now. Yeah, and you know, to
have an experience, [it is] an experience issue. (Betül,
Facilitator)

Betül provides the visual image of how there is a nuance with grammar, that slight changes can result in different meanings, and you need to have the immersive experience in the language to start grasping those subtleties.

For several participants and facilitators, the online nature of the program was a motivating factor for involvement. It provided access to an exchange program that was not possible when the program required physical travel. Mohamed reflected on his journey to joining Soliya that he had been looking for an opportunity for an exchange program, but coming from Libya restricted his participation, the online venue provided a means of joining in an exchange:

So the first thing was because it's under Erasmus+[4] so I
was looking for an exchange program that was sponsored
by Erasmus, but unfortunately due to the security issues
here they kind of don't operate in the country, so this
program I found online virtual dialogue so I was like, why
not? Let's give it a try and see how it goes. It's really
interesting so far for me. (Mohamed, Facilitator)

Some participants and facilitators spoke of the practical benefits of skill development that comes from being involved in the Soliya program. Several talked about the online facilitation skill development as an appealing factor for joining, and as a way to use skills across their various professional roles or future careers:

---

[4] "Erasmus+ is the EU's programme to support education, training, youth and sport in Europe" ("Erasmus+ ," n.d.). Erasmus + Virtual Exchange is a partnership with Soliya and other organizations ("Erasmus+ Virtual Exchange," n.d.).

> I am not going to need it for my studies. But just for my personality, my career, it's very important to communicate with others from multi-nationalities, and I am thinking about one day if I am going to work in a multi-national company where I am going to work with others, and it's very good to have such an experience. I think that's going to help me in my career, more than my studies. (Sarra, Participant)

For Sarra, the opportunity to interact with international people is vital for future job opportunities. She hopes to work abroad or for a multi-national company, where having inter-cultural skills will be valuable.

"Was Not Voluntary for Me"

Following along with the practical motivations for joining the Soliya program are academic requirements. Three of those in the participant role group cited school as the impetus to join the program. Hassan and Nicolas, both facilitators now, mentioned that they initially joined as participants as part of their respective schools. Soliya offers partnerships with universities whereby their programs may be integrated into courses so that students receive credit for participation ("Connect Program," n.d.). Jacob (Participant) mentions that "this program was not voluntary for me; it's a part of one of my courses at University… So, it was obligatory for me to join the program, but I didn't mind it at all."

"Itsy Bitsy Teeny Weeny Little Constructive, Positive Thing"

Finally, an undercurrent to the motivations many of the facilitators I spoke with was a sense of altruism. This altruism was heard in Nicolas's earlier comment of "a goal that was meaningful," and Amanda's mention of her draw to work related to civil rights and creating "a better way to deal with this from a people-to-people connection," previously in this chapter. Others, such as Rianne, raises those same sentiments as she talks about her motivation for the work being her "medicine" against the broader negative narratives that dominate the public discourses of the day:

> But generally, it's really like, when you hear bad news
> in the media and stuff, it's like "oh the world is going,
> you know, whatever" And then you have a session, and it's
> like "oh but there is hope!" So, it's kind of like my, well
> medicine sounds like a strong word, but it's, well, even
> if people are having difficult discussions, it's really
> like, yeah, but this is the way forward... I guess the main
> thing is that I am doing my itsy bitsy teeny weeny little
> constructive, positive thing because otherwise, I would
> just curl up in a corner and cry, the way the state of the
> world is going. I think that's a big part of my motivation.
> ... So, it's like, my personal rebellion, antidote, to the
> doom and gloom in the world. (Rianne, Facilitator)

Amongst both facilitators and participants, there is a range of motivating factors that lead them to Soliya. As seen above, for facilitators, their decision to be involved tends to stem from their career journey or to a sense of enacting positive change in the lives of others. For participants, the chance to join is more often related to the opportunity for new experiences, or they view it as practical decisions related to school or developing their skill sets. However, these are not strict distinctions but rather broad strokes and, as seen above, there is intermingling between motivations and the role individuals have in the program.

4.3 "I Expected To..."

As with any new experience, people came into the Soliya program with expectations of how the encounter might go or who the other participants would be (Maoz et al., 2002; Saguy et al., 2009).

"The Muslims, the Americans, and Us"

Individual expectations included the backgrounds or demographics of the people who they might meet. For example, Jacob shared that because he filled out a questionnaire in advance, he knew to expect people from Muslim backgrounds and Americans in the group,

> Yeah, because there was some kind of, not a test, but some
> kind of form we had to fill before we joined the program
> where there were questions about are we okay to chat with

> Muslim people, so I thought there would be people from Muslim countries definitely. Our teacher mentioned that there would be people from the United States, so I thought that as well. I might have thought that there would be another participant from my country, but apart from that, I didn't have any perceptions. But basically, that's it… The Muslims, the Americans, and us from my country, I guess. (Jacob, Participant)

While many, as Jacob illustrated above, had ideas of the demographic mix that might be present in their group, it was more common for individuals to reflect their expectations of what might happen or unfold in the space, including what the topics of conversation might be. For Asma, she anticipated the opportunity to share life experiences, perhaps discover commonalities and differences:

> I expect to have relationships with these people and because my teacher told us that they are all, the participants, are like us, students in the University. So, I thought that we could discuss about our studies and some things like that. (Asma, Participant)

As reflected by Asma, if the program was an academic requirement, or if the University was the connection point into the program, some expectations were then formed by the information provided by the University. Other expectations were generated by the individual based on their past experiences, or what they hoped might happen.

"Disagreement Is Natural"

Other expectations related to group dynamics and how the encounters across differences might unfold. Several anticipated agreements or disagreements. For example, Anna thought there would be disagreements about religion and different beliefs:

> I thought there would be more arguments regarding religion…because I see that sometimes, even at University, when we are speaking with some people coming from other places who believe in different things, we tend to be quite, I would say, (*pause*) we tend to judge

a lot more, and we tend not to understand their point of view because we are so firm in what we believe... And I thought that sometimes there are arguments, even where I live, people are coming from other places, we have a lot of immigrants coming here right now. So, I see that sometimes people are arguing over that. And, even in high school I had experiences like this one because we used to have people coming from other places, and we saw that sometimes they have different ways of behaving and we tend to judge them, and they tend to judge us as well, so it was a bit difficult for us to understand them... And even on the internet I guess I see that sometimes people, even on Facebook, there are people who are arguing a lot. (Anna, Participant)

For Anna, her previous experiences across differences shaped how she anticipated the Soliya encounters to go; she was used to having tension when there was dissimilarity. Overarching cultural narratives shaped these tensions around her regarding immigrants—people coming into her community who were perceived as *other*. Similarly, Souhail expressed that he also expected to have disagreements, he thought that specific topics such as religion would provoke strong opinions, and there may be clashes as a result which, unlike Anna, was something he welcomed:

I expected to have a number of disagreements; I don't think we disagree a lot... But we have not spoken, we have not discussed any religious matter where we can disagree, so I think if we discuss, maybe in the future, some religious matter as I said, we will disagree. Especially, we come from different religions. I am Muslim ; I am sure that other people who are Christians, I am not sure if there are other religions, but there are a number of disagreements between Christianity and Islam. It's natural to have disagreement... discussing some political issues in the world nowadays, we will have disagreements. Some people agree with one political party or one political region, or other people agree with another political party or political region, so disagreement is natural in this kind of situations. (Souhail, Participant)

Souhail's comments came a few weeks into the program, as he is sharing that he hopes future weeks will yield the opportunity to discuss more contentious topics to provoke a more heated conversation. You can sense that he finds the possibility of disagreement to be exciting, as a chance to spark intellectual debate. However, not all participants expected there to be conflict. Some, such as Karoline, anticipated that there would be an avoidance of potentially prickly topics to keep the interactions pleasant:

> Yeah, actually, I was completely surprised, and as I said before, it was my first time facing this program. So, I wasn't expecting too much discussion. I was like, okay, we are going to have this program talking about different topics but not in that deep part. (Karoline, Participant)

As Souhail, Anna, and Karoline's comments reveal, many participants mentioned that they anticipated encountering different viewpoints. The assumption that there would be differing views was predicated, to some extent, on preconceived notions or stereotypes of what opinions people from different religions, or parts of the world, might carry. For example, Jacob comments that he held some stereotypes of people from the United States—stereotypes which, to some extent, were confirmed for him during the Soliya encounter:

> Well, I had some kind of perceptions of what they might think about the world. Especially I have some stereotypes about students from the States. But, well, I can't really say a concrete example about that, mostly I thought that my perceptions and their perceptions were going to be different; my ideas will be different from theirs. And yeah, that's something I found true because we had really good conversations about the different views we have so I found it to be true. (Jacob, Participant)

While the quotes above reflect some of the assumptions and preconceived ideas of people entering into the online encounter, others shared that they did not have specific expectations entering into the program. For example, Layla (Participant) commented, "I didn't have many expectations, really. I thought it would be an exchange of ideas and learning something." Her comments reflect similar sentiments from others who indicated, what they perceived to be, an absence of expectation to what could emerge. However, while Layla states that she "didn't have many expectations" she also mentions that she imagined an "exchange of ideas and learning." These remarks signal that Layla did expect the program to provide certain opportunities, even as she maintained low expectations to what those experiences might be.

4.4 "The Source of My Knowledge"

As discussed earlier in this chapter, participants expected certain things out of the encounter. Some of these expectations were based on their pre-existing narratives of *other*. These narratives were shaped by varying factors including media and the cultural discourse of their community.

"Of Course, the Media"

Media, and specifically news media, has a significant role in the discourse that constructs narratives and perceptions of *other* (Hammack, 2011; Psaltis, 2016). For example, Karoline (Participant) points out that "of course, the media… since I am studying political science and I read a lot of newspapers so sometimes I just read some news about these, for example, political problems in the Arab Union" impact her views and assumptions. Similarly, Souhail comments that reading literature, be it fiction or the news media, significantly shapes his view of the world:

> I read. I read a lot; I read a lot of novels, a lot of books. I tend to watch the news a lot; I tend to read news articles a lot from different newspapers, The Guardian, all kinds of newspapers. I do this every day; I know what is going on in the world. And I read novels, because novels make us know places, know rituals performed by people in a remote place that you didn't know before. So, you can only know that I think, from novels, novels are the source of my knowledge. (Souhail, Participant)

Jacob reflects on his expectations and how the national media, along with what he sees online, influenced them:

> Probably because I have never been in those countries, neither the States nor Morocco or any other Muslim countries. Probably most of it comes from the media and the internet, there is some kind of…. And we discussed that topic in the group as well, that there is some kind of national ideas, national perceptions about other places in the world, in all countries including in my country. So, my perceptions, my stereotypes probably come from the general view of these countries in my country, or these stereotypes that exist in the media here in my country. (Jacob, Participant).

His ideas have formed through his cultural narrative, and he comments that there has not been an opportunity to challenge those views as he has not travelled to some of the countries he has preconceived ideas about.

"Like a Taboo"

Narratives are often informed by a cultural context, the discourse that surrounds us and informs our views and perceptions of the world (Dessel & Rogge, 2008; Ron & Maoz, 2013; Ross, 2014). Participants reflected on how their societal discourse shaped their attitudes towards others. For example, Karoline mentioned the rising populism in Italy that she identified as responding to the immigrant crisis and economic concerns:

> Nowadays, it is sort of rising populism in our society. So, immigrants are considered as the main cause, the main reason for our financial crisis. Because our government should do something, and of course, they have the power to accept other immigrants, or even take them back to their home. But nowadays, it's just rising racism, especially for the amount of people who are using social media. … There is a rising populism and a kind of hate speech online, so it is basically something that I can say is not a good thing. Because, of course, people used to trust television, and now they trust more in social media. (Karoline, Participant)

Karoline reflects a view that she positions as somewhat counter-cultural to the broader narrative, that she sees driven through social media usage. She demonstrates a view that is more concerned with the moralistic imperatives of the immigrant and refugee crisis Italy is facing and that she sees the populist message as ethically problematic.

Cultural norms also dictate appropriate conversation topics, and as Oldez identifies, there are topics such as religion that are avoided even amongst family:

> things like religion, we don't have that opportunity to talk, even with family, my family, our friends, we don't talk about those things that much. We can… not in deep conversation, you can say that we don't get into deep conversations in that… I don't know, maybe it's a habit… like a taboo. (Oldez, Participant)

Similarly, for Mostafa, there is a sense of taboo topics in his culture:

> I would say that we don't really have that freedom of expressing different ideas….Like in the West countries, in Egypt, we (*pause*) are taught to have one thing right, like you are in "my way or the highway"… yeah, that is how things are here. That is why I feel a little bit exhausted when I try to express myself to others from my same community because it's not really a common thing. It's like we have one identity, one thing that you have to follow and if you think in a different way, okay you have your own group, you find your own group that thinks the same way and you live alone, eat alone, it's hard to group people from different cultures and way of thinking and put them together, it will be hard. (Mostafa, Participant)

He reflects on his perception that culturally you are perceived negatively for deviating from the norms, from the group mentality and collective opinion. His experience is that it becomes socially difficult if one does not conform within those boundaries.

4.5 Cogitatio[5]

Reflexivity in qualitative inquiry, and particularly in ethnographies, is critical to an "ethical practice" (Pink et al., 2016, p. 12) of research. Pascale (2012) reminds us that, to enact ethically reflexive research, one must situate their own location "within networks of power, geographies of privilege, and the histories of experience" (p. 72). Having spent the above sections of this chapter introducing the participants and exploring their motivations, expectations and narratives, I seek to make explicit my own positionality in these conversations. My positionality undoubtably informed the research process and interpretation of the data along with the discussion I present in this book. With this in mind, I owe it to myself, the participants, and you as the reader to bring transparency to who I am and uncover my biases.

I am a cis-white Canadian woman who comes from a Judeo-Christian, settler-colonial background from a middle-class family in Canada. These identities and experiences have afforded me a great deal of privilege in my life; I have not had to confront discrimination or bias against me based on ethnicity or religion, and I have had opportunities opened to me that may otherwise have been inaccessible. I think it was my gender identity that acted as a catalyst into my journey of understanding oppression based on patriarchal ideals and structures. In beginning to uncover the insidious ways that women are disenfranchised in my cultural context of Canada, I started on a path towards understanding intersectional identities that inform experiences outside of my own. I am on, what I assume will be a lifelong 'unlearning' process—interrogating my narratives, biases, and assumptions that are so engrained they remain invisible to me until something, or someone, prompts the question of "how's the water?".

I surface here my 'unlearning' journey to reflect that, while I actively work towards an increased consciousness of how my identity positions me in varying contexts, it is also an ongoing process—I will continue to have blind spots.

My motivations for this research were both for personal fulfillment of undertaking research while also wanting to contribute useful knowledge to the practice of peacebuilding. I hope that these reflections surface some of my own motivations ("Journey to Soliya"), expectations ("I Expected To..."), and narratives ("The Source of my Knowledge") for you as the reader.

---

[5] To distinguish my personal reflections in the text, Cogitatio sections will be displayed in *italics*.

4.6 Summary

This chapter began with an overview of the overarching narrative which emerged from the findings: 'bringing into,' 'the encounter,' and 'what shifted.' This narrative will be explored through four distinct findings chapters, of which this was the first. This chapter explored the element of 'bringing into'—beginning with an introduction to the interviewees themselves, offering insight into this cohort of unique individuals who generously offered to engage in a conversation about their experiences and reflections as members of an online dialogue program. Following the initial introduction, this chapter explored three aspects of 'bringing into,' the motivations for joining ("Journey to Soliya"), their expectation of the experience ("I Expected To…"), and their pre-existing narratives and perceptions of each other ("The Source of my Knowledge"). The chapter closed with the first reflexive *cogitatio* passage, offering my own positionally as the researcher in relation to the area of 'bringing into' this dialogue journey.

References

Connect Program. (n.d). Retrieved from the Soliya website: https://www.soliya.net/programs/connect-program

Dessel, A., & Rogge, M. E. (2008). Evaluation of intergroup dialogue: A review of the empirical literature. *Conflict Resolution Quarterly, 26*(2), 199–238.

Erasmus+. (n.d.). Retrieved from the European Commission website: https://ec.europa.eu/programmes/erasmus-plus/about_en

Erasmus+ Virtual Exchange. (n.d.). Retrieved from the Soliya website: https://www.soliya.net/story/european-union-makes-first-investment-virtual-exchange

Hammack, P. L. (2011). *Narrative and the politics of identity the cultural psychology of Israeli and Palestinian youth*. Oxford University Press.

Maoz, I., Steinberg, S., Bar-On, D., & Fakhereldeen, M. (2002). The dialogue between the "self" and the "other": A process analysis of Palestinian-Jewish encounters in Israel. *Human Relations, 55*(8), 931–962. https://doi.org/10.1177/0018726702055008178

Pascale, C.-M. (2012). *Cartographies of knowledge: Exploring qualitative epistemologies*. Sage.

Pink, S., Horst, H. A., Postill, J., Hjorth, L., Lewis, T., & Tacchi, J. (2016). *Digital ethnography: Principles and practice*. Sage.

Psaltis, C. (2016). Collective memory, social representations of intercommunal relations, and conflict transformation in divided Cyprus. *Peace and Conflict:*

Journal of Peace Psychology, 22(1), 19–27. https://doi.org/10.1037/pac0000145

Ron, Y., & Maoz, I. (2013). Dangerous stories: Encountering narratives of the other in the Israeli-Palestinian conflict. *Peace and Conflict: Journal of Peace Psychology, 19*(3), 281–294. https://doi.org/10.1037/a0033686

Ross, K. (2014). Narratives of belonging (and not): Inter-group contact in Israel and the formation of ethno-national identity claims. *International Journal of Intercultural Relations, 42*, 38–52. https://doi.org/10.1016/j.ijintrel.2014.07.002

Saguy, T., Tausch, N., Dovidio, J. F., & Pratto, F. (2009). The irony of harmony: Intergroup contact can produce false expectations for equality. *Psychological Science, 20*(1), 114. https://doi.org/10.1111/j.1467-9280.2008.02261.x

University Partners. (n.d). Retrieved from the Soliya website: https://www.soliya.net/about/university-partners

CHAPTER 5

The Setting

Having introduced the research participants—including what they carry into the encounter, their motivations, expectations, and pre-existing narratives in the previous chapter—I now turn to the setting of the dialogic encounter. I include here, in Fig. 5.1, an updated version of the visual representation to indicate where, in the overall narrative, this chapter is located.

This chapter first explores how the Soliya Connect program aligns with the characteristics of dialogue identified in Chapter 3. I then provide an overview of four key influencing factors in the dialogue encounters: the facilitator role, program design, social dynamics, and power dynamics. Finally, I will look at the benefits and limitations of the online program.

Soliya identifies the Connect program as its "flagship virtual exchange initiative" ("Connect Program," n.d.). The program is described on the Soliya website as:

> An online cross-cultural education program integrated into curriculum that provides young adults with a unique opportunity to: Establish a deeper understanding for the perspectives of others around the world on important socio-political issues [and] develop 21st Century skills such as critical thinking, cross-cultural communication, and media literacy. ("Connect Program," n.d.)

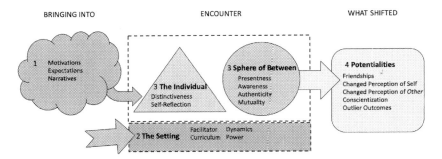

Fig. 5.1 Location of Chapter 5 in overarching findings narrative

The Connect program aims to provide students with "the opportunity to engage in facilitated and substantive dialogue, and build meaningful relationships across national, cultural, religious, and ideological boundaries" ("Connect Program," n.d.). Mai (Facilitator) describes Soliya as "very good, quality time with other people from different places [and] cultures to have a cultural exchange, discuss important topics and exchange ideas." Hassan comments on what, from his perspective, some of the objectives within Soliya are:

> In Soliya, we are not there to change people's ideas, we are giving people an opportunity so they can get in touch with each other. They can know more; we are not trying just to change ideas. Yes, change happens, but we want people to know more, to be more aware of what is going on around, how cultures look like on each side of the world, and that's the change, that's the impact. The impact of maybe erasing a little bit of our ignorance towards other cultures, you know. So, this is the change; it's not just "okay you have some ideas, and we came to change these ideas," no this is not what Soliya is doing or what I am doing as a facilitator, no it's not that. (Hassan, Facilitator)

Hassan and Mai reflect the shared view that Soliya is a space where individuals are exposed in meaningful ways to other ideas and perspectives. There is a sense that the program aims to increase the awareness of each participant of what diverse cultures and other forms of experiencing the world could be. As Hassan indicates, the aim is not a radical transformation of each participant, but rather the facilitation of an encounter that decreases ignorance, builds meaningful connections, and shifts perspectives.

5.1 Connect Program and Characteristics of Dialogue in Community Peacebuilding

As previous chapters have emphasized, this research project is concerned with sustained dialogic encounters between individuals in online settings. As such, the research setting ideally encompasses the five characteristics commonly found in community-based peacebuilding practice (identified in Chapter 3). These characteristics are: encountering *other,* establishing a safe space that addresses issues of inequality amongst participants, attending to issues of identity both within in-group and out-group contexts, an examination of truth and narratives, and creating relationships with *other* that enable a movement towards change or action. In that chapter, I commented—and it is worth noting again here—that while these characteristics are common, they are not universal to all dialogue practices. In setting out to identify the research setting, I was not exclusively looking for all of these characteristics to be present; instead, I hoped to partner with organizations pursuing at least several of these elements in their online peacebuilding work. In the following section, I explore how each of the five characteristics relates to the Soliya Connect program to illuminate how the program aligns with and differs from the features of dialogue practice in community peacebuilding. In proceeding with this discussion, it is essential to note that Soliya does not identify itself as a community-based peacebuilding organization. Instead, they function at an international level and see themselves as "operat[ing] at the intersection of technology, peacebuilding, and global education to foster local awareness and global perspectives" ("About Us," n.d.).

Encountering Other *and Exploring Identity*

The notion of encountering *other* and exploring identity are essential in community-based peacebuilding practice. As aspects of *otherness* are often revealed when identities are uncovered in the group, the two characteristics of encountering *other* and exploring identity are reflected together within this section. The Connect program presents opportunity for both of these dialogue characteristics by bringing together diverse groups to specifically engage across facets of identity and topics that bring differences to the surface. Broadly, this encountering of *other* is based on an East–West binary, encompassing both nationality and religion, bringing together participants from geographical locations such as the Middle East, North Africa, Europe, and North America.

As Soliya notes on their Curriculum Overview:

> As East-West identities will continue to play a role in discussions, they should not be the only focus. Facilitators are encouraged to transcend these categories and help students reflect on which part of their identity is playing a role at different times, why this is, and how this impacts the prospect for successful working relationships and effects social change within and between societies. ("Curriculum Overview," n.d., p. 10)

Rianne commented on how the formation of groups across an East–West binary identity can ignore the nuanced and intersectional identities of group members:

> What I feel is that it's still, to some extent, clear that the Soliya program, and obviously that's the one I am referencing, was set up post 9/11. And it's very much like, Muslim versus Western, or Islam versus Western, it's now being changed, some of it is semantics, and some of it is this. But it's like, I am a Western Muslim, so if it's Islam versus the West, like which camp should I go in? Like born Western, chose to be Muslim, did I then leave the Western camp? So, I have some issues with that, where already in the program itself we're having these biases, unintentionally built in. And I know they're being written out a little bit, but still, I find that hard to get that over my lips, Western versus Islamic. Because it could entrench differences which aren't actually there and could widen the gap of Muslims living in the West, or Western Muslims, be they converts, but also migrants, that Islam is something that is not Western, is something that is maybe showing up through migration but is still an alien thing. ... I don't doubt the well-meaning thing, but like unintentionally, it does seep through, and that is a secret wish if that could

be explored more consciously that in the effort to do well, it could also unintentionally actually entrench or reinforce difference. (Rianne, Facilitator)

While the East–West distinction is the most evident categorization of *otherness*, the intention of having further diverse identities is built into the program curriculum. Intra-regional differences, such as politics, gender, religion, and communication style, are included as dimensions of *otherness* along with the inter-regional encounters that occur within Soliya's programs.

As explored in the previous chapter, many interviewees commented that the program provided them with the opportunity for first-time encounters. The encountering of *other* is not restricted to Connect participants but occurs for facilitators as well. While there may be perceptible indicators of *otherness* that appear readily in the group, such as ethnicity or religious dress, many other individualities are not as readily visible. Differences emerge as the group delves into aspects of their identity, such as sexual orientation, religion, and ableness (Tapper, 2013). The Connect program intentionally explores the topic of identity so that group members may consider how their various identities influence and shape their interpretation of the world as well as their perception of *other* in a safe setting.

Safe Space

Dialogue-based peacebuilding work seeks authentic representation and vulnerability from participants (Chaitin, 2012). In asking participants to reveal themselves truthfully, there becomes an ethical imperative to provide a physical, emotional, and psychologically safe or brave space (Arao & Clemens, 2013) for the dialogue to unfold. The Connect curriculum and platform design intends to establish a space for the group members to discuss openly topics that may be sensitive or culturally taboo. Facilitators go through two training programs to equip them in the role so they can thoughtfully and skillfully facilitate the group. The facilitator training emphasizes how the facilitator themselves informs the dynamics and the safety of the group with their own identity and biases. By equipping facilitators with the skills to be "multi-partial and neutral process leaders" ("Facilitation Training," n.d.), Soliya aims to lessen the influence of the facilitator's identity on the group so that all members feel supported equally and without bias.

While the design of the Connect online space is meant to ensure the wellbeing of group members and to minimize power dynamics that would contribute to feelings of being unsafe (Maoz et al., 2002), some factors are difficult to mitigate. These considerations, such as power imbalances amongst group members and infringements on anonymity, are explored in greater detail later in this chapter.

Examination of 'Truth'

Investigating the dissonance between narratives is essential to the work of dialogue (Bryn, 2015). The act of remaining open while encountering what *other* holds to be true, even when it is at odds with your understanding, is where the opportunity for authentic change and growth occurs (Ellis & Maoz, 2012; Hammack, 2008). The Connect program allows for the examination of truth and narratives as the participants move through topics each week. The group members select the issues and topics for discussion themselves, and the facilitator is there to move the group into more in-depth explorations and ask probing questions.

Relational Movement

The characteristic of relational movement in dialogue practice relates to the shifts, both internal and external, that occur through the formation of relationship with *other*. This characteristic occurs in the individual through authentic connection with *other* and is less inside the control or influence of the organization in question, in this case, Soliya. In Chapter 3, I outlined an understanding of how action is inherent to this characteristic, that participants in dialogue can experience a widening around their boundary of *self* that becomes inclusive of *other*. How this particular characteristic of dialogue practice was evidenced in the data for this research will be examined in Chapter 7 (Potentialities).

5.2 Program Design: Influencing Factors

Having looked at the goals of the Connect program, along with how it encompasses the characteristics of community-based dialogue for peacebuilding, I will now move to the intentional design elements which shape the dialogue encounter. While there are multiple factors which impact the online dialogue space, there are two particularly noteworthy ones included here, the role of the facilitator and the program curriculum.

The Facilitator

The facilitators' role and function are essential influencing dynamics in shaping the dialogue encounters (Frantell et al., 2019; Gurin et al., 2013). The facilitator role is there to "sustain dialogue and support an environment where students can comfortably explore perspectives, uncover biases, and arrive at a better understanding of cultures, with the goal of developing the global competence essential to thriving in an interconnected world" ("Connect Program," n.d.).[1]

Facilitators must complete an introduction and advanced training before becoming a facilitator with Soliya. While completion of facilitator training equips individuals with the skills and insights to support a Soliya dialogue group, facilitators indicated that they experienced unique development opportunities each time they began with a new cohort:

> As a facilitator and working in this field, you never stop growing and never stop learning from one discussion to the next. From one group to the next, everything is different, everything is new, and it's never the same. So I think that… there was this one coach that I had when I first started out, and he was telling me, and I still use the same analogy in regard to a stream, that you can work with the same group every week for eight weeks and each week you're walking into a new stream with new current and new waves and new temperatures, and it's the same way with facilitation I think, that preparing myself for it to always be different and always to have surprised, is just what we need to do. It's part of being prepared

---

[1] Each Connect group has a facilitator. Most commonly, there are two facilitators per group; however, in some cases, Soliya provides one senior facilitator instead of two.

> as a facilitator, so even where there are big surprises, and I still say, "wow, that really surprised me," there are usually always different gifts and surprises from every single group that you work with every week, and that's what makes it exciting. I think that's what makes it exciting, because that's what's always changing, it's always different. So it's not like someone who is working in a job where day-in and day-out they're going in, and they're doing the exact same thing over and over again, and it goes in one side and out the other, and all looks the same, this is always different. (Amanda, Facilitator)

The dynamism experienced by Amanda and others indicates the need for facilitators to be self-reflective and constantly incorporating new learning into their practices.

Facilitators are coached in how to maintain multi-partiality and appear as neutral as possible to the group. In doing so, the group members will ideally perceive the facilitators as there to guide the process but not to pass judgement or interject their own agendas. This appearance of neutrality is not to say that facilitators are, in fact, neutral. Facilitators must be attuned to the bounds of their neutrality and cognizant of the power they wield in the group that can shape interactions. A component of facilitator training is to manage and self-regulate when topics and perspectives are raised by group members, which may be emotionally triggering for facilitators (as discussed later in Chapter 6 "Think about my identity and my values and beliefs."). Challenges can also arise when the conversation is particularly stimulating, as Arji (Facilitator) comments: "Yeah, I mean, at sometimes I really feel jealous of them and I really want to participate, and I feel like it's a really interesting discussion, but then I go 'I am a facilitator, I should not engage." In our conversation, Mai spoke to the skill required to ensure she does not reveal any bias:

> Because I know my role very well, so I try to, for example, get others to reflect. For example, "this person said such and such, do you agree or disagree? Would you like to have the same approach in your country or not?" I think that it is something if you have a very strong opinion it can be very difficult to keep your neutrality, but I am very happy that I did! (Mai, Facilitator)

A tactic aimed towards keeping facilitators seemingly separate from the group is that they do not share personal details about themselves beyond their names and what is visible to participants on the screen. As such, facilitators do not reveal where they are logging in from and are thoughtful about what is displayed in their video camera background. Not revealing personal details can prove especially challenging when participants directly ask probing questions, as Joanna experienced:

> And one more thing that was really hard was to not engage with them on a personal level because sometimes they would ask us personal questions. And they were so nice, and they were making Facebook groups with one another outside of Soliya, they were kind of like "you can also participate" and I was like, "no, I am sorry, I can't, I wish I could, but I can't! (Joanna, Facilitator)

The Soliya program's ethos builds towards an 'activation' component, wherein, ideally, participants move into some form of action as a result of their engagement in the dialogue program. Nicolas shared how he perceives this dynamic:

> So activation, the way I see it, is the final step before you move forward post-Soliya. So you know, in the last, final session, you're not going to start anything new. You're not going to try to start a new, how can I phrase this... basically what I am trying to say is that the development of the participants themselves is there throughout the eight weeks or the four weeks, and you're not going make it all happen in the last session. So it's a gradual development, basically. And in that activation stage, you're focusing on the conclusion, so basically ensuring that everyone has achieved what they wanted to achieve in the program, so you are finalizing that. And you are preparing them for what is coming next. Whether it be, in my case, as a participant exchanging contact information or social media to continue the conversation and stay connected beyond. That is basically how I see activation, the conclusion and beyond. (Nicolas, Facilitator)

As reflected by Nicolas, facilitators hold this 'journey' in their minds as they progress through the sessions, looking for how group members might experience their own form of activation.

The Curriculum

The Connect program follows weekly outlines; these outlines are suggested activities, tools, and discussion guides to support the facilitators. Emphasis is placed on equipping facilitators to invite going into depth in group conversations while supporting participants to lead their discussions.

"We opened up to many topics"

Ideally, the participants will guide the conversation themselves, while focusing on issues that bring to the surface biases and divergent perspectives such as "identity, religion, culture, and social and political topics" ("Connect Program," n.d.). Duha (Participant) mentions some of the topics their group discussed, "we talked about global issues facing the world; we talked about religion, mental health." Nidhal shared examples of the issues his group chose to talk about that were relevant to their individual experiences:

> we opened up to many topics; most important of them was the relation between religion and violence. And we spoke about politics and people's decision in each country, how do we live, how do we perceive the picture of the other from the other side, and our opinions about peace and war, and a lot of these types of topics. But we focused on religion and violence, which is terrorism and the acts that have occurred lately. (Nidhal, Participant)

As Mai illustrates, the selection of discussion topics varies by the subtleties and interest of the group members:

> some groups are driven by curiosity. They have a lot of questions to ask each other, and somehow, they are not interested in politics. They are not bringing Israel and Palestine into the discussion at all. They are not interested in gender, they do not bring the LGBT community

at all, they are not interested in women's rights, and they will not bring it to the discussion at all. They are more interested in families, and norms, and in what's happening in the world in culture, in education, in other things that not necessarily will bring a strong disagreement or 'heated' argument. (Mai, Facilitator)

While Mai highlights that some groups do not demonstrate an interest in discussing "politics," or topics that may stimulate disagreements, other interviewees mentioned specifically tackling issues that may be considered culturally taboo. For some interviewees, such as Duha, it was surprising to discuss taboo topics such as religion and the Israeli and Palestinian conflict:

So, something that surprised me during this experience would be that we were allowed to discuss and talk about any topic that we are willing to talk about. Even if this topic was a sensitive topic like religion or politics, it was okay to talk about it. Unlike what happens in other student activities or other classes that we usually don't bring up these topics because it might cause conflict and tension amongst the group, or sometimes we are even told not to bring up these topics. So, I was surprised that in Soliya's discussion, we were allowed to discuss these topics. For example, as I told you before, we talked about religion, and in the last session, we talked about the Israeli and Palestinian conflict, which is absolutely a sensitive topic to talk about it. (Duha, Participant)

Similarly, Karoline mentioned that potentially sensitive issues were discussed amongst her group, which stimulated the sharing of different viewpoints. In our first interview she comments;

We had different points of view. Especially from the political side, we discussed, for example, gun protection and the LGBT community, and the religion that is present in specific states. For example, in Tunisia, the LGBT community is not recognized, so it is kind of hard to explain the differences about gender and sex. (Karoline, Participant)

Then, in our second conversation two months later, Karoline shares that her group also talked about abortion:

> I can say we had the chance to talk about abortion, which is a topic where, for example, in the Middle East, it is not common. And the girls in the group they actually didn't talk about it that much, abortion, because they didn't know the legislation and the laws in general. (Karoline, Participant)

Karoline reflects that, while she perceived an openness amongst the group members to discuss some of these potentially controversial topics, there may have been less willingness on the part of the group members from the Middle East to talk about abortion. She attributes this reluctance to a lack of awareness of laws.

Ultimately, each group will determine what topics they cover in their sessions. However, the Connect program is designed to encourage critical thinking, and, therefore, emphasis is placed on the discussion of issues that will bring to light differences and facilitate encounter with diverse worldviews.

5.3 'The Water'

Beyond the program design aspects, other facets characterize the dialogue encounters. Power and group dynamics characterize dialogic encounters and influence how the group discussions proceed, what is revealed, and what voices are heard in the encounter. In Chapter 2, I quoted from the author David Foster Wallace in his telling of two young fish who are asked "how's the water?" as an analogy for recognizing and articulating the invisible contexts that shape daily experiences and encounters. Having provided a look at two tangible influencing factors on dialogue (facilitators and the curriculum), I now turn to an exploration of the intangible factors (the water) that also shape the setting in which the dialogic encounter occurs.

"We Thought the Group is Stuck"

The social group dynamics in the Connect setting contributed to how conversations developed, along with the topics and opinions that surfaced.

Within Soliya, and other dialogue-based programs, there is a desire to see groups move through specific phases of development, with the intent that they will reach a group stage where each member can share with transparency while listeners hold open to difference with curiosity and respect ("Curriculum Overview," n.d).

The social dynamics commented on by interviewees encompassed a range between positive and negative experiences. However, interviewees most frequently employed warm terms to discuss their groups. For example, Nidhal's (Participant) description of his group connotes friendly and enjoyable dynamics "there was no aggression, no hate, no anger, or anything, and everything went great." Similarly, Oya found that her group was easygoing and enjoyable,

> Our group was really easy going, and we didn't have any challenging group dynamics at all. We occasionally had some silent participants, but later on, they started opening up, they started sharing too. …The group was open and really respectful from the beginning until the end. At first, I had some doubts, I was biased that maybe it was a politically correct group. It turned out that they are just nice people, actually. (Oya, Facilitator)

While initially, Oya thought perhaps the group was being "politically correct" and avoiding conflict, she felt in the end that the group was being authentic in their interactions. A familiar group dynamic in dialogue settings is when the group does not move past a degree of social nicety, preferring to focus on commonalities rather than differences (Phipps, 2014). Others, such as Betül, raised this "politically correct" dynamic as well:

> Betül: we thought the group is stuck somewhere between, what was that politically (*pause*)
> Rachel: correct, politically correct
> Betül: Politically correct, yeah, something like that. And somewhere between that step and the next step is learning from difference. So they are, they are not fully aware of being different, or recognizing the difference, yeah, that's the word for that. They don't recognize the difference. (Betül, Facilitator)

As Betül indicates, moving a group into potential areas of contention by surfacing differences is vital, as this is where dialogic moments can occur (Phipps, 2014). While some interviewees enjoyed the likeability of their group, there are risks if the group does not move into spaces of disagreement. When a group stays in the dynamic of political correctness or social politeness, there is a risk of normalization or negative contact (Saguy et al., 2009).

"An Expression of International Power Dynamics"

One of the sharpest identifications of 'the water' that emerged from the data relates to power dynamics. Power influences why specific identities and voices experience privilege over others, and yet it can be challenging to discern (Tapper, 2013). As power dynamics are often insidious, and, therefore, infrequently questioned or verbalized, they become normalized. Even when efforts are made towards establishing a neutral environment for dialogue to occur, power is evidenced (Senesh, 2012). In the conversations I had with participants, along with my observations, the most common forms of power in the dialogue space related to language, technology, and gender.

"English…it's the most powerful language in the world"

The Connect program is held in English, although other language programs are in development with Soliya. Souhail (Participant) remarked on the significance of the English language: "English is, as you know, it's the most powerful language in the world." As explored in Chapter 2, language and power are intrinsically linked (Ahearn, 2001; Hermans & Dimaggio, 2007). The inherent power that comes from speaking English fluently in the dialogue setting can, as with any issue of power, be hard to identify (Wood, 2004). This difficulty in discerning power is especially challenging for those who hold power in the group (Hammond et al., 2003), as Rianne illustrates:

> When an American girl was saying "oh, the others are so quiet and I wish they would participate more" and then one, I think it was Moroccan or Tunisian girl said "yeah but it's your mother tongue, and you're the only one who's got English as a mother tongue, so we're all speaking our second or maybe third language" and that was where the

> American girl was like "oh I've never thought about that." You know, so I think the language part, especially for like the Westerners, to put it crudely, it is very helpful to know that English is an international language, but it is at the same time also an expression of international power dynamics. (*continued later in the interview*) This Moroccan girl explicitly mentioned, "we need more time to think because it's not our mother tongue, so sometimes we're about to say something because we've thought the thought and then translated it into English and then you've already intervened." (Rianne, Facilitator)

In this instance, the native-English speaker was unaware of how the other people in the group experienced power related to language and was critical of other members' participation because she viewed it through her own experience and not with an understanding of the reality for other group members.

For group members who do not speak English fluently, they will likely encounter difficulties, depending on their level of fluency, when it comes to participation in the conversations:

> I think it's [the role of language] the most important next to a good internet connection. If you cannot talk, it doesn't matter how you talk, or what accent, or what level of language you have, if you don't feel like you can express yourself if you think that your English is bad, or you don't have the same vocabulary as other participants it, I think, creates a barrier for students, and they just give up. And I noticed a lot of small signs from students like they try, they will start, they build up their argument, and then after a while, they cannot go to the next level and they just say "that's okay, okay," and they just leave the mic. And sometimes, they don't continue, and I think that language is the most important part of the dialogue. (Burcu, Facilitator)

As Burcu notes, there will often be a level someone might reach where their ability to express themselves or further articulate the point they are making becomes hindered, and they will pull back or cut themselves off.

This limit of language fluency hinders self-expression, which relates to both the facilitators and the participants in the group. Other research participants similarly noted how language constrained their participation because of the limits on expression:

> Well yeah, actually, I think that language plays a role. For me, I think that if the program was in Arabic, I would express myself in more detail, I'll talk more, and it will not be difficult to find the words or find the phrases of what I want to say, but in this program sometimes it's been difficult for me to express what I am thinking or what I really feel and sometimes I say things that other people understand it in a wrong way. So, I think yes, for me, English is kind of a barrier to me in communicating with my group. And I experience that when we were talking about something and one of my group mates, we didn't have the time to finish our conversation during the session, so we completed it on our own on WhatsApp, and he is Egyptian as well so we talked in our mother language, and it was completely different for me to talk in Arabic in the same topic, I felt like I said a lot more and I expressed myself in a better way than in English. (Duha, Participant)

Mohamed also noted that the ability to express oneself in English could correlate with the amount of active participation group members were exhibiting:

> Yeah, the vibe of the group is still kind of shy somehow, because there seems to be a language barrier. We have some participants who can't speak or understand English very well, so you will find them silent most of the time. But we keep calling them, their names, sometimes out to join us, help them to deliver the perspective they are trying to approach and expose to other participants. (Mohamed, Facilitator)

While language can restrict the expression, and therefore the participation of the speaker, the level of fluency of others can impact the experience for the listener as well. As Souhail shares,

> Some people, I think they sometimes have difficulty with expressing ideas, with (*audio cut out*) I get distracted, I cannot focus, I cannot even understand what they want to say sometimes. Different levels of fluency effects, I am speaking about myself, when I hear a person who is struggling with expressing a certain idea, I get distracted and I cannot even focus on what he is trying to say. (Souhail, Participant)

Souhails' reflection of how other group members' language abilities relate to his experience stresses how the dynamics of power compound. Group members who have a higher degree of fluency with the English language are afforded a higher degree of power in the group as they can more readily convey their viewpoints. Whereas other group members, who may struggle to be precise in their comments due to language limitations, can face additional barriers to being understood if the listener becomes disengaged due to their frustrations relating to language skills.

While many interviewees spoke to the issue of power in terms that illustrated how it weighed on dynamics within the group, there were a few who commented they did not feel language was a factor in the group experience:

> I think that it doesn't impact the session because generally participants who are there, they speak English very well. And also, if they don't speak English very well, we can understand them, so it means we go slowly and we give them the possibility to talk, so it doesn't impact the session that much. (Marjus, Facilitator)

Nidhal added:

> It seemed pretty much that people who decided to participate in the Soliya program knew already that they were capable of speaking the language; they knew what they were coming into, what was required of them. Which is being or having a good level in language in speaking English. Still, some people didn't have the accent like it is meant to be, but most of them really had some really good English speaking and understanding. …We do not only speak and hear, but we also type, if someone missed something, he can just read it in the conversation below. I think we pretty

much didn't have that barrier of the language difference. (Nidhal, Participant)

Both Marjus and Nidhal's comments have an embedded acknowledgement that language skills in the group had a bearing on comprehension for some group members. They felt these limitations could be remedied by group members speaking slowly or by typing in the chat bar. So, while their comments reflect a view that language was not an issue, there is an internal reconciliation between the limits experienced by some group members with the degree to which it factored into the encounter.

"They don't have access to resources so you can expect several tech issues"

Technology plays a pivotal role in accessing and participating in the online dialogue as a stable connection is crucial, along with audio and video capabilities. Access to both the physical technology, such as a computer with a microphone and camera, and the technical infrastructure such as the internet, varies by factors such as socio-economic status, gender, age, and nationality (Ghobadi & Ghobadi, 2015; Johnson, 2010; Royal, 2005). As Beatrix identifies, issues with technology stability can result in participants having significant challenges, and, in some cases, forcing them to withdraw from the program:

> Definitely, it's a disadvantage that we can only do it in countries where you have a stable internet connection because without internet connection it's not going to work and there's a lot of computer issues. They try to do it at the Universities, so the Universities should have a stable connection, but it's still not always possible, that's a disadvantage. And I know, in my facilitation group, there was this guy that had to do it a second time because of the tech issues. But at least the second time he managed to do that, so he had a borrowed everything, a computer and new headphones and he did so many things just to make it work because he was so interested, and he liked it so much. (Beatrix, Facilitator)

Her comments also reflect that participation is, by the necessity of the online context, restricted to those individuals who have the stable internet and technology tools available to them and would exclude anyone not meeting those requirements from participation. Many interviewees noted that those facilitators and participants who more frequently experienced technology barriers to participation were from similar geographic locations:

> Some students have several tech issues, and people from Palestine, of course, have tech issues, people from Libya, Pakistan. I would say there are some people from countries in conflict; they don't have access to resources so you can expect several tech issues. Some countries have several tech issues, and it is challenging. (Mai, Facilitator)

These technical challenges meant that, for some participants, the ease of joining and participation was more significant than for those who encountered ongoing technological barriers.

> Yeah, it was from different regions, they kept disconnecting, and they had some issues with their mic. But people from, let's say, from the West region and the East region were more like let's say, comfortable as they didn't have any tech issues because most of the tech issues that are related to participants are from the Arab region. (Mohamed, Facilitator)

Individuals who are joining from locations that encounter obstacles related to technology, such as from the MENA region, are also participants who typically are not native-English speakers. This overlap is necessary to note as it is one of the ways in which power differentials can compound for certain identity groups.

"It means that you are a dominant male"

Gender, as a dynamic of power, was not as prominent in the findings. This may have been due in part to the fact that I did not specifically raise it in conversations as I did with the role of language. However, I was surprised that participants or facilitators did not more readily note it in their reflections of their experience as it was something that I observed in the group I facilitated. I noted that, in my group, the most dominant and vocal voices were male, whereas the majority of female participants required prompting by a facilitator to join in the conversation. However, only one interviewee specifically referred to it as a dynamic they experienced,

> I saw this strange dynamic; I remember a participant, a man from I don't know, maybe an Arab country, he said he was from Iraq, Kurdistan, I am not sure. And it was so surprising the way he sits, the way he talks to people, he was you know, with open legs and in our culture, let's say in this area, it means that you are a dominant male. And whenever… a female participant was speaking, this man, he was like looking around and watching TV, doing other things. And whenever I asked him a question, he just doesn't want to be asked a question by me. I don't know if it was a bias, but it was a gut instinct. It was a feeling; I had that feeling because it didn't happen when the male co-facilitator was facilitating. (Oya, Facilitator)

While this is an outlier finding, I believe it is essential to include as a dynamic as there is a significant body of literature that demonstrates how gender relates to issues of power in social settings and therefore is undoubtedly a consideration in these encounters (Crenshaw, 1995; Riddle, 2017; Tapper, 2013).

These findings align with the existing literature on dialogue in face-to-face settings on how power emerges and shapes group interactions. Even in considering power dynamics within the program and platform design, they remain ubiquitous in the encounters (Amichai-Hamburger et al., 2015; Senesh, 2012).

5.4 Benefits

Considering the implementation of dialogue practices into online settings, it is valuable to spend some time exploring the benefits and, later on, the limitations that were surfaced in this research. The benefits included broadening participant accessibility, and in doing so, increasing the diversity amongst group members, and cultivating boldness (or greater willingness to be vulnerable), as a result of the online setting.

"There Are No Barriers of Borders, or Religion, or Anything."

Having a cross-cultural dialogue opportunity available online, such as the Connect program, addresses issues of accessibility. Barriers to accessing in-person exchange or dialogue opportunities were raised by research participants; the two most often cited obstacles related to cost and logistical restrictions.

Often the costs of attending an in-person exchange program are prohibitively high. As Beatrix explains, most commonly, the participants are students who may not have disposable income to support the travel costs involved:

> The value is definitely that you don't have to travel and then you meet people. Because to have a meeting between someone from the US, and someone from the Middle East, and someone from Europe, and they don't always have the possibility to travel. And these people are normally students, so they are on a low budget, it's very interesting that they have the chance to meet. So that's also a positive thing, I think, to give them a platform where they can meet others, and really basically break stereotypes and talk. (Beatrix, Facilitator)

Another barrier to accessing in-person programs that require travel is the travel restrictions that some potential participants face. Mohamed mentions the benefits of online programs when participants are living in a dangerous location, or there are visa limitations related to their nationality:

> So yeah, the main thing I remember is bringing people from different cultures, from different backgrounds, and different countries. Also, reaching out to people who are in some dangerous and risky regions, like here in Libya and Yemen. … So, there are no barriers of borders, or religion, or anything. (Mohamed, Facilitator)

Oya also mentions travel restrictions as to why online space allows for greater accessibility. However, she also brings in cultural norms related to gender as an important consideration:

Yes, well I think that it's a great opportunity, especially for people who have troubles when it comes to travelling. Even myself, from Turkey, also people from North Africa. So, it is a great opportunity. I also realized that I remember this girl from Mauritania, saying while we were talking about gender equality, she said: "well it's okay for me to be here, to talk to you online from my computer it's okay, but when it comes to travelling I have to take permission from my father, or my husband, or my brother, etcetera." So, especially for such people, I think it's a great opportunity because they are becoming a part of something. (Oya, Facilitator)

"You Can Make It a Very Inclusive Environment"

The topic of accessibility as a benefit to the program being online was intimately connected to the view, for many interviewees, that greater convenience contributes to greater diversity amongst the participant groups:

It just opens up the door for so many more people to participate, if it were physical, the logistics of getting ten folks in a room once a week, over eight weeks, that's just not going to happen. Or the numbers are going to be so teeny tiny and the self-selection of people who've got the money, let's be honest, the diversity is going to be totally lost. Whereas with the online version, there are participants joining in from locations they would never ever be allowed to leave. I mean, in the case of, again, the Libya's of this world, or Palestinians, for pure visa reasons, they're not going to be able to leave their place. They wouldn't be able to participate were it not for it being online. Or for cultural reasons, I mean Tunisian, Moroccan, Egyptian girls I don't see them jumping on a plane and meeting face-to-face. Or even in America, we don't know everything about them but, from the participation, you know that some people are living on studentship and you know, the first one in the family to go to Uni etcetera, so it's like, they would never ever have the opportunity to get this exposure to other cultures through any other means, realistically speaking. So, even though it's not like 100% the real deal, it is coming very, very close to it, looking at the realities. (Rianne, Facilitator)

Rianne pulls together many common threads across the interviews that, by avoiding the financial, cultural, and travel obstacles that hinder an in-person dialogue program, the online space allows for increased representation of diverse groups. Amanda was another individual who raised comments about how diversity leads to an essential element of the Soliya program, that it can open people up to others whom they may not otherwise encounter:

And it's richer because of it because you can connect, the whole global piece really matters, it really matters. Even if I have a group here with students from different backgrounds, nationalities, it works. However, in this online environment, you can reach people in areas that you're not able to reach if you do it physically, even if you are in a diverse neighbourhood here in the US... you can make it a very inclusive environment. It's not exclusive to only what's accessible around you. (Amanda, Facilitator)

With the increased inclusivity, bringing people who may not be able to meet under other conditions, the online space can add richness to the issues discussed in the group conversations:

Well, one of the positive things is, of course, outreach. You can't reach all the people who are able to join us in these online sessions. And that's the beauty of it because we are talking about nationalism, newcomers, migration, and all these things, it doesn't really pay well only to have representation from Europe or the West. You need people that come from the other side of this modern issue. And that really enriches the discussion and everything that is transpiring in the session. (Joanna, Facilitator)

Joanna's comments bring up the added value that comes from having diversity represented in the dialogue space. By allowing access to participation through having it online, a more extensive range of experiences is brought into the conversation, thus bringing further nuance that comes from multiple ways of viewing, understanding, and interpreting a topic or issue.

"I Think That This Makes People Brave to Speak"

Finally, many research participants shared that the online setting allowed for an increased boldness amongst group members when sharing about their lives and their viewpoints:

> Because it's online, there are a lot of benefits for people who are shy, for example. ... So, it means that I don't know you, so who cares? I am on the other side of the world; I am just here within this screen, and what can happen? If I don't like these people, I just turn off the camera! (Marjus, Facilitator)

Marjus reflects a sense of safety in the anonymity that being in dialogue online allows if something uncomfortable happens or if you realize that you do not want to be a part of the conversation any longer you can always exit the room abruptly. So, not only are participants potentially bolder in an online space, but that the boldness comes from the degree of anonymity that is afforded online along with the sense of security that comes from discussing potentially culturally taboo topics with people outside their daily life:

> There is something good about it being online, and with people that we don't have a relationship with, they are not our colleagues, they are not in the same physical space. So I think that this makes people brave to speak, so I don't know you, I just got to meet Rachel for one time or two times, and I don't know if we will meet again after that so why should I be somehow afraid of expressing myself, no I will express myself no matter what. I will say my ideas. I don't think I would be afraid of saying things that I usually don't say in my environment. And this is something that some people mentioned, "we share ideas about ourselves, thoughts about our life, our relationship with our family members, our religious beliefs, our political affiliations and stuff like that, with us, in the group." While they say that it would not be safe to speak about these topics in a face-to-face environment. (Hassan, Facilitator)

Souhail adds:

> Yeah, you can speak yourself; you can speak your mind freely and openly. But when you meet people in person, sometimes, maybe our group, if we meet in person, I am not sure what will happen, but sometimes people tend to be shy when they meet people in person, right? So, if they are shy, they cannot really speak a lot, they cannot express their minds a lot, they cannot say what they want. For me, I have no problem whether we are online or meet in person, but I think meeting online gives people the opportunity to speak and express themselves more. ... Maybe sometimes you can say some things that people may not agree with you, or they may not like. So, when you speak about, especially when you have people from different backgrounds, sometimes you will say something about your cultures that people from your culture do not agree with, or speaking with people from different backgrounds gives you the courage to express your ideas because they will not judge you, they will not disagree. (Souhail, Participant)

Both Hassan and Souhail share the observation that engaging with people from different cultural backgrounds in online spaces allows for greater honesty than might exist with people from the same culture and location. They believe that, because the background or cultural context is different, there will be less judgement. The lack of familiarity makes it so that people will accept one another more readily than if they share the same culture.

5.5 Limitations

While the identified benefits of the program were plentiful, there were also limitations to the experience being online.

"Technology Tends to Fail Us"

The most commonly commented upon limitation by interviewees was technology; as Joanna (Facilitator) put it, "one of the negative things is that we rely heavily on technology, and technology tends to fail us." Facilitators and participants both experienced challenges themselves, and with other group members, due to the dependence on stable internet connection, video and audio capabilities, and the Exchange Platform stability—with which some individuals experienced unreliability. The reliance on technology for access can lead to frustrations amongst the group members; if a critical piece of the technological equation that allows someone to join the virtual space fails, such as a faulty internet connection or an updated operating system, it can result in missing an entire session. These challenges with technology perhaps reflect the double-sided coin of online dialogue: the technology that allows the program to exist in the first place can also place obstacles to participation. While the reliance on these technological components can create obstacles to participation if an individual does not have access to the requisite infrastructure, this research suggests that interviewees viewed the online nature of the program to provide greater accessibility than exclusion.

"We're in the Car!"

When meeting virtually, challenges can emerge related to the physical location that each group member is in when they join the online space. Mai shared an example of a participant from one of her groups:

> She logged in from her phone, and she was driving her car, and she was laughing with her friends, and she was like, "we're in the car!" and she was laughing out loud. And, I don't know if she was busy having fun, she shouldn't come to the session and be that destructive, logging from her car and doing this. (Mai, Facilitator)

In Mai's experience, this participant was behaving rudely to the rest of the group, by joining in a manner that seemed inconsiderate and disregarded privacy concerns for other members by having her friends in the physical space with her when she joined. These environmental distractions were also something that I observed while facilitating my Connect group, certain group members often had third parties in the room with them; we could see them occasionally in the background or observed that the group member was talking to someone offscreen. As a facilitator, I found these distractions challenging to contend with, especially when it seemed there could be other people who were not part of the group listening in to the conversation without the knowledge of other group members. While we tried to mitigate this challenge by reminding our group of the need for privacy and respecting one another by finding a quiet place or using headphones, if it was not possible to seclude themselves, it remained an issue through the duration of the program.

Participants joining from disparate locations also presents challenges for facilitators to connect with unengaged participants, as Burcu illustrates:

> We had some participants who were kind of shy or seemed uninterested in the topics and discussions. So, we really tried to get them involved, we wrote them in their native language, we asked them all the time, "how are you" or "is there something we can do to help?" but I think it missed them somehow. And it's kind of the obstacle in this kind of environment because when you are not in the room you cannot have, for example, an energizer for people to get more active or participate. Sometimes they fall into their corner and there are only some things that you can do in the online world if the participants don't reply to you when you try. (Burcu, Facilitator)

Burcu highlights a unique challenge within the online space of not being able to connect directly with participants who may be disengaged or facing barriers to participation. If the participant chooses, in the online environment, to ignore messages and chats from a facilitator, or if those prompts are somehow missed in the technical environment, there is not a clear path for the facilitator to discuss further with those individuals.

"There Is a Kind of Spirit that You Miss"

Many of the limitations that were raised by interviewees were presented in contrast to the benefits of face-to-face settings. This comparison between virtual and in-person was something I raised specifically in our conversations, as I was curious about what might be gained or lost in the online space versus in-person encounters. There was a common refrain about the physical nearness to another person, which allows you to perceive them or understand them in a nuanced way that might not be possible in an online setting. Arij shared a story from a group she facilitated whereby a group member likened the experience to attending church:

> Some part that we can miss in this experience is the human contact, the physical contact, like the spirit of the person. And this is something that I have seen some participants comment on, and one of them had a brilliant question because one of them said, "it's the same having a discussion online or offline," and this person was Christian. So the other participant asked them, "okay so what if you go to the Church but online, you don't go to church on Sunday or Saturday, you go to church to have this kind of meeting, and they are singing," and then he told him "what if you had church online? Would that be the same kind of experience for you?" And he said "no," and he was laughing so hard, and that explained that it does not, that there is a kind of spirit that you miss in the online communication. (Arij, Facilitator)

Some interviewees associated this idea of capturing the spirit of someone with the body language and facial expressions that are present when meeting someone in person:

> So, the online, you know you can't use the body language while online, only the facial expressions. And if you don't have a good connection, then you lose that detail as well. And already you have a very small icon appearing on the screens, so it's already far from the camera you already lose them. So, it's, of course, never something that's like face-to-face communication, but, anyhow, better than nothing. I mean otherwise…they won't be hearing anything from such a different person at all. (Betül, Facilitator)

Nidhal connects the lack of human connection within an online space to the inability to physically interact with each other:

> Of course, I used to think that meeting face-to-face is always better than online because, in face-to-face, you get to see the partner in HD, no pixels, no internet issues. And in real life, you can take the expressions more honestly than online, and besides you can shake hands, you can kiss each other; there is this physical interaction

that is added to the conversation or the experience of exchange. (Nidhal, Participant)

The physicality of being in-person with another dialogue participant was a commonly-cited limitation of the online program, something that many interviewees missed in the experience. Others felt that the lack of being face-to-face translated into a reduced level of participation, underscoring the idea that being in-person obligates you to a different level of participation than perhaps being online necessitates.

While the limitations here illustrate some considerations that are ultimately outside of the influence of facilitators and the Soliya organization itself, such as environmental distractions in the location of the group member or local internet service failing, many limitations can amplify existing dynamics amongst group members.

5.6 'The Setting' and Positive Peace

The above findings aid in illuminating our understanding of how positive peace might emerge from online dialogue encounters. There appears to be a reach available due to the online nature, creating possibilities for individuals to encounter other across a breadth of society. This range and diversity are valuable in crossing over the dimensions of cultural, direct, and structural peace, as the more accessible dialogue encounters are, the greater the opportunity for holistic influence, action, and transformation. Additionally, the sense of bravery that can emerge presents an increased likelihood that participants will be open to discussing systemic and structural issues of oppression and violence.

However, this chapter has also surfaced that, while people feel bold, power dynamics remain. One of the prominent ways in which issues of social dominance and power evidenced themselves was within language. Language is not neutral; it is imbued with subconscious meanings and subtle nods to systems of advantage and persecution. Therefore, when in dialogue, it is not only the speaker's words but also the inherent meaning or interpretation of those words that dictate the encounter's power dynamics (Hermans & Dimaggio, 2007). These findings align with the literature on dialogue encounters and dialogue theory. As Wood identifies, between oppressors and the oppressed, there is a privileging of language and speech that can remain invisible:

Whereas members of marginal groups often learn to communicate in ways approved by dominant culture, the converse seldom occurs. How can people enter into dialogue on equal bases if the preferred communication style of only some participants is regarded as legitimate? (Wood, 2004, p. xxi)

Power imbalances can be indicative of broader issues whereby violence has manifested in myriad structural ways. These structural forms of violence diminish opportunity and equity for the oppressed and marginalized (Galtung, 1996). Structural violence is often insidious, and as such, it can pose a challenging obstacle on the path to positive peace, as it is difficult to recognize and articulate. Galtung identified this as especially problematic for the oppressed: "the object of structural violence may be persuaded not to perceive this at all....Structural violence is silent, it does not show - it is essentially static, it is the tranquil waters" (Galtung, 1996, p. 173). Given the power imbalances that language presents, reflection must be given to how effectively a program such as Soliya, which operates in English and therefore privileges specific demographics, can contribute to positive peace.

While these online conversations may take place more readily and boldly, there remain risks of avoidance and negative contact. And, while the reach of such dialogue programs increases with the online format, there is a strong perception illustrated in these limitations that the impact diminishes due to the virtual nature and that face-to-face encounters remain more powerful. These are significant challenges in connecting the emergence of positive peace and online dialogue encounters and essential to consider as we move into Chapter 6 (The Encounter).

5.7 Cogitatio

In the previous chapter, I reflected on my positionality in the research. Looking now at how the experience of data collection unfolded, from facilitating the Connect group to conducting interviews, I see ways that my position and identities shaped my interactions, my collection, and my interpretations.

'Insider'

My role as a facilitator lent me an 'insider' view of the experience. In this regard, whenever I was functioning in my researcher role, I was also navigating the insider perspective that came from holding a facilitator role. Being a facilitator meant that I had an internal perspective on the Connect program, and I knew how the design and intent might be contributing to the experience for participants. I also drew on some of my own experiences in prompting questions for the facilitators I interviewed. For example, in my experiences as a facilitator, I felt that even though I wasn't contributing content to the group discussions, I was still part of a learning journey by being in the space of encounter where dialogue was unfolding. Based on this personal experience, I was curious if other facilitators shared this experience and raised the question with them in our interviews.

However, having an experience as a facilitator also meant that my instinct was to speculate or assume what an interviewee might share—particularly if they were also a facilitator. I had to actively step back, internally, when someone would make a comment or share a story of how they approached a situation in their group that was at odds with how I would view it or react in their place.

In other moments, when I was enacting my facilitator role in group settings, I was negotiating the balance between that role and my motivations as a researcher. I raised this experience in my fieldnotes following the last group session in May 2019:

```
Being part of the facilitated sessions is a very
different experience. As a facilitator, I felt a lot of
responsibility, and I think rightfully so, that I didn't
want my research to interfere with my role as facilitator
and helping to enable a process that was useful for the
participants and valuable for them. But I also am aware
I wanted to see certain things happening, to observe
certain things. And the group that I was with didn't move
through the group stages the way that I think that I would
want. (Fieldnotes, May 1, 2019)[2]
```

This fieldnote reflects the internal negotiation that was taking place each time I was facilitating: there was the researcher agenda interacting with my facilitator capacity. I always felt that my role as a facilitator took precedent in those sessions; I didn't want the group to lose valuable opportunities

---

[2] To distinguish research data, fieldnotes will be displayed in Courier font.

for dialogic moments because of my dual agendas. However, it was a negotiation within myself. As the weeks went on, I had to ensure my facilitation choices were driven by how the group was organically developing and not based on what I wanted to see happen for the sake of the research.

Power

I want to pause here to contemplate how power informed this research process. I was actively aware ahead of time from my literature review, and personal experiences, that power dynamics might surface during the dialogue encounters in the group setting. What I was less attuned to in advance was my own position of power in the group and interviews. My field notes from the third group session reveal my increasing awareness of how my positioning as a native-English speaker had given me power to that point in the group:

> Today's conversation about language reinforced for me the power dynamics in the group around language. Until today, I have been the only native English speaker in the group, today, an American native English speaker joined. As a Caucasian, English speaker, who is the facilitator and who they know is [an academic] I feel a lot of power in the group that I need to be aware of. (*Fieldnotes, March 25, 2019*)

Having the dynamic of language in mind from my group sessions, I was able to carry that awareness into my interviews, paying extra attention to my word choice, and making sure I was checking in that what I was asking was clear. The challenge came when interviewees were searching for a word in English, and I wanted to offer a suggestion but recognized that doing so would presume that I already knew what they were going to say.
*I also had the impression that power was at play in some interviews because of my position as an academic researcher. A few interviewees commented that they had responded to my invitation because it can be beneficial to connect with internationals from English speaking countries. One interviewee answered a question and then asked, "*is this what you wanted to hear?*" which immediately raised a flag for me that they were responding based on what they perceived I wanted them to say. From that point on, I was especially attuned to how I was presenting my questions so as*

to avoid leading them towards any specific answer. It also raised my awareness of the need to ask robust follow up questions to probe deeper into responses that may have been catered to what the interviewee thought I wanted to hear.

During the data collection and analysis, I actively attempted to interrogate how my position was shaping what was unfolding and what I was seeing. However, the experiences of power surfaced above raise the concern that power was at play, even when I was trying to mitigate it.

5.8 Summary

This chapter is one of the largest in this book due to the importance of providing a thorough and nuanced description of the setting for this online ethnographic inquiry. I began by giving an overview of the Soliya program aims, and by situating an understanding of the program within the previously identified characteristics of face-to-face dialogue, as discussed in-depth in the Chapter 3. The chapter then followed in three thematic sections: the program design, the intangible dynamics, and the benefits and limitations. Together, these three sections establish a full picture of the setting and context in which the online dialogue unfolds. There are both tangible and intangible factors at play in shaping the experience through the dialogue program. The tangible factors relate to the role of facilitator and the program design, while the intangibles reference the social and power dynamics which can be insidious and, as such, challenging to articulate the myriad ways in which they shape the dialogue encounters. The exploration of the benefits and limitations contributes knowledge to the existing literature on online peacebuilding practices. As discussed in Chapter 3, this current knowledge primarily relates to other peacebuilding models predicated on the Contact Hypothesis, peace education, and games for peace. Musings on the connection between the setting and positive peace are offered. Finally, the chapter provided a reflexive passage on how my positioning as an insider, and dynamics of power, influenced and informed the data collection and analysis of this research inquiry.

References

About Us. (n.d.). Retrieved from the Soliya website. https://www.soliya.net/about/about-us

Ahearn, L. M. (2001). Language and agency. *Annual Review of Anthropology, 30*, 109–137.

Arao, B., & Clemens, K. (2013). From safe spaces to brave spaces. In L. M. Landreman (Ed.), *The art of effective facilitation: Reflections from social justice educators* (pp. 135–150). Sterling, VA: Stylus.

Bryn, S. (2015). Can dialogue make a difference?: The experience of the Nansen dialogue network. In S. P. Ramet, A Simkus & O. Listhaug (Eds.), *Civic and uncivic values in Kosovo* (pp. 365–394). Central European University Press. Retrieved from http://www.jstor.org/stable/10.7829/j.ctt13wzttq.21

Chaitin, J. (2012). Co-creating peace: Confronting psychosocial-economic injustices in the Israeli-Palestinian context. In B. Charbonneau & G. Parent (Eds.), *Peacebuilding, memory and reconciliation: Bridging top-down and bottom-up approaches* (pp. 146–162). Routledge.

Connect Program. (n.d.). Retrieved from the Soliya website. https://www.soliya.net/programs/connect-program

Crenshaw, K. W. (1995). The intersection of race and gender. In K. W. Crenshaw, N. Gotanda, G. Peller, & K. Thomas (Eds.), *Critical race theory: The key writings that formed the movement*. New Press.

Curriculum Overview. (n.d.). Retrieved from the Soliya website. https://www.soliya.net/sites/default/files/pdfs/CurriculumOverview.pdf

Ellis, D. G., & Maoz, I. (2012). Communication and reconciling intergroup conflict. In H. Giles (Ed.), *The handbook of intergroup communication* (pp. 153–166). Routledge.

Facilitation Training. (n.d.). Retrieved from the Soliya website. https://www.soliya.net/programs/facilitation-training

Frantell, K. A., Miles, J. R., & Ruwe, A. M. (2019). Intergroup dialogue: A review of recent empirical research and its implications for research and practice. *Small Group Research, 50*(5), 654–695. https://doi.org/10.1177/1046496419835923

Galtung, J. (1996). *Peace by peaceful means: Peace and conflict, development and civilization*. London: Sage Publications. https://doi.org/10.4135/9781446221631

Ghobadi, S., & Ghobadi, Z. (2015). How access gaps interact and shape digital divide: A cognitive investigation. *Behaviour & Information Technology, 34*(4), 330–340. https://doi.org/10.1080/0144929X.2013.833650

Gurin, P., Nagda, B. (Ratnesh) A., & Zúñiga, X. (2013). *Dialogue across difference: Practice, theory, and research on intergroup dialogue*. New York, NY: Russell Safe Foundation.

Hammack, P. L. (2008). Narrative and the cultural psychology of identity. *Personality and Social Psychology Review, 12*(3), 222–247. https://doi.org/10.1177/1088868308316892

Hammond, S. C., Anderson, R., & Cissna, K. N. (2003). The problematics of dialogue and power. *Annals of the International Communication Association, 27*(1), 125–157. https://doi.org/10.1080/23808985.2003.11679024

Hermans, H. J. M., & Dimaggio, G. (2007). Self, identity, and globalization in times of uncertainty: A dialogical analysis. *Review of General Psychology, 11*(1), 31–61. https://doi.org/10.1037/1089-2680.11.1.31

Johnson, V. (2010). Women and the internet. *Indian Journal of Gender Studies, 17*(1), 151–163. https://doi.org/10.1177/097152150901700107

Maoz, I., Steinberg, S., Bar-On, D., & Fakhereldeen, M. (2002). The dialogue between the "Self" and the "Other": A process analysis of Palestinian-Jewish encounters in Israel. *Human Relations, 55*(8), 931–962. https://doi.org/10.1177/0018726702055008178

Phipps, A. (2014). 'They are bombing now': 'Intercultural Dialogue' in times of conflict. *Language and Intercultural Communication, 14*(1), 108–124. https://doi.org/10.1080/14708477.2013.866127

Riddle, K. C. (2017). Structural violence, intersectionality, and justpeace: Evaluating women's peacebuilding agency in Manipur, India. *Hypatia, 32*(3), 574–592. https://doi.org/10.1111/hypa.12340

Royal, C. (2005). A meta-analysis of journal articles intersecting issues of internet and gender. *Journal of Technical Writing and Communication, 35*(4), 403–429. https://doi.org/10.2190/3RBM-XKEQ-TRAF-E8GN

Saguy, T., Tausch, N., Dovidio, J. F., & Pratto, F. (2009). The irony of harmony: Intergroup contact can produce false expectations for equality. *Psychological Science, 20*(1), 114. https://doi.org/10.1111/j.1467-9280.2008.02261.x

Senesh, D. (2012). Restorative moments: From First Nations people in Canada to conflicts in an Israeli-Palestinian dialogue group. In B. Charbonneau & G. Parent (Eds.), *Peacebuilding, memory and reconciliation: Bridging top-down and bottom-up approaches* (pp. 163–175). Routledge.

Tapper, A. J. H. (2013). A pedagogy of social justice education: Social identity theory, intersectionality, and empowerment. *Conflict Resolution Quarterly, 30*(4), 411–445. https://doi.org/10.1002/crq.21072

Wood, J. T. (2004). Foreword: Entering into dialogue. In R. Anderson, L. A. Baxter, & K. N. Cissna (Eds.), *Dialogue: Theorizing difference in communication studies* (pp. xv–xxii). Sage.

CHAPTER 6

The Encounter

The previous two chapters provided an immersive understanding of the participants as well as the environment of the Connect program in which the dialogue unfolds. As a reminder of where this chapter is situated within the overall narrative, I include Fig. 6.1.

This chapter turns to the dialogue encounter itself, exploring findings related to two phenomena occurring during the dialogue. The first of these phenomena is what unfolds within the individual, and the second is what happens between participants in dialogue—what Buber (1947) identifies as the "sphere of between" (p. 241).

6.1 INDIVIDUAL IN ENCOUNTER

There are two predominant themes to explore which reflect what was happening for the individual in the dialogue process. The first of these themes is distinctiveness—the desire of individuals to present themselves and aspects of their identity in ways that added dimension and subtlety. The second theme is self-reflection, wherein individuals considered their own identities, perceptions of self, and reactions to others.

© The Author(s), under exclusive license to Springer Nature
Singapore Pte Ltd. 2022
R. Nolte-Laird, *Peacebuilding Online*,
https://doi.org/10.1007/978-981-16-6013-9_6

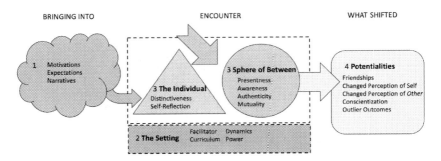

Fig. 6.1 Location of Chapter 6 in overarching findings narrative

Distinctiveness

Amongst interviewees, there is a sense of wanting to convey nuance within their national identities and bring dimension to potential views others may have of who they are and where they come from. Participants were aware that others in the dialogue might have preconceptions of them linked to their nationality, and they wanted to raise information that might contradict or add fullness to those opinions. For example, Oldez wished to share in her group that the youth in Tunisia were involved in the revolution, and that they cared about implementing change in their country:

> I remember when we talked about politics, I talked about the revolution in Tunisia. And I said that young people they are the people who made the revolution, and they want to change things in Tunisia, and they want to have a better future, they want to change their life. And that people that didn't really (*pause*) they found that very important and nice that people in Tunisia care about these things. (Oldez, Participant)

Similarly, Karoline was aware of stereotypes that might exist amongst other members of her group when they thought about Italy. She wanted to bring gradation to those views by sharing what she perceives to be the more complicated aspects of Italian society:

> Yeah, I would say that, especially from the United States, I had this feedback where they used to think of Italy like;

> dolce vita, pizza, pasta. So, I had the chance to talk about even our policies and the immigration issues that we have. So, it came up always like, "okay, I am doing a vacation in Italy, so it should be fine," but of course, we have different issues, for example, the immigration problem. And, of course, other cultures, sometimes they don't get interested in a country where you are like, "okay everything is fine over there, I don't want to read something in the paper in Italy." But of course, they had the opportunity to listen from me the bad kind of things of the society which is not always good. And they didn't know about the problem of immigration, for example. And also, for myself, I thought that Italian people were just like, "okay, we are so friendly and stuff, and so we are just here to talk about it freely." But of course, we have problems over here, so it was something that I wanted to give information to other girls if they wanted to. (Karoline, Participant)

It was important to Karoline that she raise aspects of her culture she viewed as negative because she wanted to demonstrate that what is commonly presented on the surface about her country can hide issues that she finds troubling.

While Oldez and Karoline wanted to share information that reflected political topics in their country, Nidhal sought to bring awareness about cultural norms in Tunisia:

> We had the chance to share something strange about your country... I said, "in my country, everyone is friendly, to the point where you are, for example, in the taxi or something like that and you just start speaking trash to someone beside you, and he doesn't find it offensive and he will start laughing and making jokes with you." Everyone was like, "oh, really, you curse someone, and he doesn't reply to it?" I said, "everyone feels okay with it." (Nidhal, Participant)

There is a sense that Nidhal was sharing a part of his culture he is proud of, something that might illuminate for the group how his own personality and disposition is informed by his wider culture.

For other participants in the dialogue, such as Sarra (Participant), the conversations brought in information beyond what she had been aware of previously, "well, little things… for example, in Syria, they are in the transition phase after war, and you know, so I am discovering their lifestyle now and their situation, which is not normal for others, you know?" Sarra's exchanges with group members enabled her to perceive the reality of others with greater nuance and awareness after hearing about their experiences. For participants, the opportunity to demonstrate one's distinctiveness, and being open to seeing the distinctiveness of others, was a significant aspect of their experience.

"Think About My Identity and My Values and Beliefs"

While group members were conscientious about how they were presenting themselves and their nationality to the group, there was also an internal act of self-reflection occurring. Amanda expresses this act of reflection as awareness and self-examination:

> I think that it's really the piece on awareness. Who is willing to re-examine and become more aware of what has shaped their lives? And then, they are able to really begin to open other windows to understanding what has shaped others, and what that means. I think that we have a group of people that are interested in dialogue that are more willing to put themselves into dialogue where it is attractive to people that have a propensity to open those doors. (Amanda, Facilitator)

In Amanda's view, there is a connection between the act of self-reflection and openness to exploring the identity of *other*. Hassan comments on the opportunity to consider and understand his identity and beliefs when he was a participant:

> And myself, I think that I had stereotypes of myself, I discovered this when I came to Soliya. … So, it was a good opportunity for me to focus on myself and to think about my identity and my values and beliefs and things like that. (Hassan, Facilitator)

As Hassan's comments signal, the act of self-reflection can lead to an increased understanding of self. For example, Mostafa commented several times in our conversations that he found himself identifying with a "Western" view and disposition more than his own culture:

> I felt like I am not thinking that way, I felt like I am thinking maybe in a more Western way, I am not really close to Arab countries also, not just Egypt, I felt I am not really close to what Arab countries often think. (Mostafa, Participant)

Mostafa's experience reframed how he viewed himself—his personality and disposition—within a wider societal and cultural context. Others, such as Layla (Participant), found themselves noting parts of their personality or character traits they had previously been unaware of, "yes, (*pause*) I learned that I am the kind of person who doesn't like conflict. I try to avoid conflict in relationships, so I felt that I should change that." Layla comments that, having learned that she tends to avoid conflict, she wants to shift her behaviour to address that trait.

Others similarly noted how the act of self-reflection translated to intentionality in behaviour. For example, Nicolas mentions that, when he was a participant, he already knew that he was someone who loved to experience other cultures. He wanted to be intentional about how he engaged with other group members to take advantage of the diversity that was present:

> I am someone who loves to travel, not just to break the routine, but also to explore different cultures and see a new world basically. And just to know that I was in a room, an online room, with people from different regions, different cultures, it felt so cool in a sense. So, I really forced myself from the first session on to jump in the conversations and break the ice from the beginning and take full advantage of the opportunity. (Nicolas, Facilitator)

While Nicolas shares how he intentionally was present in the dialogue, others also commented on the intentionality that came from self-reflection.

The practice of self-reflection and intentionality in the dialogue encounter is not limited to participants; facilitators also shared how self-reflection occurs for them. Commonly, for facilitators, this reflection related to triggers—topics or situations that, when they arise in the group, could elicit an emotional reaction. Triggers tend to be individualized; each person may feel more emotionally attached or invested in specific topics over others. A component of the Soliya facilitator training relates to self-awareness regarding triggers and how to manage them when something surfaces in a group you are facilitating. Arij shares how initially she thought that, because she does not see herself as a "hot-tempered person," she would not be triggered in the groups she was facilitating. However, through her experiences and practice of self-reflection, she realized that there are dynamics that elicit an emotional reaction from her:

> Watching my triggers, I am not a hot-tempered person. I am at the opposite side; I am the coldest person ever. And I thought I don't have triggers, but it turns out I have them (*laughter*). And so this is something I have learned about myself, and I have learned to deal with it and the last time I felt triggered or not really comfortable was when I had the Express group that I told you about, with the participant who cannot communicate in English, I was explaining again and again and again, and I feel like there are participants who were starting to feel bored and they wanted to talk. And I didn't know what I should be doing at this moment, and it was a total mess, and I had to step back and watch myself and watch my reaction because I really got worked up and said: "Oh look at you, you are really nervous, look at you, what kind of reaction are you having?" So yeah, I had to step back a little bit and reflect on my reactions, and after that session, I tried to think about what got me to this level, and how I can deal with in a more relaxed way and not being carried out about this. So yeah, I am reflecting a little bit about my reaction and my triggers. (Arij, Facilitator)

While bringing awareness to her reactions, Arij reflects on what is happening in the dialogue that is eliciting an emotional response from her. By articulating her triggers, she can then bring greater intentionality to how she reacts in future group sessions. Burcu also comments on learning to manage her emotions when particular dynamics emerged in the group conversation:

> I learned that I can control triggers when I feel like… how can I say, I can shut it down. I will explain it without giving names, but in our facilitation group, we had a lot of people from my country, and sometimes I didn't agree with what they were saying about the current issues in the country. Political or socialaspects or how they, for example, when you asked them something special about Turkey, and they reply with something that you really don't agree with. I felt that I can just continue with smiling and (*laughter*) don't make any gestures or shocked faces or looking like I am pissed off or something. So, that was something that was good. (Burcu, Facilitator)

The comments from Burcu and Arij reveal the common experience in dialogue of reflecting on one's emotions without allowing those reactions to restrict the ability to facilitate dialogic encounters. The themes of distinctiveness and self-reflection illustrate some of what was occurring within the individual. The following section will examine what was happening between individuals in the dialogue space.

6.2 The Sphere of Between

While Buber's philosophy of dialogue is Chapter 2, it is valuable to pause here and revisit a few important constructs. Buber identifies dialogue as the definitive humanizing act—that it is through the I-Thou relation that both self and *other* become fully human (Buber, 1947, 1970). He identifies the "sphere of between" (Buber, 1947, p. 241) as a third space where the individuals in dialogue encounter each other, a space distinct from each separate person or the shared physical setting. I draw on Buber's articulation of the sphere of between to construct an understanding of where the dialogic encounter itself unfolds in the metaphysical sense.

While the previous chapter described the physical platform along with the intangible factors and dynamics that shaped, informed, and contributed the context for the Connect program, dialogue itself is not a continuous occurrence. Dialogue happens in moments (Baxter, 2004;

Cissna & Anderson, 1998), such that the sphere of between represents a shared third space that dialogue participants inhabit for an indeterminate amount of time.

As established in Chapter 2, there are noted characteristics of dialogue as identified through the work of Martin Buber: presentness, awareness, authenticity and mutuality. These dialogue characteristics emerged when looking at what unfolded in the sphere of between during the dialogue.

Presentness

To be present in the dialogic moment is to give full attention to how one's self is embodied and represented in the shared space while being present to hearing and considering what the dialogue partner is sharing. Within presentness, the "dialogic person listens receptively and attentively and responds readily and totally. We are willing to reveal ourselves to others in ways appropriate to the relationship and to receive their revelation" (Johannesen, 2000, p. 154). To enable presentness, the individual in dialogue actively minimizes distractions and reflects upon what is being shared.

For many interviewees, the characteristic of presentness was evidenced in how they intentionally listened to others, as Mohamed articulates:

> I learned how to listen to people more carefully and understand why they are saying. And what is the idea behind what they are saying and discovering their cultures and sometimes their beliefs and what they think about other countries and cultures also breaking some stereotypes sometimes. (Mohamed, Facilitator)

By enacting presentness, Mohamed allows himself to interrogate his assumptions and stereotypes, reframing how he understands the *other*. Karoline echoed these comments as she spoke about the difficulty in hearing challenging opinions while intentionally listening and acknowledging what the other person is sharing:

> It was challenging for me because, of course, it is something that you're supposed to discuss together because Soliya was born as a platform where you discuss about different topics. And at first, I was kind of shocked because I didn't know that even young people think the way

> that old people used to think, so it was challenging, of course. But Soliya, for that site of the conversation, gave me the opportunity to wait, just because we had this press button to talk, so you have to press, and then you talk. So, I had the opportunity to listen to all the point of views of the girls, so I can analyze every single point. ... So, it is very sensitive stuff, so I had the chance to respect their point of view and, of course, listen, because that is something we don't do, especially with our conversations physically. We tend to interrupt other people because we think that "you are saying something that is not correct," so we have to stop you and then talk over you. And that is not something that you can do on the Soliya platform because you have to wait and to listen to all the points of view of the other person. (Karoline, Participant)

For Karoline, the immediate reaction to the comments from her peers is shock, but she responds by listening to them rather than moving into a debate. The comments from Karoline raise the connection between the technical platform and the characteristics of dialogue. In this case, she notes how the talk button functionality caused her to be attentive in listening to others and not rushing in with her own comments. Nidhal also raised the flexibility required to be present to hear what the *other* is saying:

> I mean, if you have just the ability to listen and to respect the idea of the other and to hear their answer and do not tilt and try to adapt. And be flexible in mind, you don't just be convinced that your idea is the ideal and the true. There is always a place for wrong in your idea. There is always a chance for fixing and changing the mind and understanding, and so on. That's how we learn, that's how we improve, that's how we change for good. (Nidhal, Participant)

Nidhal reflects on his belief that being present in dialogue opens the opportunity for individual change and growth. For facilitators as well as participant, presentness existed in their encounters:

> And one of the things that really got me into the idea of being a facilitator was that I was very curious to

explore what other people thought of issues. So nowadays, we sometimes get lost in the discussion, and we don't pay attention to what the other person is saying; we care more about what we will say afterwards. And being a facilitator definitely helped me tone down that and pay more attention to the other people when they are talking. (Joanna, Facilitator)

Joanna reflects on how her experience as a facilitator required the practice of intentional listening to hear what others in dialogue might share and to silence the internal voices that would rush to debate or counterarguments.

Awareness

Awareness occurs when an individual attempts to see the *other's* perspective and "imagine an event or feeling from the side of the other. ... attempt[s] to understand factually and emotionally the other's experience" (Johannesen, 2000, p. 153). Just as with mutuality, the person in dialogue does not give up their own beliefs but can hold them while "imagining the reality of the other" (Cissna & Anderson, 1998, p. 64). Awareness connects to intentionality, as several interviewees commented on their need to be attuned to their focus in the dialogue:

> Well, I think that when I started being interested in the program, I knew that I had to be open-minded, and I knew that I had to reflect on what I was going to say and what people were saying. ...I think that when I was in the program I didn't want to start an argument and I was just curious to know what people thought and what they believe in, so it was a chance to get to know them rather than starting a debate and just telling my point of view, it was a bit different I guess. (Anna, Participant)

Karoline adds:

> We had different points of view, of course, and sometimes it was really hard to get into their shoes. Understanding a hundred percent their view because you are grown in a specific society, so you are grown with that, so understanding the different culture made me realize it is a completely curious thing to do. Because if you are just

staying in your country and you don't develop a curiosity
of the culture, of course, you are just, like "okay the
LBGT community is fine, and I don't recognize you and blah
blah blah." (Karoline, Participant)

The comments from Anna and Karoline illustrate that they were purposely attentive to what might happen in the dialogue. They knew that other perspectives and opinions would likely arise and, instead of moving into a debate or closing the door to the conversation, they wanted to remain curious and open to what was shared.

The intentionality behind awareness can be particularly important when contentious or political topics are discussed. For example, Nidhal found the conversation about Israel and Palestine to be a significant moment:

Actually, while having the conversation and exchanging
ideas, we changed our minds about people and how other
people think. And I can tell you an example, we had three
Muslims and one Jewish person, and we talked about the
conflict in Palestine and Israel, and we heard how the
Israeli was experiencing the war, and how a Palestinian
experiences the war and we literally saw how the same,
everyone is living in fear, and there is no concern,
(*pause*) I am not talking about military or politically,
but the people are both harmed and live in fear, and both
are experiencing the bad times.
  So (*pause*) before we were expecting that the other side
is living in peace and it's just one side with the war.
(Nidhal, Participant)

In Nidhal's story, the group opens up to "imagine the real" (Johannesen, 2000, p. 153) of the *other* in such a way that allows the possibilities for multiple experiences of the same context to exist. Duha also shared a story about their group discussing the Israeli and Palestinian conflict in a way that embodied awareness:

So, of course, everything has its drawbacks, like it might
cause some kind of tension among the group members. But
I think the benefit we are gaining from this is even
more since we are able to hear different opinions about
these topics that we usually don't discuss. So, it's like

> talking about it, it widens our field of thinking and field of knowledge about it, and it enables us to hear others' opinions about it, which we usually don't.
> Like for example, in that session, when we talked about the Israeli and Palestine conflict. There are a lot of things that I really did not expect, but I heard during our discussion like, for example, most of the Arab group members did not hate Israel or did not think Israel was a racist country. And that is totally against my expectation since I thought that most Arabs actually are not on good terms with Israel or even hate Israel. And I was also surprised when one of the American group members said that the media there, in the US, most of the media, is actually with the Palestinian side not with the Israeli side, and that was also against my expectations since I had this idea and I believe most of the people here have the idea that in the West most people, and the media and everything, they support Israel and not Palestine. So, talking about this topic, that we usually don't talk about, widened my field of knowledge about it and made me know things that I really did not know about or corrected some thoughts that I had about these topics. (Duha, Participant)

Duha's group approached a topic that is politically contentious and can be taboo and was able to surface different perspectives and experiences, allowing for expanded knowledge and viewpoints.

Awareness between individuals in dialogue can also allow for personal self-reflection in the encounter. For example, Oldez shares how she learned about herself through enacting awareness while in dialogue:

> Like I said, it's very important to have that feeling that you want to be open to people, and you want to share about your thoughts, and you are safe to say what you want. And that helped me to discover that I can go into a deep conversation with people, and I can accept different thoughts and different people and also to have that high estimate of yourself. (Oldez, Participant)

As Oldez shares, as the characteristic of awareness was present in her group, she turned that experience into an opportunity for self-reflection and identified her capacity to hold in-depth conversations with people across difference—accepting their difference while still holding her views and beliefs.

Authenticity

A characteristic of dialogue is authenticity. The existence of authenticity does not presume radical transparency; participants are not required to reveal everything about themselves in the dialogue. What authenticity does signify, however, is that what is shared is a truthful representation of the speaker, there should not be a persona or façade that would inhibit the listener from seeing and understanding who their dialogue partner truly is (Cissna & Anderson, 1998; Hammond et al., 2003; Westoby, 2014). Amanda (Facilitator) described this dynamic of authenticity with connotations of bravery, "so when you see those bridges that people dare to walk across and bring a piece of themselves forward. It's amazing when they take the risk to do that."

In our conversations, interviewees articulated moments that occurred in their dialogic encounters in terms that indicated the characteristic of authenticity. Some reflections illustrated how the authentic presence of other group members became impactful within the dialogue. For example, Mostafa mentioned how another group member shared openly their sexual orientation:

> He was a gay person, and that really shocked me about Tunisia. Yeah, because I felt it was different than I imagined, like now after the meetings and what I heard, I started to focus more on the news in Tunisia and what the people are doing and how they think. (Mostafa, Participant)

For Mostafa, this willingness on the part of another group member to reveal their sexual orientation signalled an openness and transparency which sparked curiosity.

Layla shared a story of how her sister's authenticity and vulnerability were impactful in the group's dialogue. Layla's group had brought in interviews they conducted with people outside the group to share, and Layla had interviewed her sister. Her sister shared about her experience fleeing Syria and moving to Germany. Layla comments:

> Because she felt that she is afraid of losing who she is and her family, her son—she has a son now, but she didn't have a son at that time. But as a group [the Syrian community in Germany], she felt that they have that sense of fear of losing touch of their own selves, own cultures. And I was really surprised because I was thinking in like an integrated and building [way], why we don't come with something new and better from both cultures? And I felt like all the [Connect] group was really shocked by the fear. …That fear of losing oneself also surprised me in terms of how they deal with that. And I think that I don't know how they will deal with that. (Layla, Participant)

Her sister's authenticity in sharing her experiences and fears was meaningful, both for Layla herself and also for others within the dialogue group because it brought in real emotion and vulnerability. By revealing her fears, Layla's sister offers a different lens through which Layla can view her and her experiences.

With authenticity in dialogue, while it does not mandate full disclosure, it does imply an act of boldness and willingness to share comments that may be at odds with others in the group or feel incongruent with the conversation. Amanda shared a story of a Connect group where members were surprised and impacted by specific participants' willingness to contribute their own experiences:

> There was this group where everyone was talking about women's movement and women's rights and the men in the group you would not necessarily expect to speak up as much; these men were from the MENA region. They said, "women do not realize that in other parts of the world how lacking it is also for men in regard to some of these issues." So I think that there are always surprising moments where a group begins to see a different picture than what they envisioned before. Where they didn't, they wouldn't expect for men from Egypt and Tunisia and Syria and these different countries to come up with just how devastated their lives have been in regard to rights or privileges when this group was having a discussion about women's rights and the MeToo movement and all of this information. It just came flooding in that changed the whole conversation in a wonderful and surprising new

direction where tenfold was learned. …The dynamic was absolutely wonderful because the reflections were; "I just can't believe where this discussion went, if anyone had told me what we'd end up talking about (*pause*) and it was just amazing. I've learned so much." …They were very happy with what they all learned out of it, their awareness had dramatically increased, and everybody felt really comfortable with the direction, surprised, and they were pleased. (Amanda, Facilitator)

Amanda's story highlights how a truthful representation from group members can inform and open up unexpected space in the dialogue. In this case, the authenticity of group members led to greater awareness and learning amongst others in the group. Duha also shared a story of how they authentically represented themself,

Something that I think that surprised my groupmates is when we were talking about our identities, and we were asked to mention seven aspects or seven items that we think constitutes our identity. So, one of the things that I mentioned was that I support the rights of minority groups in my communities like non-Muslims, either Christians or Atheists or also minority groups like gay people or the LGBT community. So, I think that surprised them because it's not usual for someone who is Muslim from an Arab country like Egypt to support these rights, especially the LGBT community rights. (Duha, Participant)

In Duha's experience, revealing their beliefs and opinions that perhaps challenged pre-conceived ideas others might have had of them, held significance for Duha and created a facet of surprise for others in the group.

Mutuality

Intimately related to the trait of awareness is mutuality. Mutuality is indicative of when individuals in dialogue see and respect each other as full persons (Cissna & Anderson, 1998; Hammond et al., 2003). As Johannesen (2000) explains,

We express non-possessive concern for the other. The other person is valued for his or her worth and integrity as a human being. A partner in dialogue is affirmed as a person, not merely tolerated, even though we oppose her or him on some specific matter. (p. 154)

The characteristic of mutuality embodies the ability to hold open to the *other* and appreciate that each person will contain their own views, beliefs, and opinions that will likely differ. While respecting that each person is able to hold their beliefs, mutuality does not suppose an approval of those opinions.

Many interviewees spoke about the feeling that their group members were not judging them:

> I think that fact that I knew I wasn't going to be judged, they were really interested in what I wanted to say and what I was saying, they were curious about it. And I saw that when someone wasn't speaking, they were like, "just say what you are going to say, you are not going to be judged," so that made me feel at ease. Whereas sometimes I can feel like I will be judged for saying something, but it didn't happen. (Anna, Participant)

This sense of lack of judgement led to individuals feeling they could share their views, and that they would be respected and heard even if those views were different from other members in the group. For example, Asma spoke about being able to discuss her religious views even when others in the group had different beliefs than her:

> Especially about the religion, we are not from the same religion. So, when we open this discussion, we are not agreeing, but with respect, we didn't fight at all. We respect one another, but everyone has the freedom to choose his religion, but everyone talked about his religion, and there was some question about my religion. …Okay, I shared something, I don't know, but there is a girl, the Italian girl, asked how I am Muslim, and I don't wear the hijab? I explained to her that it's an obligation for Muslimgirls, but I don't because I have some health problems. But it's not just me; there are a lot of girls who are Muslim, but (*pause*) it's obliged from the religion, but it's up to you if you want to wear it or not. So, your

parents and your people will never oblige you to wear it; it's referred to you; it is your relationship between you and God. So, it's up to me to wear it or not. ...They found that surprising how I am Muslim, and I didn't wear it. (Asma, Participant)

Asma shares in her group about her religious views and is open to the questions that other group members pose to her because she feels that each opinion is heard and respected. While this story reflects mutuality, it also relates to distinctiveness, being able to bring her unique perspective into the group. Asma was asked a question about not wearing the hijab, which may have been a question predicated on a presumed homogenous identity. Yet, she was able to express her individual perspective within her broader cultural context.

Duha shared a story which embodies mutuality as they encountered unexpected viewpoints from other members in their group:

I remember the last session we talked about religion, and two of my classmates who are from the USA, they both said they are Christians, and they are religious, but they are not like anti-Muslim or anti-gay. Because I had this idea that all religious people, whether they are Muslims or Christiansor Jews or whatever, they would be hating, or not hating but not liking, people from another religion or they are, for example, against gay rights and stuff. So, it was surprising for me to know that they are religious, and they are believers, but at the same time, they respect people who are different, and they are fighting for their rights as well. So, it was kind of surprising for me because it's different here in Egypt. If you are religious, it's like you don't fully accept people who are different from what is common in the society. That's what I see in my community, that they don't fully accept difference. So, it was really interesting and good to hear that. (Duha, Participant)

While respecting and hearing the differing opinions of others in the group, Duha moves into reflection regarding their own narratives and understanding of these issues. There is a recognition that the views of their group mates who identify as religious differs from those of their religious community and they begin to question the tension between these perspectives.

When mutuality is present, there can be a validation that occurs when a group member shares authentically, and they are received with respect and affirmation by others. For example, Arij shared this story from one of her recent groups where participants from an Eastern background appeared hesitant to share:

> I feel that they are not talking, I know that especially the people who are from an Eastern background, and the people who do speak in English it is easy for them to be outgoing and to talk and to not hesitate before taking the mic, but for the others, I know that they are thinking about what they are going to say, and before they have the mic they would have a scenario in their heads and then try to say it when they take the mic. And so, I tried to send them a private message telling them, "please express your opinion, and if you want to talk in Arabic, that is fine as well."
>
> They were also a little reluctant to express a different opinion. Because I think we were talking about marriage, and those Western people, participants, were saying, "it's a ridiculous thing, why do people get married? I mean, you can be loyal to another partner, but you don't have to get married." Which is really something that the Eastern people, like the people from the Muslim religion background, do really cherish and look to marriage as a sacred thing.
>
> So, they were thinking about it, I know that they were not okay with that, I know that they have different opinions, but we had silence in the room. And I know that they had something to say about that. And I was texting them, private messaging them in the chatbox and then they started to talk, and they started to show a different opinion. And the other participants were really happy to hear them and were really happy to discuss and to explain why they think this way. So it's not just imposing their opinions, they are open for the discussion and so on, and it was really a great opportunity for them to talk. And at the end, we do this recognition activity where I ask okay

> "so write the name of one person who made you laugh, write the name of one participant who you learned from." And when I asked them to write the name of one participant who they learned from, they all write the name of this participant who shared a different opinion, and I felt like it was an empowering moment for her because she didn't expect that. ...If I compare to the first session, she was not talking; she was just there sitting quiet, not willing to take any risk, just "I am here, listening to you," and that's all. But then once she started to engage, and once she started to see that the others were appreciating her difference, and appreciating her way of looking at things, she felt really empowered, and it was a great moment. (Arij, Facilitator)

Arij's story illustrates how, in the sphere of between, validation and encouragement contribute to mutuality. This group member was reluctant to share a different perspective; however, after doing so, she received validation from the group that they heard her and learned from her. This story represents mutuality, but it also incorporates elements of power dynamics related to language, and how power can influence the opportunity for dialogue to occur. If the participant had not been prompted and encouraged to share, they may have remained reluctant, and the different views of the group members may not have surfaced, or perspectives been shifted.

While, as illustrated above, the presence of mutuality allows for validation in sharing about opinions and beliefs, it can also open the possibility for personal vulnerability relating to life experiences. Joanna shared a story from her dialogue group:

> One of my participants had to go through some difficult periods of time in her life, and she, around the fifth week, she started opening up about her own personal life. And as time went by, she became so accustomed to having people around her who would listen to her and not criticize her in any way because they had already built this safe environment for them to express themselves freely. And so, she confided in us that she felt in a way liberated by this experience and that it was the first time that she felt like she belonged in a group of people. (Joanna, Facilitator)

Joanna's story reflects that, by feeling accepted and respected in the group setting, this individual felt she could share about difficult aspects of her life. The group member experienced a sense of belonging and community. As the findings above illustrate, the presence of mutuality in dialogue occurs alongside a feeling of safety in the encounter.

The above section highlights that, while the sphere of between can be elusive and challenging to describe, the characteristics of presentness, awareness, authenticity, and mutuality occurred in the experiences of interviewees.

The above findings provide insight into the existence of the sphere of between in dialogic encounters online in relation to presentness, awareness, authenticity and mutuality. These characteristics are of particular interest to the online nature of the encounter, as existing literature suggests that dialogue must occur face-to-face to be effective (Kelleher & Ryan, 2012; Lefranc, 2012; Roy & Kundu, 2017; Senesh, 2012). The findings discussed here provide a counterargument to the belief that dialogue must occur in person, demonstrating that online dialogue, within this specific setting of Soliya, can indeed provide meaningful encounters that embody Buber's characteristics of dialogue, and, in turn, provide an opportunity for humanization and transformation to occur.

6.3 Cogitatio

It occurs to me, as I reflect on this research journey, that my interview conversations with research participants are, themselves, an expression of dialogue. There is a sphere of between where I must be present to what unfolds. While the voice of the research participants is, hopefully, more evident than my own, I am undeniably a partner in the conversation. What I hold coming into the encounter—my motivations, narratives, ontology—all inform what can emerge in the conversation. And, ultimately, what does appear in the interview is data. That data is analyzed and interpreted by me—so I am very much a voice in dialogue with the research itself.

In sitting with these reflections, I am attempting to bring my own awareness to how the characteristics of dialogue interacted with the experience of collecting data through interviews and observations. A moment that comes to mind is from a group session I was facilitating, where the topic for discussion was related to conceptions and understanding of beauty. It was a topic that had been chosen by the group, suggested by a female participant. And the conversation went in a different direction than I expected:

We then moved into an open conversation about conceptions of beauty around the world. …the opening question "how do you define beauty?" took the group towards a more philosophical conversation (dominated by two voices, I would say). A few people inputted in ways that might draw the conversation towards social norms and ideals, but it kept getting pulled back to philosophical and artistic interpretations. …As a facilitator, I felt I struggled a bit with how to make the conversation cohesive without being too directive. ... It was the most I have felt that I wanted to contribute to content and ask leading or more confrontational questions than I have before in this setting, I think, because I felt they weren't getting to the meat of the conversation. (Fieldnotes, April 15, 2019)

Looking at my fieldnotes, I can see how I was not present to the dialogue that was happening and instead was fixing my attention to the imagined dialogue I had expected to take place. There were competing elements in my mind, most pressing was that women had raised the topic, and yet they were not speaking (Is it because the men are directing the conversation? Is this the conversation that the whole group wants to be having?). Also evident from my fieldnotes was that I was biased to there being a specific direction the discussion would take, I wanted it to be about beauty norms and patriarchal ideals. It raises the question for me now, in hindsight, of what might also have been happening in the space that I missed because I was not embodying presentness or awareness.

While these reflections bring to mind what I might have missed in the research from not engaging dialogically, I am also aware of how the qualities of dialogue positively informed how I held myself in interviews. I knew when I entered into the data collection process that I never wanted my views to influence the interviewee and what they shared. I was very conscientious that my external demeanour remained warm, invitational, and curious. This intentionality caused my internal self to move away from disagreement and into curiosity when interviewees shared a different view on a topic than what I would hold. In those moments, I needed to consider what was shared and how I could move more in-depth in the conversation. Bringing intentionality as an interviewer caused me to hold each conversation with mutuality, presentness, awareness, and authenticity.

6.4 Summary

This chapter moved into an exploration of the dialogue encounter itself, as understood through two phenomena. The first of these phenomena incorporated occurrences unfolding in the individual, recognized as distinctiveness and self-reflection. Findings indicated the desire for participants to represent themselves and their nationality, cultures, etc., as unique in order to transition others away from a simplistic perception. Also occurring within the individual was self-reflection, a prodding of their pre-existing understandings of themselves, their intentionality within encounter, and their triggers.

The other phenomenon examined the sphere of between, the third space occurring amongst those within dialogue. The sphere of between was presented through an understanding of Buber's characteristics of dialogue, which emerged in the findings. These characteristics were: authenticity, mutuality, awareness, and presentness. Finally, a closing cogitatio passage reflected the experience of the sphere of between, and the associated characteristics of dialogue, within my own experiences as researcher.

References

Baxter, L. A. (2004). Dialogues of relating. In R. Anderson, L. A. Baxter, & K. N. Cissna (Eds.), *Dialogue: Theorizing difference in communication studies* (pp. 107–124). Sage.

Buber, M. (1947). *Between man and man* (R. G. Smith, Trans.). Routledge.

Buber, M. (1970). *I and Thou*. (W. Kaufmann, Trans.). Scribner.

Cissna, K. N., & Anderson, R. (1998). Theorizing about dialogic moments: The Buber-Rogers position and postmodern themes. *Communication Theory, 8*(1), 63–104.

Hammond, S. C., Anderson, R., & Cissna, K. N. (2003). The problematics of dialogue and power. *Annals of the International Communication Association, 27*(1), 125–157. https://doi.org/10.1080/23808985.2003.11679024

Johannesen, R. L. (2000). Nel Noddings's uses of Martin Buber's philosophy of dialogue. *Southern Communication Journal, 65*(2–3), 151–160. https://doi.org/10.1080/10417940009373164

Kelleher, A., & Ryan, K. (2012). Successful local peacebuilding in Macedonia: Sustained dialogue in practice. *Peace Research, 44*(1), 63–94. http://www.jstor.org/stable/23607918

Lefranc, S. (2012). A critique of "bottom-up" peacebuilding: Do peaceful individuals make peaceful societies? In B. Charbonneau & G. Parent (Eds.),

Peacebuilding, memory and reconciliation: Bridging top-down and bottom-up approaches (pp. 34–52). New York, NY: Routledge.

Roy, S., & Kundu, D. V. (2017). Promoting youth participation for peace and intercultural dialogue through new media and digital literacy. *Research Expo International Multidisciplinary Research Journal, VII*(VII), 48–55.

Senesh, D. (2012). Restorative moments: From First Nations people in Canada to conflicts in an Israeli-Palestinian dialogue group. In B. Charbonneau & G. Parent (Eds.), *Peacebuilding, memory and reconciliation: Bridging top-down and bottom-up approaches* (pp. 163–175). New York, NY: Routledge.

Westoby, P. (2014). Theorising dialogue for community development practice— An exploration of crucial thinkers. *Journal of Dialogue Studies, 2*(1), 69–85.

CHAPTER 7

Potentialities

The previous three chapters have provided an immersive look at: who the research participants are, a descriptive overview of the setting for the dialogue program, and what occurs within individuals and the sphere of between in dialogic encounters. This chapter explores potentialities, which is to say: what emerges out of the encounter and program experiences. The term 'potentialities' comes from Aristotle's philosophy of metaphysics. The original word from Aristotle is *dunamis* and has two aspects within it, the first being *kinésis*, which is related to movement. The second element is *energeia*, which is connected to actuality:

> In Aristotle the concept of 'dynamis,' as a complementary term to 'energeia,' plays a central role in his metaphysics. It was primarily introduced to explain phenomena of identity and change. …there is a merely modal sense by which 'dynamis' can be translated by possibility or probability. And there is a predictive sense by which 'dynamis' means 'capacity,' 'faculty,' 'disposition' or 'power.' (Engelhard, 2018)

The term 'potentialities' is therefore indicative of both the modal sense of 'possibility' while also encompassing a predictive understanding of the "capacity to be in a different and more completed state" (Cohen, 2000). I have elected to use this term as a reflection of the evolving nature of dialogue, and that what shifts for people out of their encounters with *other* is dynamic, infused with a sense of both possibility and capacity.

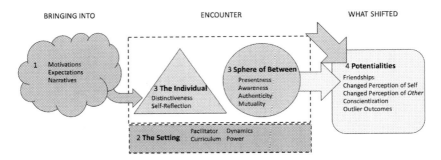

Fig. 7.1 Location of Chapter 7 in overarching findings narrative

As illustrated in Fig. 7.1, the overarching narrative of the research findings has been: bringing into, the dialogue encounter itself, and what shifted out of the encounter experience.

The following chapter will delve into three sections related to 'what shifted': friendships ("New and Beautiful Friends"), shifts in perceptions of both self and *other* ("To See Something Different"), and conscientization ("How's the Water?"). I will also discuss outlier findings ("I Don't Change Easily").

7.1 "New and Beautiful Friends"

In line with common outcomes of dialogue-based peacebuilding practice (Dessel & Ali, 2012; Nagda et al., 2012), many interviewees commented on the relationships they formed during the program. The majority of research participants felt the Connect experience enabled them to develop friendships with other members of their group:

> I like that the program helped me make friends with people from other places and the fact that I am still in touch with them. And I think that the program creates such a beautiful environment for us to get to know each other. So, the fact that we are still friends. I really like it. (Anna, Participant)

Souhail added:

> I think the experience of meeting people, foreign people, is nice. And the people we met are nice; I am in contact with some of them. So, they are nice people; in fact, when I speak to them now, I don't feel like I am talking to a person from another country. I feel like I am speaking to my friend, for example, a friend who lives in Morocco. (Souhail, Participant)

Both Anna and Souhail reflect that they met and formed friendships with people they otherwise may not have had the opportunity to meet. Their comments also reveal their experience of continuing a connection with friends after the program ended. Many interviewees, especially those who held a participant role in the program, shared that they had connected with group members on social media platforms such as Facebook and Instagram, which contributed to sustained contact:

> When we first met, we didn't know each other but week after week we are getting closer and now, we are friends, we share our Facebook, and we talk with each other, and I have new friends from different nationalities. (Oldez, Participant)

Asma commented:

> Okay, we still keep in contact, we can speak on Facebook. And I get new and beautiful friends; I like them. ...to get new friends, from different cultures, from different countries in the world, it's great, and I like it. (Asma, Participant)

While interviewees reflected their feeling of enthusiasm for creating new friendships, there were varying degrees of skepticism that the relationships could be sustained, as Mostafa illustrates:

> I already added some of them on Instagram; we made a small group on Instagram and added some of them on Facebook. But are we going to keep in touch and try to make more online meetings through the social rooms on Soliya or any other application we can connect through? I don't know if we're going to do that in the future. (Mostafa, Participant)

I spoke with eight of the 11 interviewees who held the participant role in Soliya for a second interview following the completion of the program. Of the eight participants who had a second interview, five of them specifically mentioned that they were still in contact with people from their group. Three of them did not specify if they remained in touch with members of their group. And one individual commented that they were connected to people on social media but not actively in communication. Several of those interviewees who were still in contact with group members reflected uncertainty about how sustained their connections would be, "but now, everyone has a program, so we don't talk a lot. So, I think the relationship will be less… we talk but not like in the program" (Asma, Participant).

While those who had been recent participants were unsure if they would maintain ongoing connections, a few of the facilitator interviewees shared that they had longstanding friendships from their involvement with Soliya. For example, Hassan comments that he is still in contact with some members of his group from when he was a participant:

> I would say that one of the good things was that I got to have different friendships with people from different parts of the world. People who did the Connect program with me at the very beginning when I joined Soliya in 2015, I am still in touch with these people, we are still talking from time to time. That's something really great. We got to learn more about our cultures when we connect to each other on Facebook or different online platforms. Because you know, sixteen hours was not enough time to explore everything about their cultures, but it is where we started, it was the beginning of our journey to learn more about different cultures, so I think that was really great.
>
> As facilitators, you know that we need to stay neutral, so many people were interested in knowing more about the Egyptian culture, but I was not able to participate, of course, so that I can have a successful semester with people. So, they asked if they could stay in touch with me via email, Facebook, or whatever platform would help. So, they got to, after the semester, they got to ask me so many things about my culture and my country, so that is something that is really great. Also, I have so many African friendships that are only virtual, I got to meet

> some of them later but some of them I didn't meet so far, but I am planning to travel to these countries, maybe, and of course, I believe I will meet them one day. (Hassan, Facilitator)

In addition to the connections he made when he was a participant, Hassan also formed friendships with individuals from groups he has facilitated, connecting with them on social media after the end of the program. He was unable to make these social media connections during the semester while in the facilitator role to maintain his neutrality and multi-partiality.

Amanda also shared that she formed friendships from her involvement with Soliya over the years:

> It's highly impactful, in my own life, and in others that I meet along this journey. It's an unbelievably diverse group of people that I've come to meet that I, many of which I consider my friends and acquaintances that still continue. (Amanda, Facilitator)

Several participants mentioned that they hoped for the chance to meet friends face-to-face by hosting them in their home country. Nidhal (Participant) revealed that he had invited a friend from his group to visit him, "one of my group members I have invited to come to me, to Tunisia, and he accepted yes, so I am hosting him from Turkey." Karoline (Participant) was also expecting someone from her group to visit, "one girl actually told me she is going to visit me here in Milan, so she is planning something around August, I guess. And yeah, I am going to be her personal guide." Similarly, Oldez was expecting a fellow group member to visit soon:

> My friend from Italy, she is planning to come to Tunisia (*laughter*), and I am really happy to meet her. She is coming with her family. Yes, and she wants to come to my city to Sousse, it is very great. I am very happy to meet her…she is coming next month. (Oldez, Participant)

Nidhal, Karoline, and Oldez, all exhibited excitement at the opportunity to host their new friends and show them their home, their culture, and their communities.

"Not Friends in Reality."

While many interviewees commented on the friendships formed and the desire to remain in contact with each other, a few reflected that they did not feel they had developed friendships from their experience. For Mohamed, his involvement as a participant did not result in what he would consider being "friends in reality":

> I can't consider them my friends, because I believe that friendship needs some face-to-face process if that makes sense. Because I am kind of selective (audio glitch), you know, I consider them 'mates' and let's say virtual friends, but that doesn't make them, not friends in reality, that opens an opportunity to maybe becoming real friends. It's initiative for friendships. (Mohamed, Facilitator)

Mohamed's comments are illustrative of discourse occurring in the literature regarding the strength and depth of relationships that are possible when formed in online communities. That perhaps "the Internet is effective in making possible social relations at a distance; these are relations that otherwise would not be sustained due to the effort involved and perhaps because of the value of the relationship" (Delanty, 2018, p. 212).

Layla expressed that the relationships formed in her group had not sustained over time,[1] that others in the group who were from Europe were not as interested in staying connected after the program had ended:

> I felt that many of them, some of them, wanted this experience just as a course. ...they didn't get involved after the discussion was ended. Maybe it is an experience in other groups as well. Because I think maybe people from, I mean refugees, from North African and the Middle East, from MENA, would expect them to continue at least a relationship. But they had other commitments, and they appreciated the time and the insights they have and most of them were really supportive. (Layla, Participant)

---

[1] Layla was the only interviewee in the 'participant' role who had completed her involvement before the current semester. She had participated in Connect in the Spring 2018 cohort, while all other 'participants' were in the Spring 2019 cohort.

The longevity of friendships reflected in the findings is variable based on the role of the research participant. Facilitators, who had been participants previously, or were involved for several years, can reflect on the lasting nature and dynamics of friendships they created in the Soliya community. While others who had just completed their Connect program experience as participants could only comment on their experience of sustaining relationships a few months after the program had ended.[2]

7.2 "To See Something Different"

The above findings reflect an external potentiality: the formation of friendships amongst group members. Another significant body of findings conveys an internal potentiality: a change in perception. These changed perceptions relate to both views of oneself ("I Never Thought of Myself As...") and an understanding of *other* ("These People Are Not Monsters").

"I Never Thought of Myself as..."

Many interviewees reflected on how they had grown or changed through their experiences in Connect. Specifically, their perceptions of self were altered in some way. Most commonly, their comments revealed a shift in how they perceived themselves, often around the issue of confidence:

> Maybe sometimes I can be quite shy, so it was great to see that I could engage in the conversation and just speak. So, sometimes I was just like, "am I really talking? For real?" (*laughter*) And also maybe, I don't know, I think that at first, I was quite scared because I thought that it would be difficult to represent my country while talking with other people and then I realized that I am able to do it, and if I want to I am able to speak and just say what I think. So maybe that's what really surprised me, the fact that I am quite shy but was able to just be me and feel at ease. (Anna, Participant)

---

[2] Except for Layla, who had completed her program 12 months prior.

Anna anticipated feeling uncomfortable voicing her opinions because she considered herself to be shy. She then surprised herself by sharing openly and with confidence what she wanted to communicate in her group. Similarly, Duha shared how they had an increase in confidence through their experience:

> How this affected me in my daily life is that I think that it made me more confident in sharing my opinions and thoughts. And sharing whatever comes to my head even if I think that it's not important to share, but some of these thoughts and some of these opinions end up really important or good ones to share with others. (Duha, Participant)

Duha discusses learning to trust that what they have to share and contribute is worthwhile and that their viewpoint holds value. This change in perception of self was not limited to participants but also occurred amongst facilitators:

> The most important thing that I think I am taking away from this is the type of confidence that facilitating these sessions gave me. So, as I told you, at the beginning, I never thought of myself as a facilitator, and I am kind of introverted person who doesn't express themselves easily… so I never thought that I could do something like this. …Yeah, so the most important thing I think Soliya gave me is confidence. (Arij, Facilitator)

As Arij shares, the experience of facilitating over time and many sessions increased her confidence and the way she viewed herself and her capabilities.

The dialogue program created the opportunity for individuals to self-reflect, and, through self-reflection, shift the ways they perceived their own identities or beliefs. For example, Hassan shared how meaningful it was for him to connect to the "African part of [his] identity" as an outcome of being involved in the Connect program:

> I am a person who feels very African; the African part of my identity is one of the main parts for me. It's hard for us to get in touch with everybody, I get in touch with so

many African people in my country but other people I might not be able to get in touch with.

So, I, with other African people, got to develop a program so that we connect African people. It's just an African-to-African initiative, just for African people so they can get to know each other. I was ignorant about Cameroon; I was ignorant about Ghana; I was ignorant about so many African countries. I just know where these countries are and have very few information about the people, the life, the culture, and so on. But when I got to talk to these people in online sessions, it was really great for me. I got to learn so many things, and I got to understand about things that I always see, but I don't understand about our continent. That impacted the way I see my people here in Egypt because many people say that people in North Africa are not that African, they are immigrants, or they just came from so many different countries, that was not true. (Hassan, Facilitator)

Hassan's involvement with Connect enabled him to recognize part of his identity and articulate cultural factors which had caused him to be "ignorant" about other "African people." The boundary around Hassan's understanding of himself widened to become inclusive of the African part of his identity.

Nicolas also experienced an expansion in how he viewed himself. He shares how, coming from a conservative social group, he wanted to push himself to be more "open to the world" when he first joined Soliya as a participant:

A few people from my entourage are more, are those you think of as the classic conservative, narrow-minded personality or characteristics. And so, I've always, all my life, I've tried to break away from that and tried to remain an individual who remains open-minded and open to the world. So, the Soliya Connect program kind of… it made me leap into this whole new experience. To expose me to different perspectives, and its kind of helped me to carve my own path and break free from my own familiar environment. And to just get out there and see new perspectives and new cultures and through this, from the first session onwards, I felt so much more open-minded, so much more critical thinking skills were through the roof. (Nicolas, Facilitator)

The Connect program provided the opportunity for Nicolas to explore how open-minded he truly was. Through his experience he began to perceive himself as more responsive to new perspectives and capable of critical thinking than he had previously recognized.

"These People Are Not Monsters."

While the previous section explored changed perceptions of self, the other shift in perceptions related to views of *other*. Many interviewees shared how their experience in Soliya had shifted their perceptions of fellow group members by having their assumptions and biases challenged. For some, these assumptions were of group members from their own community or perceived "group" outside of the program. For example, Burcu shares how she unconsciously assumed that cultural norms would dictate who exhibited leadership in the groups she facilitated:

> I think I am surprised that the discussions were led, in both of the groups I facilitated, by North African participants. We had native speakers of English, Canadian or the US. Before that, I was always thinking that they would talk more because you know it's their first language, or their education system, or something else, that European or Western participants would be more active. But in both groups, we had a lot of people from Tunisia and Morocco, a lot of participants who were leading the discussions.
> I think it's maybe a stereotype, but because I am also from, you know, the developing world or predominantly Muslim country and so on. I felt that people on this side of the world, they don't talk so much or they don't try to express themselves as much. Because this program is built around exploring 'Why? Why?' and that is something I don't usually associate with the cultural environment. (Burcu, Facilitator)

For Burcu, there was an underlying belief that people from a similar cultural background to her would behave more reservedly in group settings. Her experiences in the Connect program challenged those assumptions. They caused her to reconsider how she believed people from those locations and cultures would act in a group dialogue setting like Soliya. Hassan shared his experience where, similar to Burcu, he was confronted with assumptions about people from his own culture:

> They always say that people from the Middle East, or maybe what has been called the Arab Countries, the countries speaking Arabic, they have high religious standards, so they are too religious, things like that. …So, they always think that, okay, these are the religious people, these are the people who put religion first, and everything else comes after. I myself used to think that yes, we are like that, and we are a religious people and so on, but I had to dig deeper, so it was not religion, it was more habits and traditions, things like that.
> On the other hand, they always say that people in the West don't care about religion, they are not interested in religion, it does not come as a priority for so many people, but I don't think that was the case with the people that I met. …It got me thinking in a different way; I don't look at people as people from the West or people from the East because you could be in the Middle East, and you could have the same idea that someone in the West has and vice versa. So, after that, when I meet someone from the West, I don't think that they are not religious, they could be religious, and they could not be. And it's the same for people from the Middle East and things like that, you know? So, it just helped me to get rid of so many stereotypes that I used to have. (Hassan, Facilitator)

As Hassan highlights, interrogating how he perceived people from his own culture opened the possibility for him also to reconsider how he viewed people from the West.

In some cases, the encounter with *other* added complexity to assumptions. Arij shared a story from her group in which a student from Tunisia had her expectations challenged by the experiences of another group member:

> They were all students in their twenties; I remember a participant saying something like, she mentioned family

or a son or something, and then another participant commented on that saying, "do you have a son? We are all University students, and you mentioned a son, so is this something because you have a son or just something you had in mind?" and she said, "no, I have a son he is like three years old, and I am still a student, and I have to go through hard times, and I quit education, and I did many things, and then when I got my child I felt like I wanted to be a better person for him, so I went back to University, I want to get my degree to have a better life and to make my son feel proud of me."

And these kinds of experiences really click with some participants, I wouldn't say with all of them, but I see that it really clicks with some of the participants. And because I know for a fact that this participant who asked the question would never expect a student at this age having a child. Because she was from Tunisia, and I am Tunisian, and I know that in Tunisian Universities, especially at twenty to twenty-three, it's just studying, and you don't think about something beyond that. So, once you have heard that another student, in another part of the world (*pause*) so she was thinking that everyone would have the same, and that made her think, that made her reflect a bit on things. I always tell them we look the same, but sometimes we are not the same, so we should ask questions; we should explore our differences. And maybe this assumption of similarities hides many questions. (Arij, Facilitator)

Arij highlights here that expectations can be subverted in many ways. In Arij's example, the student expected similarity and found difference; however, in most of the stories shared by interviewees, it was a case of discovering similarities where they expected difference. For example, Jacob found that his experience both confirmed and challenged his perceptions of what people from Morocco might be like,

There are two people from Morocco, or three, in the group. And one of them I found as a person I can imagine as a person from Morocco; a little bit traditional, a little bit conservative, and more of a religious kind of a person. But one of the other Moroccan people was a big surprise for me because we talked a lot and, as far as I know, him now, he seems more like an open-minded, Western type of person for me with mostly liberal ideas as I see it. So that was a kind of surprise. I didn't think that before. (Jacob, Participant)

For Jacob, the encounter reshaped how he perceived someone from Morocco to be. These shifts in perceptions of *other*, through confronting stereotypes, were echoed by many other research participants. Nicolas recalled his experience as a participant with Connect:

It was mainly; I would say, the Muslim participants from the Middle East mainly. Because you go back two years, you hear on the news almost on a daily basis, or on social media; you hear the word terrorist, you hear about something going on whether it's local or abroad. Every day we heard something about that. …And then I come to Soliya, as a participant, and I see fellow Muslim friends from the Middle East and what I know because before this I maybe had one or two Muslim friends outside from elementary and high school, but apart from that, I didn't have much knowledge previously. I don't know what to expect; I don't have much knowledge except what I hear on the daily from the news and on social media. And you sit there through Soliya, and you see that "wow these people are not monsters as we hear or see online." And so that helped me, it was kind of transformative I would say, to expose me to the reality of "we have more in common than we think." (Nicolas, Facilitator)

For Nicolas, the experience of being in a dialogue group with people who were Muslim provided the opportunity to confront the narratives he heard in his community. For him, the encounter was "transformative" as he gained access to more knowledge about who they were and what he held in common with them. Similarly, Oya expressed how her experience as a facilitator challenged her biases and caused her to rethink how she formed her assumptions:

I really rethought about my biases, my prejudices, a lot. …I also realized that I am 33 years old, and I don't have any younger siblings. I cannot say that I am really close to, let's say, millennials or twenty-year-olds. So, I have prejudices about them, so it just broke it. I realized that my biases about them were totally wrong; they were aware of everything going on in their environment. Many of them they were even more mature than I am about some things. (*laughter*) So it was one of the things that I wrote down, it was my takeaway. (Oya, Facilitator)

Oya's story illustrates how confronting her biases caused her to consider how she had formed those assumptions, reshaping her understanding of *other*. Rianne shared a story from one of her groups where two group members, in particular, had a meaningful encounter:

There were two particular participants, one from South Libya and one from somewhere in the US who had never, a white guy, who had never left his village. And it's like when they came in, and they introduced themselves you could almost see their faces like "oh, they are supposed to be 'the enemy'" because the American had like, proper strong accent, so it's like it was the stereotypical enemy *other* type of thing. The icebreaker was like "what's happening in the background," and the Libyan was like, "well, you know, it's bombs," and it was bombs. So, the look on their faces, they didn't say anything but just how they initially looked at each other like "oh my god, you're like the enemy personified," and at the end of the semester, they were like "but we think so much alike…" I don't know whether they'll stay in touch or not, but it had completely changed their lives, and it's like; obviously, that's not enough to counter all nasty stuff, but those are like the glimmers of hope. (Rianne, Facilitator)

Rianne's story illustrates how she perceived the encounter between two group members, who through their experience of encounter with each other, there was a humanizing shift to their view of the other person. Beatrix shared a similar account from her group:

They were into cultural differences and stereotypes; that was what they were very interested in how the others see each other. And basically, that's what they wanted to do like almost all the time, so kind of we talked a lot about stereotypes. And at the end, they said that they broke their stereotype because they didn't think this could be something or that they could (*pause*) like an American because we had participants from the US, and from Tunis, and from Italy and it was very divided. And you have most of your stereotypes of people, and they really got to know each other in the four weeks, and then they said at the end they really broke the stereotypes that they thought initially about people from the other part of the world, and it really helped them to see something different. (Beatrix, Facilitator)

The findings above reflect how, through dialogic encounter, individuals question and interrogate their beliefs and pre-conceived ideas of *other*, in ways that can alter those perceptions.

7.3 How's the Water?

The third category of potentialities which emerged was the articulation of previously unseen social realities, the naming of 'the water.' For some interviewees there was also a connection between this critical consciousness of their social reality into deliberate action. This potentiality is understood through Freire's concept of conscientization, in which individuals become aware of their social reality (Freire, 2000). As Bebbington et al. (2007) describe it,

> conscientization is a process of becoming dialogically aware of social reality… [it] requires exposing and reflecting on "invisible" or "silenced" factors that oppress specific groups, re-examining situations in light of new understandings, problematizing existing situations, re-presenting and re-narrating existing situations…and identifying solutions to transcend existing situations of oppression. (pp. 363–364)

As discussed in the Chapter 2, Freire evokes the language of *emergence* and *intervention* when he describes the process of conscientization, "humankind *emerge* from their *submersion* and acquire the ability to *intervene* in reality as it is unveiled" (Freire, 2000, p. 109). *Emergence* is the naming of 'the water,' an articulation of the social reality, while *intervention* is the action taken in response to that named social reality. The following subsections examine both *emergence* and *intervention* related to the findings of this research.

"The Circumstances and the Situation and the Differences."

For many interviewees, there was an *emergence* from submersion—beginning to identify and name their social reality. For example, Nicolas illustrates how his experiences in the Connect program have reframed how he understands his societal context:

> I'd say in real life; it's much more related to my own personal critical thinking skills. So, if I hear something on the news, I am not just jumping to conclusions, trying to analyze situations as a whole, trying to naturally (*pause*) it's become a habit now to just think of all possible or potential perspectives before making a conclusion. Making informed decisions has become part of my life. (Nicolas, Facilitator)

Nicolas no longer automatically accepts the narrative he is presented with, rather, he interrogates the underlying assumptions embedded in the narrative to arrive at his own interpretation.

Other interviewees reflected on moments within the dialogue experience that surfaced an alternate lens through which to view the structural or systemic influences on their lives. For example, Duha raised a specific conversation that had taken place in their group:

> Once we were talking about the global challenges that are facing the world, and our facilitator asked each one of us to mention two challenges that they think their country suffers from more. And then she asked us if solving these issues is more often an individual responsibility or governmental responsibility. So, all of them from the United States said it's more of an individual responsibility, while all of us from the Middle East or North Africa said that it's a government responsibility. So, this situation kind of reflected the circumstances and the situation and the differences between a first world country and a third world country. In a first-world country everything, or not everything, most of the facilities and things are provided, but it's needed from individuals to keep it and not to destroy it, but it's different for us who live in a third world country because things are not provided anyway, so this situation

reflected what everyone is experiencing and living in their own country. (Duha, Participant)

The conversation in Duha's group raised how systemic challenges related to global issues of power influence and inform societies differently. For those coming from the United States, there appeared to be an assumption of what constituted basic living standards. In contrast, participants from MENA had a different expectation of what role the government should have in providing services because they did not assume the same standards would already be in place. The conversation highlighted how one's context informs one's beliefs, understanding, and assumptions about the world more broadly. Karoline shared a story of an experience she had after the program had concluded when she became aware of a cultural norm she previously had not identified:

> I went to Rome just last month, and I saw how people, for example, just near the Vatican state, for example, we say "okay, European people they dress like they want; a skirt, t-shirt, that's fine," but once you go inside of a church you have to wear something that covers everything. So, we just say, "okay, Muslim people, they cover them up every single day, oh they are just limited, limiting women's freedom and stuff," but even in Italy, there is something like that, especially in church. (Karoline, Participant)

For Karoline, her experiences within her group shifted her perspective to allow her to see what was previously unseen. She identified that within her cultural context there was judgement towards those who would dress conservatively according to their religious views if they were Muslim. She saw this judgement as a double standard as conservative dress was culturally expected if the religious norm stemmed from Catholicism.

Two interviewees articulated an identification of global power dynamics by contrasting their experiences with that of others in their group. Their descriptions held connotations of discouragement or an increased dissatisfaction with their own lives. Asma shared that:

> from our conversation (*pause*) I think that their life is beautiful, more than my life, and it's very dramatic (*laughter*) it is just like the films, the movies. So I think that if I try it [live in those countries], maybe

> I will find something negative or something doesn't work with me, and I will like more my life in my country, maybe I will like more the life, I don't know, it's just, I am just confused and curious about their life, I want to try it; to have the decision. (Asma, Participant)

Asma left her Connect experience with a desire to experience the type of life as others in the group; she felt that their lives were more 'beautiful' than her own. Similarly, Mostafa shared how his experience shifted how he thought about his own country:

> If we spoke about the big things that we discussed, like in Europe or the US, that the problems are different. So, when I look at my country now, I feel like we are so far from these countries. More than I felt before, we are talking about small problems, we are still a third world country, and we are not going far from that. It is a little bit depressing if you can say that. It made me; I used to think more about these problems before the meetings, now I am not really thinking more about it because I feel that we are far from solutions and I fear that we are having a twenty-year from getting anywhere near these countries. They have their own problems, and we have our own problems; we look like we have things in common. ... And it makes me more convinced that I need to leave my country if I want a life, I won't say better because we have people who live a better life in Egypt, they have more money. But I would say more evolved and developed life, like a country, not just living in a place that is for rich people, that is not what I mean. (Mostafa, Participant)

Both Asma and Mostafa reflect a shift in how they view their country in terms that relate to privilege. They see themselves and their nation as less privileged, less "evolved and developed" than others. These comments illustrate a 'naming' of the water as it relates to systemic power. For some, this was the extent of conscientization, as reflected in our conversation; there was an *emergence* without *intervention*. For others, there was a connection between the identification of social reality and a perceived change to their actions and behaviour.

"I Won't Hold My Tongue."

While the above section illustrates an *"emerg[ing]"* from their *submersion"* (Freire, 2000, p. 109), there is the second component of conscientization: "the ability to *intervene* in reality as it is unveiled" (p. 109). Out of the dialogue experience, several interviewees reflected a shift in their intentionality when engaging people with different views. For some, this intentionality related to how they internally positioned themselves in a conversation. For example, Layla mentioned that she deliberately tries to hold herself open to hearing differences of opinion:

> I feel less need for responding now. If someone had an opinion, so I feel I appreciate it, I try to understand it, and just to think of it. I am working on having that long-term view of opinions and discussion and arguments. (Layla, Participant)

Others, such as Nicolas, reflected similar sentiments:

> There is a whole part, you know, in training [as a facilitator] we go through being neutral and multi-partial, and I felt like the discussions, whether it be in class or even with family members, I tend to be much more calm, less impulsive. If I hear something that I don't agree with, I try to understand where they are coming from instead of just disagreeing as I did perhaps in the past. So, I try to piece out the different arguments and understand the why, not just the what. (Nicolas, Facilitator)

The comments from Layla and Nicolas demonstrate how being a part of the Soliya experience has influenced their behaviour in other parts of their lives. Their intentions when holding conversations across difference had shifted to a posture of openness and attempting to avoid initial judgements of the other person.

For others, there was a clear correlation between the identification of their social reality and the action they wanted to take in response to that reality. Anna shared how her experience with Connect shifted her perception of the normative narratives in her community related to specific identity groups:

> I realized that we were really different when we were discussing our countries' problems. And I realized that when we think about a problem we just think about what is related to our world, to what we live, and it was nice to understand that there are really a lot of problems and even if they don't regard us, we should just recognize them and act in order to solve them. …But when I hear people talking in the street about people coming from other places, mostly from Africa, and they all classify people with their religion. And I know people tend to do this a lot, and I am starting to say something like "why do you think about the religion when you are talking about them, there is more to know about the person, why do you think about that?" So, I just think that all the stereotypes that I have, I mean they don't make much sense, they are just stereotypes. I think that because of terrorism, there is that stereotype going around that everyone who has a different complexion or a different religion, must be a terrorist, and it's not true. And I don't know, it's really mean, and people tend to say it out loud, so I really hate it, it's not something I really want people to say when I am near, I don't want to hear it. (Anna, Participant)

Anna reveals her journey of beginning to identify and name the social reality that informs her perception of the world and *other*. From there, she moves into a reflection on questioning the accepted narratives within her social reality, and how those narratives should be interrogated. Anna's comments surface a dimension of action related to this potentiality—intentional conversations. She mentions that she has begun to say something when she hears comments that are rooted in stereotypes. This action of intentional conversation and questioning arose amongst others, including Amanda:

> I think that for me, although I have always been an advocate and stood firmly against different stereotypes and assumptions, I tend to (*pause*) do more of that discovery with people outside of this facilitation. Like new people that I meet or family that I don't see very often, I'll start to maybe challenge or approach those issues in a much different way than I did years ago. I think what I do is, I am much more, I don't even like using the

word challenging (*pause*), I am much less likely to walk away from the table without bringing it to the attention of an assumption or of a stereotype. Where before I may have kind of said something or shrugged my shoulders or kind of (*pause*), I wasn't really one that tended to do that (*laughter*). So, I don't want to give the impression that I was; however, I do it very differently now. I do it much more deliberately, and it's like "this is my mission in life," I don't care whether I am doing dialogue or not. I hear someone talk about a news article, and then I'll say, "really, where did you read that?" and "what did you learn about that" and "have you looked at any other sources? this is what I have learned; this is what I have heard first hand, maybe you don't want to hear this but, etcetera etcetera etcetera." So, yeah. I will be much more forthright with my ideas and opinions, in a very (*pause*) I don't do it in an aggressive way, I try to do it very diplomatically; however, I won't hold my tongue. Even though I was trained in conflict resolution and did mediation for years, I have always had a propensity to do that. But now the spark is much brighter and much deeper, such as "do you understand the damage that assumptions like this do to people's lives all over the world?" This is not something (*pause*) this is very serious; it's not something to be taken lightly. (Amanda, Facilitator)

Amanda reflects on how, through her role and involvement with Soliya, she has become more intentional about engaging with people when differences arise, or when she notices an assumption she feels should be challenged. She goes so far as to say that "this is [her] mission in life."

Others shared that, out of their dialogue experiences, they are now intentionally opening conversations with members of their community about topics or issues that would be considered taboo. For example, Oldez mentioned how important it was to approach difficult subjects that she previously would have avoided amongst her peers:

I am more open to talk about those topics, even with friends. And I found that the opportunity helped me to get out from that thing and to try to talk about that. I talk about the whole experience, about the topics that we talk about, and I really share my experience. I said to them that the people that I met, they were very open and very warm to me. We should talk about those issues; we have to talk about these subjects, it's nice to talk about these subjects in a safe way. (Oldez, Participant)

Oldez describes her journey from understanding certain topics to be taboo, into an articulation of why she feels conversations on those topics are important, to intentionally raise those subjects with her peers. Duha (Participant) also raised this intentionality of surfacing controversial topics. Specifically, they revisit the impact that other group members had on them when "they both said they are Christians and they are religious, but they are not like they are anti-Muslim or anti-gay." Duha comments that they have now raised these topics, and viewpoints, with people in their community:

> Duha: I would also mention to them the thing when my Christian classmates said that they can respect people who are different from them and who are having things that are wrong in their religion, but they respect them anyway, and they don't mistreat them or anything, so I would mention that to my community to tell them that it's good to be this way. I had this conversation with my siblings actually because they are the closest to me and some of my friends. But I would never bring up this thing in front of my parents, for example, or in front of other relatives or other people who I don't know well because it's kind of sensitive thing to bring up here. And you know, they will end up thinking of me that I don't respect Islam, or I don't belong to Islam and I don't want to bring these things up.
> Rachel: What was the reaction from your siblings or your friends? What were their thoughts about it?
> Duha: Well it depends, some of them accepted that, and they thought of it as a good thing, but others who are a little bit religious actually said that it's wrong and they will never do that, and they just objected to the idea. (Duha, Participant)

The topic of LGBTQ+ and religious minority rights, and the views of their group members who identified as Christian, appears as a significant moment for Duha, one that they call back to several times in our conversations. This encounter translates into action as Duha intentionally raises the topic with their siblings and friends, with the awareness that others may reject their viewpoint.

7.4 "I Don't Change Easily"

It is important to note that a feeling of being changed by the program was not universal for all interviewees. I include this section of outlier findings to emphasize two interviewees in particular who commented that, while they enjoyed the experience, they did not feel a personal change had occurred. For Jacob, he thought that his views of himself and his culture had not shifted:

> because I went through this experience before when I was [on exchange], so I have a general impression, or deeper knowledge, about our culture, so now talking with people from different cultures do not make any change in my perception about mine. (Jacob, Participant)

Jacob felt that he had already experienced personal growth during his exchange program in a different country, and so this experience did not influence his perceptions of his country or culture. While Nidhal felt that, for change to occur, something monumental needed to happen:

> I don't change easily. I feel like only hard moments and harrowing moments, the moments that I am low and have to really think about things, are the moments that change me and not the moments that I feel comfortable in. But I don't know, maybe if I had more experiences like exchange experiences or I did in real life, it might be more change in my life, but still, that doesn't mean that Soliya isn't capable of making the change in someone. (Nidhal, Participant)

While there are only the two specific reflections on the issue of not being changed by their involvement, they are significant to note to ensure transparency that not all individuals in the online dialogue leave feeling the experience has altered them.

7.5 Cogitatio

A question I returned to, as a reflection point for myself, throughout this research journey was 'what is changing for me?' I asked myself this because I wanted to be aware of alterations in my own perceptions and understanding as I engaged in the research. The desire to stay connected to the evolution of my thinking stemmed from an acknowledgment that I needed to be intimately aware of how the research was developing, and also because I knew that I was motivated to change and grow personally through this process.

One moment of asking the question 'what is changing for me?' occurred around the mid-point of my data collection. I asked a trusted individual to engage in a conversation (that was recorded and later transcribed for my field notes), where they prompted me to reflect on what I was learning and what was taking shape within my thinking. Some of my reflections from that conversation are captured here:

> I think one of the things that, for me, has been more of a challenging of my own subconscious assumptions or stereotypes… I have had several conversations with women, young women, from the Middle East, from Muslim countries who are… very devout in their faith. And I guess I have been aware that in my conversations, I am being struck by what they're reflecting back to me in terms of their own ambitions and identity and career paths. And so that's at a very superficial level, realizing that if someone asked me, I would say "sure, women in these countries want to do these things," but I am realizing that I am being surprised in these conversations by what I [subconsciously] assumed.
>
> I am very aware that women go to school and get degrees but pursuing degrees in fields that might be keeping them out of the home in the long term… I guess what I thought was that women who would be in those cultures and pursue these things wouldn't be as devout in their faith.
>
> I think that intellectually I know these things, I don't view all Muslim countries as being oppressive to women, although more broadly in our culture there is that narrative. I think of myself as having a certain awareness of the world and being a critical feminist who understands that agency looks different for each woman, but I can also

tell that I am being surprised. So, there is obviously a narrative that I have still been buying into or thinking would be confirmed in some way that it has not been. So, for me, that has been interesting in continuing to expand my boundaries of *other* and not just lumping together a homogenous idea of what that looks like. (*Fieldnotes, May 1, 2019*)

What I am realizing, in these reflections, is how subtle and insidious assumptions and biases can be. I "intellectually" knew that Muslim women pursue professional careers and qualifications. However, in pausing to reflect, I realized that I was still surprised in some of my interactions and that the feeling of surprise was something to take note of and investigate further what inherent beliefs were being challenged. Reflecting on my own experience highlighted for me, as a researcher, that even the small shifts in perceptions are meaningful. And being honest with ourselves about our assumptions, even if admitting them feels like an act of vulnerability, is vital in moving towards a fuller, more complete, and more realized comprehension of self and other. My fieldnotes signal this progression of thinking:

Now that I am aware that this is something that is happening for me, I guess I have a belief that these things that seem insignificant, or we don't want to put words to because it feels like "oh, that is silly I should have known better." That those things, I believe, are happening for people... I would love to know if those small things are happening for people. (*Fieldnotes, May 1, 2019*)

After this conversation, I began to intentionally ask questions in my interviews related to what, if anything, was surprising for people to bring to the surface assumptions or beliefs that may otherwise have remained hidden.

7.6 Summary

This chapter examined 'what shifted' for interviewees out of their dialogic encounters. The term *potentiality* was deliberately selected to signify these shifts to represent the evolving and dynamic nature of dialogue. Three themes within these potentialities were discussed: friendships, changed perceptions of self and *other*, and conscientization as *emergence* and *intervention*. Friendships surfaced as a common potentiality out of the dialogue experience. The majority of interviewees indicated that they felt they had developed friendships out of the program. At the same time, skepticism was raised amongst a few participants regarding how these relationships might be sustained. Several individuals expressed that these were "not friends in reality." The second theme of potentialities encompassed the experience of many interviewees who reflected their changed views of self and their altered perception of *other* out of their dialogue encounters. The third category of potentialities was conscientization, encompassing both the articulation of previously unseen social realities as *emergence* and *intervention* as intentionality in conversations and taking deliberate actions. Finally, outlier outcomes were shared, which signal that the experiences and impact of the dialogue experience vary amongst individuals, and there is no universal narrative or experience for every participant in dialogue.

References

Bebbington, J., Brown, J., Frame, B., & Thomson, I. (2007). Theorizing engagement: The potential of a critical dialogic approach. *Accounting, Auditing & Accountability Journal, 20*(3), 356–381. https://doi.org/10.1108/09513570710748544

Cohen, S. M. (2000). Aristotle's metaphysics. In E. N. Zalta (Ed.), *The Stanford encyclopedia of philosophy* (Winter 2016 ed.). https://plato.stanford.edu/archives/win2016/entries/aristotle-metaphysics

Delanty, G. (2018). *Community* (3rd ed.). Routledge.

Dessel, A., & Ali, N. (2012). The minds of peace and intergroup dialogue: Two complementary approaches to peace. *Israel Affairs, 18*(1), 123–139. https://doi.org/10.1080/13537121.2012.634276

Engelhard, K. (2018). Introduction. In K. Engelhard & M. Quante (Eds.), *Handbook of potentiality* (pp. 1–11). Springer.

Freire, P. (2000). *Pedagogy of the oppressed* (30th anniversary ed.) (M. B. Ramos, Trans). Continuum.

Nagda, B. R. A., Yeakley, A., Gurin, P., & Sorensen, N. (2012). Intergroup dialogue: A critical-dialogic model for conflict engagement. In L. R. Tropp (Ed.), *The Oxford handbook of intergroup conflict* (pp. 210–228). Oxford University Press. https://doi.org/10.1093/oxfordhb/9780199747672.013.0007

CHAPTER 8

The Conditions of Positive Peace

The previous four chapters have explored the results that emerged out of a qualitative research inquiry into online dialogue, while providing some preliminary discussion on how these findings inform our understanding of how dialogue unfolds within structured online settings. This chapter presents a discussion related to the overarching question on which this book is predicated: can engaging *other* through dialogic encounters within an online environment enable conditions for positive peace? This discussion is explored through the conditions identified by Galtung (2015) as friendship and love.

Prior to diving into a discussion on this overarching question, it is useful to revisit the understanding of positive peace provided in Chapter 2. According to Galtung's theory, negative peace refers to the absence of violence and outright conflict, whereas positive peace connotes the presence of something—equity and social justice (Galtung, 1990). As Galtung presents a triangle of violence, he also presents a triangle of positive peace inclusive of cultural, structural, and direct dimensions. These three contributing aspects inter-relate and are self-reinforcing, establishing a tripartite and holistic view of positive peace (Galtung, 1990).

While the terminology of negative and positive peace can imply a binary opposition, in actuality, a conceptualization of positive peace encompasses a continuum on which negative peace also resides. Negative

© The Author(s), under exclusive license to Springer Nature Singapore Pte Ltd. 2022
R. Nolte-Laird, *Peacebuilding Online*,
https://doi.org/10.1007/978-981-16-6013-9_8

Table 8.1 Tiers of positive peace, adapted from Galtung (2012, p. 58; 2015, p. 1)

0. Negative (2012)	"Dissociative: Passive coexistence" (2012)
1. Symbiosis (2012) OR Equity (2015)	"Associative, Active coexistence Joint projects" (2012) "cooperating for mutual and equal benefit, aka friendship" (2015)
2. Transcendence (2012) OR Harmony (2015)	"New actors, old projects" (2012) "sharing joys and sorrows, high on empathy, aka love" (2015)
3. Suigeneris (2012) OR Organization of equity-harmony (2015)	"New actors, new projects" (2012) "aka transcendence-institution" (2015)
4. Fusion (2012; 2015)	"absorption, nirvana" (2012) "total peace, aka pax omnium cum omnibus, sui generis" (2015)
5. Afterlife (2015)	"in others, in Heaven, aka as Mutual Assured Bliss, MAB" (2015)

peace is required to facilitate the actualization of positive peace. In addition to Galtung's conception of a triangle representing the three aspects of positive peace, he also provides an understanding of positive peace through tiers (2012) or levels (2015) as illustrated in Table 8.1.

Table 8.1 demonstrates how positive peace builds upon itself, with negative peace as the fundamental first tier necessary for further progression. While Galtung's conceptualization of tiers indicates ordered steps, the theory of positive peace posited in this book encompasses an understanding of positive peace as a process on a holistic continuum. I draw from Standish's (2020) language when she describes her model of relationships as peace praxis as:

> a circle with continuous processes because it may be useful to think of 'first steps' for the model…but in reality, this is a continual and circular process that resists discreet categories and instead, overlaps and reinforces connection and reconnection. (p. 267)

Similarly, in a discussion of positive peace, we can understand it as self-reinforcing, requiring progressive motion towards what could be envisioned as the ideal embodiment. The preceding steps, or movement, towards that ideal state are not irrelevant simply because they come before; rather, they are necessary conditions through which positive peace can evolve. Therefore, a discussion of the conditions for positive peace necessitates a recognition of the value of small, incremental movements within a continuous process.

8.1 Positive Peace: The Conditions

In returning to the overall question explored in this book, it is necessary to identify what is meant by the 'conditions' for positive peace. As this research inquiry did not seek to identify the conditions themselves, these emerge from the existing literature. The first section of this discussion will therefore introduce further theoretical material related to positive peace to lay the groundwork for a discussion on the findings themselves.

The following discussion is predicated on an understanding of the conditions for positive peace, as what Galtung recognizes as "the building blocks for positive peace [which] are friendship and love…one behavioral, one attitudinal;" he further adds that "generally, friendship precedes love" (Galtung, 2015, p. 2). These two building blocks, or conditions, for positive peace—friendship and love—are intimately related to what I have previously discussed as aspects of dialogue: *humanization* and *transformation* (Cissna & Anderson, 1998; Friedman, 2004; Westoby, 2014). *Humanization* is the I-Thou relation (Buber, 1970), moving from an I-It relationship of *other* into an I-Thou in which both self and *other* are humanized. The second condition, *transformation*, is understood as the awakening of critical consciousness such that reflection upon one's social context becomes action against oppression within that context (Freire, 2000). Godden succinctly articulates this linkage as, "love as emancipatory practice through interconnectedness and relationship" (Godden, 2017, p. 413). In the following sections, I discuss key research findings as the conditions for positive peace: *friendship as humanization* and *love as transformation*.

Condition: Friendship

Galtung identifies friendship as one of the building blocks of positive peace (Galtung, 2015). There are discussions across disciplines regarding the definitions and theories of friendship, without a unified and cohesive consensus on what is meant by the term (Devere, 2014). It is important to note that there are criticisms throughout the literature on contact and dialogue encounters that identify friendship's problematic nature if such relationships encourage an erasure of social identity and inequalities (Devere & Smith, 2010). Given these concerns, it is appropriate and useful to frame a conception of friendship from the literature related to positive peace. In offering an exploration of friendships in association to positive peace, Devere (2018) argues that:

> The sorts of relationships between people that might contribute to positive peace… might be classified as 'good relationships' – the sorts of relationships that help to reduce violence and increase justice; that might help to create environments and societies where positive peace is possible. (p. 60)

In her exploration of these 'good relationships,' Devere (2018) offers four relationship categories for exploration: "relationships based on emotion; relationships based on cognitive awareness; relationships based on social conscience; and relationships based on trust" (p. 60). Across all of these categories of 'good' friendships, there are characteristics that indicate a humanized relation, such as: affection, kind-heartedness, respect, acceptance, justice, generosity, honesty, integrity, and trustworthiness (Devere,). As Buber reminds us, the I-It relation indicates the objectification of the *other*, while an I-Thou relation implies humanization and mutuality. An I-Thou relation is required for a good relationship to exist, one that contributes to positive peace.

Friendship as Humanization.

For Buber, dialogue is a humanizing act as the I-It relation becomes the I-Thou. As humanization occurs between those in dialogue, there is a relational connection: "in dialogue we overcome our separateness, for everything 'permeates everything else,' and we encounter the other's being or actuality in the timeless present moment" (Czubaroff, 2000, p. 172). The separateness described here is both from the *other* as well as within one's self. As Buber articulates, the humanization of both self and *other* requires one's whole being:

> The basic word I-You can be spoke only with one's whole being. The concentration and fusion into a whole being can never be accomplished by me, can never be accomplished without me. I require a You to become; becoming I, I say You. All actual life is encounter. (Buber, 1970, p. 62)

In overcoming this separateness, there is a change in the substance of the relationships between those in dialogue. A shift that Hustvedt identified as "a change from communication to communion" (as cited in Westoby, 2014, p. 74). This communion between individuals encountering one another in the sphere of between (Buber, 1947) is representative of what Buber (1970) describes as "true community:"

> True community does not come into being because people have feelings for each other (though that is required, too), but rather on two accounts: all of them have to stand in a living, reciprocal relationship to a single living centre, and they have to stand in a living, reciprocal relationship to one another. (p. 94)

Within this conception of community as "living, reciprocal relationship," Buber understands "community as a humanising experience (with people not treating one another as objects)" (Westoby, 2014, p. 74). Buber constructs an understanding that through dialogue, the notion of 'we,' or of community, becomes possible (Gill & Niens, 2014). As illustrated by Fig. 8.1, community, or friendship, necessitates humanization—it cannot occur in union with the objectification of other persons.

It is often hard to illustrate what is meant by 'humanization,' so articulating an understanding of its opposite form, dehumanization, can be useful in constructing an understanding. Freire (2000) discusses dehumanization as used to validate unjust actions:

> For the oppressors, "human beings" refers only to themselves; other people are "things." For the oppressors, there exists only one right: their right to live in peace, over against the right, not always even recognized, but simply conceded, of the oppressed to survival. (p. 57–58)

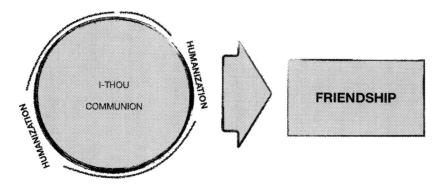

Fig. 8.1 Representation of humanization in relation to friendship

Dehumanization is the classification of certain people as non-human (Bar-Tal & Hammack,). Dehumanization can occur through a process of *othering* based on difference. As Gergen et al. (2001) explain:

> The problem of difference is intensified by several ancillary tendencies. First, there is a *tendency to avoid* those who are different, and particularly when they seem antagonistic to one's way of life... With less opportunity for interchange, there is secondly a tendency for *accounts of the other to become simplified*. There are few challenges to one's descriptions and explanations; fewer exceptions are made. Third, with the continuing tendency to explain others' actions in a negative way, there is a *movement toward extremity*. As we continue to locate "the evil" in the other's actions, there is an accumulation; slowly the other takes on the shape of the inferior, the stupid or the villainous. Social psychologists often speak in this context of "negative stereotyping," that is, rigid and simplified conceptions of the other. (*italics* in original) (pp. 680–681)

As one moves further into the simplification of others, such that their identity becomes a stereotype or classified by generic labels that encompass entire people groups, those individuals become dehumanized. The process of dehumanization is often likened, or linked, to moral exclusion. Opotow describes moral exclusion as when people are placed "outside the boundary in which moral values, rules, and considerations of fairness apply. Those who are morally excluded are perceived as nonentities, expendable, or undeserving; consequently, harming them appears acceptable, appropriate, or just" (as cited in Bar-Tal & Hammack, 2012, p. 31).

We can begin to articulate what humanization or moral inclusion looks like based on their opposing constructs of dehumanization and moral exclusion. As someone becomes humanized, their perceived identity moves from a simplified construct into a nuanced and dynamic individual. The person who is engaging with them travels from the I-IT relation embodied by stereotypes into the I-Thou relation of comprehending their unique and individual personhood. The I-Thou similarly reflects a moral inclusion, whereby "an expanding scope of justice widens the applicability of justice and supports mutual respect, constructive approaches to conflict, and the potential for peaceful intergroup relations" (Opotow, 2012, p. 72).

While this book considers moral inclusion on an individualized basis, there is considered to be a link between moral inclusion on an individual level and cultural change more broadly. In discussing the perspectives of Galtung and Lederach regarding transformative peacebuilding, Gill and Niens (2014) comment, "Mitchell considers such transformation as located within structural, personal and relationship changes towards engendering the moral growth of the society" (p. 12). Therefore, it is useful to consider that the interconnection between what occurs at an individual level, such as within community-based peacebuilding practice, as a potential link to cultural changes more broadly within societies.

So, friendships, as a condition of positive peace, are understood as the humanization of *other*—the inclusion of *other* within one's moral universe (Hansen, 2016). With the view of this kind of friendship, we understand more clearly how Galtung views friendship as a condition for positive peace (Galtung, 2015; Westoby, 2014)—as friendships become the foundation for enacting "constructive social change" (Lederach, 2005, p. 75). Friendship can be the precursor to love in the establishment of positive peace and, as will be explored in the following section, love is action towards changing systemic oppression. As such, we are reminded that "friendship has had an important theoretical and even practical role in the resistance of power and the fight for justice" (Devere & Smith, 2010, p. 342), which is central to an understanding of positive peace.

Findings: Friendships & Changed Perceptions

Out of the online dialogic encounters, two key areas of potentialities emerged related to friendship as humanization: friendships ("New and Beautiful Friends") and changed perceptions of *other* ("These People Are Not Monsters").

The findings presented in "New and Beautiful Friends" indicate that interviewees felt they created relationships which fit their own understanding of 'friendship.' These are individual definitions of friendships, and not necessarily indicative of a humanized I-Thou relation. These findings on friendships reveal varying degrees of both intimacy and sustained connection amongst individuals who engaged in the online dialogue. For the majority of participants, there emerged feelings of friendship from their encounters—a sense that they had made connections that were meaningful to them in some way. However, for a small number, their experience did not result in the sense that friendships had formed. As Layla (Participant) shared in her reflections, there was a lack of interest from other members of her group, specifically those from Europe, to sustain contact, "they didn't get involved after the discussion was ended." The degree and depth to which these friendships will be sustained, and if they are of the substance required to translate to emancipatory action, remains unknown and out of the scope of this research inquiry.

These findings suggest that participants in the online dialogic encounter leave their experiences with the emotions or connotations that they associate with a friendship relation. Which is to say that a universal definition of friendship was not provided to interviewees, as such, we can assume variation in what each individual perceives and understands 'friendship' to mean. These findings are in alignment with the existing research about friendship formation online, which shows that friendship formation can and does occur in general in online environments (McKenna et al., 2002). The literature also indicates that friendship occurs as an outcome of computer-mediated contact programs (Hasler & Amichai-Hamburger, 2013; White et al., 2015b), online education for peace programs (Hoter et al., 2012), and in unstructured dialogue for peacebuilding online (Chaitin, 2012; Roberts, 2009; Witte & Booth, 2014). While the findings related to perceived friendships are valuable, they do not, on their own, provide insight into whether these friendships involved humanization of *other*. To understand if the dialogue encounters contributed to humanization of *other* as an expression of the I-Thou relation, I turn to the findings indicating changed perceptions of *other*.

For humanization to occur, the *other* must become more fully realized as an individual. This realization is indicated by a movement from perceiving *other* through stereotypes or reductionist identity characteristics into a more abundant, complex, and holistic understanding of the individual. The findings discussed in Chapter 7 of this book (in the section titled "These People Are Not Monsters") explore how perceptions of *other* shifted for those in the dialogue experience. The experiences recounted by Jacob, Beatrix, Nicolas, and Rianne suggest an encounter that challenged assumptions about the *other*, and, in some cases, such as with Nicolas, interrogated the dominant societal narrative of the *other*. These experiences signal a shift in perceptions, away from stereotypes, and, in some cases, such as with Hassan and Arij's stories, there was also critical thinking evident as they moved beyond surface-level assumptions of the *other*. While engaging with complicated and more nuanced ideas of who the *other* was within the dialogue space, individual participants were able to evaluate their pre-existing notions and reframe how they understood and perceived the *other* to be. The literature supports an understanding that reframing of perceptions is essential in cultivating friendships that are united in action against systemic issues. As Nagda (2006) articulates, "for the possibility of alliances across differences in the context of social inequalities to be real, both groups must 'work toward replacing judgments by category with new ways of thinking and acting'" (Collins as cited by Nagda, 2006, p. 570).

The findings indicate that, for many interviewees, there was a shift in perception of *other* that occurred through their online dialogic encounters. As discussed above, in order for friendship to occur, the 'I' must move into a relation of 'Thou.' An I-It relation cannot be a relation of friendship as it is not in communion with another person, but rather a relation with an objectified *other*. When there is an I-Thou encounter in dialogue, it brings into being a new world of relation, one which Galtung would describe as friendship. The literature regarding face-to-face dialogue for peacebuilding purposes indicates that "extended dialogue between adversarial groups facilitates mutual humanisation and acknowledgement" (Burkhardt-Vetter, 2018, p. 257). The change in view of *other* identified in this research is also in line with the literature on face-to-face programs, which find that perceptions of *other* changed as an outcome of dialogue experiences.[1] The existing literature exploring computer-mediated contact finds that programs employing the Contact Hypothesis online see a reduction in prejudice between outgroups and intergroup bias while increasing knowledge of the *other*, and changing perceptions in positive directions.[2]

Additionally, research on dialogue encounters has indicated that "the boundaries of the self are extended toward the inclusion of the other within the self... the other is included within the realm of relational moral responsibility; perceptions of and relations to the other are transformed" (Maoz et al., 2002, p. 936). So, we see from the literature that, in face-to-face dialogues, there are outcomes related to humanization and moral obligation, as well as shifts in perceptions of *other*, and reduction in stereotypes (Dessel & Rogge, 2008). The findings presented in this book

---

[1] For more on changed perceptions of *other* see: Burkhardt-Vetter (2018), Chaitin (2012), Dessel & Ali (2012), and Maoz et al. (2002).

[2] For more on outcomes of CMC see: Amichai-Hamburger et al. (2015), Harwood (2010), Kampf (2011), McKenna et al. (2009), Mollov & Schwartz (2010), Walther et al. (2015), White et al. (2015a), and Yablon & Katz (2001).

support the understanding that these outcomes are also possible within sustained dialogue encounters in online environments.

The findings related to changed perceptions extended to changed perceptions of self as well as *other* (Chapter 7, "I never thought of myself as..."). These findings align with existing literature on dialogue programs in face-to-face settings; self-reflection can occur for participants, which results in shifts in perception of self, narratives, beliefs, and identities (Dessel & Ali, 2012). As discussed in Chapter 2 ("Dialogue as Humanization"), Buber's theory of dialogue conveys an understanding that one's humanity is fully realized only when one engages with the full humanity of others (Buber, 1947), as Friedman (2004) articulates "As I become I, I say Thou" (p. 67). Indeed, the perception of oneself as able to hold open, and be changed by, the humanity of those previously *other* creates reinforces the opportunity for positive peace to emerge in allowing for awareness and mutuality to exist in the sphere of between. As the *humanization* of *other* intertwines with the *humanization* of self, it is valuable to discover that changes to how one perceives self and *other* occur as a result of online dialogic encounters.

Condition: Love

The second condition for positive peace discussed here is love. As acknowledged by Devere (2018), "love is one of the most difficult words in the English language to define" (p. 63). Similar to the concept of friendship, there are wide-ranging discussions regarding how love can be best understood. Love, in relation to a discussion of this research topic, and an understanding of positive peace, is best appreciated as a verb rather than a noun (Godden, 2017; Hooks, 2001). Freire expresses his conception of love this way:

> love is an act of courage, not of fear, love is commitment to others... As an act of bravery, love cannot be sentimental; as an act of freedom, it must not serve as a pretext for manipulation. It must generate other acts of freedom; otherwise, it is not love. (Freire, 2000, p. 89–90)

This envisioning of love presents courage, commitment, and bravery as the connotations for action towards freedom. These connotations are at odds with the more common associations of love as "naive, weak, and romantic" (Godden, 2017, p. 408); however, Godden reminds us that, within "the great social justice movements...love [was] the actualisation of the justice imperative" (p. 409). Love understood in this frame, becomes radical as it concerns itself with addressing the dynamics of oppression (Godden, 2017; Liambas & Kaskaris, 2012).

Love as action in relation to positive peace occurs within and across the three dimensions of direct, structural, and cultural:

> Positive peace...consists of direct actions of kindness, fostering the well-being of the body, mind, and spirit for oneself (inner peace) and others, meeting everyone's basic needs (including love and identity); structural actions to cultivate societal freedom, equity, dialogue, integration, solidarity, and participation; and cultural actions that legitimate both positive and negative peace rather than violence. (Hansen, 2016, p. 212)

A holistic composition of positive peace encompasses action related to structural oppression, cultural norms, and individual relationships that target systemic issues. As indicated in Fig. 8.2, the structural, direct, and cultural dimensions reinforce each other and establish an all-inclusive construct of positive peace.

In considering love as a condition for positive peace, there should be a recognition of the need for positive action amongst all three dimensions. However, this does not imply that an individual will necessarily take action

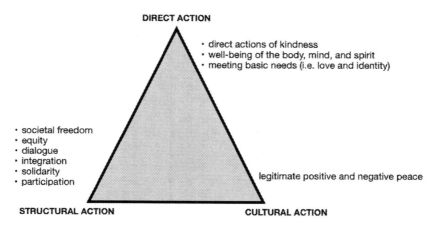

Fig. 8.2 Actions related to the dimensions of positive peace, described by Hansen (2016)

across all three dimensions themselves; it may be that they do so in only one of the areas. Rather, an envisioning of love as action encompasses a holistic view of social change—that collectively amongst a community or society, there must be action in all three dimensions to foster positive peace.

Love as Transformation.

As discussed in Chapter 2, dialogue is transformational when an individual is personally changed in such a way that sparks action. Therefore, there is an inter-relation between personal transformation and taking action, as Lederach points out:

> In the peacemaking endeavour, there seems to be a certain tension around how to pursue social change, which too often is posed as an either/or contradiction: Is social change fundamentally a process of personal or systemic transformation? ... Paulo Freire...suggests we understand social change as including both. (Lederach, 1995, p. 19)

The personally transformative is a valuable contributor in working towards positive peace. There is a reciprocal relationship between personal and societal transformation, "as individuals transform the world, they transform themselves within it" (Gill & Niens, 2014, p. 23). However, dialogue, in contributing to positive peace, must move beyond the personal, and, as argued by Freire, provide "a catalyst for social and structural transformation" (Westoby, 2014, p. 79).

As represented in Fig. 8.3, love understood as action within direct, cultural, and structural dimensions is then the outworking of dialogue as conscientization. To undertake love as action, there must be both *emergence,* an identification of the 'water' or context, which contributes to dynamics of oppression, and *intervention,* taking action against those identified systemic issues. When *emergence* and *intervention* occur across the three dimensions of positive peace, it becomes transformational.

The symbiotic relationship between *emergence* and *intervention*— reflection and action—is necessary for transformation (Freire, 2000); if there is only one or the other, they become "reduced to either verbalism or activism" (Freire, 2000, p. 125). Therefore, both the articulation of power dynamics and lived realities, along with intentional action occurring out of dialogic encounters are necessary to consider in looking at love as transformation.

8 THE CONDITIONS OF POSITIVE PEACE   189

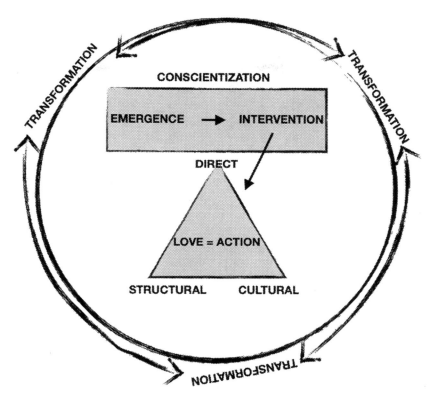

Fig. 8.3 Relationship between conscientization and love as action with transformation

Findings: Emergence & Intervention

For the building block of love to occur, there must be both facets of conscientization: the *emergence* and the *intervention* (italics in original) (Freire, 2000). *Emergence*, as the articulation of power, is exhibited within the findings of this research as many interviewees indicated an elucidation of their social realities ("The Circumstances and the Situation and the Differences"). Through their experiences in dialogue and engagement with *other*, they were able to identify previously unseen factors shaping their existence. This *emergence* is an essential component within the conceptualization of love as transformation. Reflections shared by interviewees such as Duha, Asma, and Mostafa suggested an *emergence* through the identification of international dynamics of power and privilege, which had a bearing on their individual lived experiences. While others, such as Nicolas and Karoline, illustrated how their online dialogue experiences impacted their ability to recognize and critique the prevalent narratives and social discourses in their lived context. *Emergence* as increased critical consciousness was found as an outcome of dialogue in face-to-face settings, and specifically in peace education programs employing dialogue methodologies (Nagda & Gurin, 2007; Tapper, 2013).

The second element of conscientization is *intervention*, the necessary action that embodies transformation. In Chapter 7, the element of *intervention* is evidenced in the section "I Won't Hold my Tongue." Deliberate action varied in expression, for some such as Layla and Nicolas, their action was outworked in how they interacted with others and their intentional interactions and openness across difference. For others, such as Anna and Amanda, *intervention* occurred as they heard or encountered an opinion they found problematic. If they were troubled by something that was said because it was perpetuating stereotypes or contributing to moral exclusion, they felt compelled to challenge those perspectives. In the examples provided by Duha and Oldez, their action was challenging the status quo beliefs or narratives to provide others in their social sphere the opportunity for *emergence*.

Returning to Chapter 4 ("Journey to Soliya"), there is evidence that, for facilitators, their role is their act of *intervention*. For those who have participated in the Soliya program and experienced *emergence*, facilitation provides the opportunity to *intervene*. Nicolas (Facilitator) commented, "I told myself that if I can have that same impact on other people, that would be marvellous." Similarly, Hassan said that:

> what we had in Soliya was very different, so it just got me interested in being a part of this great work, you know?...
> I just wished that I could help as many people as possible to have the same experience. (Hassan, Facilitator)

For others, who previously had not participated in the Soliya program but had felt *emergence* through other experiences in their lives, facilitation was also an act of *intervention*. As Rianne (Facilitator) articulated, "I am doing my itsy bitsy teeny weeny little constructive, positive thing." As discussed previously, if we conceive of positive peace as "a circle with continuous processes" (Standish, 2020, p. 267), we can see the act of facilitation as illustrative of this circle. An individual *emerges* and chooses to *intervene* through becoming a facilitator to provide opportunities for others to experience a similar *emergence*, and, in doing so, opens up the possibility for themselves to experience further *emergence* in the space of dialogue. Within face-to-face dialogue programs, there are examples of intentional individual or collective social action as an outcome of the experience (Bryn, 2015; Dessel & Rogge, 2008; Lefranc, 2012). The findings of this research illustrate that, as with face-to-face programs, *emergence* and *intervention* are possible out of dialogue encounters online. While these findings are encouraging regarding the potential of online dialogue for peacebuilding practice, there are necessary critiques to be considered within this discussion.

8.2 Critiques of the Findings

In discussing the findings of this research project there are cautions and critiques which are essential to consider. In the following section, I will present four of these areas for discussion: dialogue without *emergence*, *emergence* without *intervention*, friendships without *emergence* or *intervention*, Soliya as an 'ideal setting,' and variations in potentialities across participants.

Dialogue Without Emergence

The recognition and articulation of social realities as they relate to power is critical in dialogue outcomes that enable positive peace (Atkinson, 2013; Tapper, 2013). As the findings of this research demonstrate (in the section titled "An Expression of International Power Dynamics"), power is insidious; it is present even in situations where best efforts are made to mitigate its effects. In the case of Soliya and the online dialogue model in which this research took place, power related to language, technology, and gender, were all apparent. These findings confirm the significance of technology and language as dynamics of power, which have been previously identified within the Soliya setting (Helm, 2017, 2018) and in an unnamed online intercultural dialogue program (Bali, 2014). The findings also showed the majority of interviewees were aware of power differentials in their group. However, the degree to which each person articulated those power dynamics, and how much influence they perceived the dynamics had on their group varied. These variations are important to identify, as there is a potential risk if participants in the dialogue program leave having identified commonalities without recognition of power imbalances. In focusing on commonalities without addressing power discrepancies, there is a risk of normalization to occur—a further entrenchment of the status quo (Saguy et al., 2009).

Emergence Without Intervention

For mobilization towards action to occur, there must be a recognition of intergroup inequalities, particularly amongst members of the oppressed group (Saguy et al., 2009). However, if there is not an avenue for *intervention* following the recognition of power inequalities, there can be a further entrenchment of perceptions that result in discouragement from the dialogue experience (Burkhardt-Vetter, 2018; Helman, 2002).

For two interviewees, Asma and Mostafa, there appeared to be a recognition of power inequalities, which sparked a feeling of dissatisfaction. As Mostafa commented in "The Circumstances and the Situation and the Differences" in Chapter 7,

```
It is a little bit depressing if you can say that. It
made me; I used to think more about these problems before
the meetings, now I am not really thinking more about it
because I feel that we are far from solutions and I fear
that we are having a twenty-year from getting anywhere
near these countries. (Mostafa, Participant)
```

Both Asma and Mostafa signalled in their comments that they experienced feeling less privileged and advantaged in relation to some of their fellow group members. There was no indication that intentional action or *intervention* occurred for Asma or Mostafa in connection to their articulation of power dynamics. The time frame of this research meant that inquiry into any intentional action or behaviour participants might take emerging from their experiences was limited to the period between their program end date and our final interview. This research cannot answer the question of long-term outcomes of the dialogue experience for the individual or any *intervention* they might enact. However, a caveat with any dialogue program is: if participants identify power dynamics without identifying avenues for *intervention*, there remain risks of normalization or negative outcomes out of the encounter.

Friendships Without Emergence or Intervention

Intimately related to the above critique of dialogue is the issue of creating friendships through dialogue without *emergence* and *intervention* occurring. Dialogue undertaken for peacebuilding purposes, both online or face-to-face, must be concerned with outcomes that indicate critical consciousness and solidarity against systemic oppression. If dialogue programs produce friendships, on their own, without movement towards moral inclusion and action, it risks perpetuating the status quo (Phipps, 2014). As Devere and Smith (2010) signal:

> while friendship is often assumed to have a connection to an ethical concern with the Other, pointing to solidarity, care and reciprocity, some scholars have used its focus to show how 'friendship' has been used as a tool of power, or to subdue and stifle resistance. (p. 342)

Even if the stifling of resistance is not intentional, the literature indicates that dialogue for peacebuilding purposes must ensure it connects to both humanizing relationships and transformative action (Graf et al., 2014). As Jonathan Kuttab argues:

> when dialogue becomes a substitute for action, there are two results. First, it assuages the conscience of members of the oppressor group to the point where they feel they do not have to do anything else. The conscience is soothed and satisfied. On the other hand, for the members of the oppressed group it becomes a safety valve for venting frustrations. In both cases it becomes a means of reinforcing the existing oppression and therefore serves to perpetuate it. (as cited by Gawerc, 2006, p. 459)

There is a risk that participation in dialogue programs can limit personal action because people feel that they have done something positive just by participating in the dialogue encounter alone. Therefore, it is necessary, in the pursuit of positive peace, that action connected to a humanizing and morally inclusive relation occurs (Nagda, 2006).

The findings presented in this book suggest that a majority of individuals who were involved as a participant[3] in the dialogue felt they had established friends through their experience and that a majority

---

[3] I am presenting the 'participant' role only in this section because these aspects of inquiry were not explored with all of the facilitators.

of participants had a positively changed view of *other*. Several interviewees specifically mentioned they developed friendships with people they otherwise may never have met. A majority of the participants also conveyed potentialities related to conscientization, including increased critical consciousness and intentional actions. While there was overlap between participants who established friendships and participants who expressed a potentiality related to conscientization, there were individuals who only expressed one or the other. Similarly, many individuals experienced both a changed view of *other* and a potentiality related to conscientization—but some participants expressed only one or the other potentiality.

These findings indicate that the creation of friendship or a change in perception of *other* did not necessarily correlate to conscientization (increased critical consciousness or intentional action). These factors are relevant due to the associated risks of producing friendships with an absence of *emergence* and *intervention*, as explored above.

Ideal Setting

The site boundaries and scope of this research were defined such that the online dialogue encounters were structured and sustained. There were facilitators, and a dialogue process was generally followed. The technical platform was designed expressly to support the program and create a setting conducive to dialogue encounters. These aspects contribute to what may be perceived as an 'ideal' setting.

This research sought to explore dialogue for peacebuilding, predicated on similar models and ethos as face-to-face encounters in the peacebuilding field. After identifying the characteristics of dialogue in community peacebuilding in Chapter 3,[4] I intentionally sought to locate an online setting that was inclusive of as many of those traits as possible. As a result, I would argue that Soliya, as an 'ideal' setting, provided an excellent context in which to explore the research questions at hand and provide new contributions to the literature regarding online dialogue for peacebuilding. The specificity of this online setting also encourages future avenues for inquiry inclusive of varied settings and platforms in online environments.

---

[4] These characteristics were: encountering *other*, establishing a safe space that addresses issues of inequality amongst participants, attending to issues of identity both within in-group and out-group contexts, examination of truth and narratives, and creating relationships with *other* that enable a movement towards change or action.

Variations in Potentialities

Finally, I want to briefly make a note of the variation of potentialities that emerged amongst interviewees. For some, there was a clear narrative of their journey into, during, and out of the encounter. This journey indicated shifts in perceptions, increased critical consciousness, and intentional action. For others, there were perhaps one or more of these expressed experiences, but not as clear a path.

Of the 11 interviewees involved as participants, ten expressed at least one potentiality related to: changed perception of self, changed perception of *other*, friendships, critical consciousness, and intentional action. Even those interviewees who signalled they did not feel changed or impacted by their experience expressed elsewhere in our conversation at least a changed perception of *other*, changed view of self, or that they had created friendships. In the case of the single participant who did not indicate any potentialities during our conversations, it is worth noting that we encountered challenges in our conversation regarding language fluency, and therefore, our ability to understand one another was limited. I felt these challenges potentially restricted the depth and scope of our interview.

I raise these variations of potentialities to surface a few final reflections. The first is that experiences within the dialogue program were unique; there is not a universal narrative which can be applied to every individual. Additionally, the potentialities varied in how strongly associated they could be to the conditions of positive peace. However, while the potentialities varied in degree, it is significant that almost all interviewees who were participants reflected a potentiality related to positive peace.

8.3 Can Online Dialogue Enable Positive Peace?

As this book has demonstrated, engaging *other* through dialogic encounters within an online environment *can* enable conditions for positive peace. The findings indicate that friendship as a humanized relation with *other* can emerge out of sustained online dialogic encounters. Additionally, the findings suggest that love as transformative action also occurs out of these online dialogue encounters. While these outcomes are not universal across all interviewees, they are common and found amongst a majority of the research participants who held a participant role in the program.

Lefranc (2012) reminds us that "dialogue-based peacebuilding offer[s] a response to an enigma that still confounds sociologists: the enigma of the 'infinitely tiny steps' that, when repeated, form the 'grand total' and build a solid social tissue" (p. 43). This concept of infinitely tiny steps is critical to incorporate into one's thinking of how positive peace can be established. This chapter began with a reminder that positive peace is holistic and exists along a continuum, incorporating and building upon other tiers of peace. The degrees to which change occurs—and conscientization can manifest—should not be deemed irrelevant or insignificant even if it appears to be small in scale.

The actions reflected within these findings are meaningful to each individual and hold the potential to act as a stepping-stone to further *emergence* into critical consciousness and actions of *intervention* amongst the three dimensions of positive peace: direct, structural, and cultural. For some interviewees within the dialogue encounter, there emerged a new comprehension of the invisible factors shaping their lives, and the lives of others. For some, these represent the first conscious steps towards articulating previously unseen social realities and power dynamics. Anna (Participant) succinctly expressed this journey of conscientization incorporating both *emergence* and *intervention*, when she commented,

```
I realized that when we think about a problem, we just
think about what is related to our world, to what we live …
and even if they don't regard us, we should just recognize
them and act in order to solve them. …and I am starting to
say something.
```

Anna's comments highlight the journey through identifying an issue, recognizing her responsibility to act upon that issue even if it is not directly related to her, and beginning to take personal action through voicing her concerns or objections. As Hassan (Facilitator) signalled, this is "the beginning of our journey." Understanding these potentialities as an aspect of an ongoing journey frames the linkages to positive peace. Nicolas (Facilitator) reflected in our conversation that his exposure to different perspectives "helped me to carve my own path and break free from my own familiar environment." His comments throughout our conversation revealed a sense that his engagement with his social reality had shifted as an outcome of his involvement with

Soliya—shaping his interactions with others and his interpretation of his lived context.

Returning to Lederach's (2005) concept of the moral imagination, as discussed in Chapter 2, we are reminded that it is the "invisible web of relationships" (p. 75) which provide the locus for transformative action. When it comes to peace, relationships—and the quality of those relationships—are the "critical yeast… It is a question of the quality of relational spaces, intersections, and interactions that affect a social process beyond the numbers involved" (Lederach, 2005, p. 100). Out of meaningful interactions and relationships can emerge solidarity, which engenders action. The aim, therefore, is to create space for quality relational, dialogic interactions to occur.

If we understand positive peace to be on a continuum, ideally moving through tiers, we can also conceptualize the conditions of friendship and love to be on a continuum. In the continuous evolution towards positive peace, small and incremental movements are necessary, movements such as: holding open to *other* across difference, an examination of narratives and identity, and openness to the humanization of *other*.

8.4 SUMMARY

This chapter provided a discussion on the overarching question presented in this book: can engaging *other* through dialogic encounters within an online environment enable conditions for positive peace? In order to address this question, there was a revisiting of positive peace theory. There was then an exploration of the two identified conditions for positive peace, friendship and love. An understanding of what is meant by friendship, specifically that friendships are the embodiment of the humanization of *other*, was presented. As separateness is overcome, there is a change from communication to communion, in living, reciprocal relationships. In order to have these relationships, humanization of the *other* must occur. Humanization was explored through an understanding of moral inclusion, looking at dehumanization and moral exclusion to provide a contrast.

The findings of this research were then examined in connection to friendship as humanization, looking at how interviewees identified the relational outcomes of their dialogic encounters, and how perceptions of self and *other* shifted into an I-Thou relation.

The chapter then moved into an exploration of the other condition for positive peace: love. The linkage between love as action amongst the dimensions of positive peace (cultural, structural, and direct), and conscientization was presented, specifically the two aspects of *emergence* and *intervention*. The findings suggested that, out of dialogic encounters online, interviewees experienced both aspects of *emergence* and *intervention*. Finally, there was a reminder given that positive peace is self-reinforcing, occurs on a continuum, and that tiny, incremental movements are essential to establish and reinforce it.

REFERENCES

Atkinson, M. (2013). Intergroup dialogue: A theoretical positioning. *Journal of Dialogue Studies, 1*(1), 63–80.

Amichai-Hamburger, Y., Hasler, B. S., & Shani-Sherman, T. (2015). Structured and unstructured intergroup contact in the digital age. *Computers in Human Behavior, 52*, 515–522. https://doi.org/10.1016/j.chb.2015.02.022

Bali, M. (2014). Why doesn't this feel empowering? The challenges of web-based intercultural dialogue. *Teaching in Higher Education, 19*(2), 208–215. https://doi.org/10.1080/13562517.2014.867620

Bar-Tal, D., & Hammack, P. L. (2012). Conflict, delegitimization, and violence. In L. R. Tropp (Ed.), *The Oxford Handbook of Intergroup Conflict* (pp. 29–52). Oxford University Press. https://doi.org/10.1093/oxfordhb/9780199747672.013.0003

Bryn, S. (2015). Can dialogue make a difference?: The experience of the Nansen dialogue network. In S. P. Ramet, A Simkus & O. Listhaug (Eds.), *Civic and uncivic values in Kosovo* (pp. 365–394). Central European University Press. https://doi.org/10.7829/j.ctt13wzttq.21

Buber, M. (1947). *Between man and man* (R. G. Smith, Trans.). Routledge.

Buber, M. (1970). *I and Thou*. (W. Kaufmann, Trans.). Scribner.

Burkhardt-Vetter, O. (2018). Reconciliation in the making: Overcoming competitive victimhood through inter-group dialogue in Palestine/Israel. In V. Druliolle & R. Brett (Eds.), *The politics of victimhood in post-conflict societies: Comparative and analytical perspectives* (pp. 237–263). Springer International Publishing. https://doi.org/10.1007/978-3-319-70202-5_10

Chaitin, J. (2012). Co-creating peace: Confronting psychosocial-economic injustices in the Israeli-Palestinian context. In B. Charbonneau & G. Parent (Eds.), *Peacebuilding, memory and reconciliation: Bridging top-down and bottom-up approaches* (pp. 146–162). Routledge.

Cissna, K. N., & Anderson, R. (1998). Theorizing about dialogic moments: The Buber-Rogers position and postmodern themes. *Communication Theory, 8*(1), 63–104.

Czubaroff, J. (2000). Dialogical rhetoric: An application of Martin Buber's philosophy of dialogue. *Quarterly Journal of Speech, 86*(2), 168–189. https://doi.org/10.1080/00335630009384288

Dessel, A., & Rogge, M. E. (2008). Evaluation of intergroup dialogue: A review of the empirical literature. *Conflict Resolution Quarterly, 26*(2), 199–238. https://doi.org/10.1002/crq.230

Dessel, A., & Ali, N. (2012). The minds of peace and intergroup dialogue: Two complementary approaches to peace. *Israel Affairs, 18*(1), 123–139. https://doi.org/10.1080/13537121.2012.634276

Devere, H. (2014). The many meanings of friendship. *AMITY: The Journal of Friendship Studies, 2*(1), 1–3.

Devere, H. (2018). Exploring relationships for positive peace. *In Factis Pax, 12*(1), 59–79.

Devere, H., & Smith, G. M. (2010). Friendship and politics. *Political Studies Review, 8*(3), 341–356. https://doi.org/10.1111/j.1478-9302.2010.00214.x

Freire, P. (2000). *Pedagogy of the oppressed* (30th anniversary ed.) (M. B. Ramos, Trans). Continuum.

Friedman, M. S. (2004). *Martin Buber: The life of dialogue*. Routledge.

Galtung, J. (1990). Cultural violence. *Journal of Peace Research, 27*(3), 291–305. http://www.jstor.org/stable/423472

Galtung, J. (2012). *A theory of peace: Building direct structural cultural peace*. Transcend University Press.

Galtung, J. (2015, January 5). Positive peace—What is that? Retrieved from the TRANSCEND Media Service website: https://www.transcend.org/tms/2015/01/positive-peace-what-is-that/

Gawerc, M. (2006). Peace-building: Theoretical and concrete perspectives. *Peace & Change, 31*(4), 435–478. https://doi.org/10.1111/j.1468-0130.2006.00387.x

Gergen, K. J., McNamee, S., & Barrett, F. J. (2001). Toward transformative dialogue. *International Journal of Public Administration, 24*(7–8), 679–707. https://doi.org/10.1081/PAD-100104770

Gill, S., & Niens, U. (2014). Education as humanisation: A theoretical review on the role of dialogic pedagogy in peacebuilding education. *Compare: A Journal of Comparative and International Education, 44*(1), 10–31. https://doi.org/10.1080/03057925.2013.859879

Godden, N. J. (2017). The love ethic: A radical theory for social work practice. *Australian Social Work, 70*(4), 405–416. https://doi.org/10.1080/0312407X.2017.1301506

Graf, S., Paolini, S., & Rubin, M. (2014). Negative intergroup contact is more influential, but positive intergroup contact is more common: Assessing contact prominence and contact prevalence in five Central European countries. *European Journal of Social Psychology, 44*(6), 536–547. https://doi.org/10.1002/ejsp.2052

Hansen, T. (2016). Holistic peace. *Peace Review, 28*(2), 212–219. https://doi.org/10.1080/10402659.2016.1166758

Harwood, J. (2010). The contact space: A novel framework for intergroup contact research. *Journal of Language and Social Psychology, 29*(2), 147–177. https://doi.org/10.1177/0261927X09359520

Hasler, B. S., & Amichai-Hamburger, Y. (2013). Online intergroup contact. In Y. Amichai-Hamburger (Ed.), *The social net: Understanding our online behavior* (2nd ed.) (pp. 220–252). Oxford University Press.

Helm, F. (2017). *I'm not disagreeing, I'm just curious: Exploring identities through multimodal interaction in virtual exchange*. (Doctoral thesis). Universitat Autònoma De Barcelona.

Helm, F. (2018). *Emerging identities in virtual exchange*. research-publishing.net.

Helman, S. (2002). Monologic results of dialogue: Jewish-Palestinian encounter groups as sites of essentialization. *Identities, 9*(3), 327–354. https://doi.org/10.1080/10702890213971

hooks, bell. (2001). *All about love: New visions*. Harper Collins Publishers.

Hoter, E., Shonfeld, M., & Ganayem, A. N. (2012). TEC center: Linking technology, education and cultural diversity. *i-Manager's Journal of Educational Technology, 9*(1), 15–22. https://search.proquest.com/docview/1473901542/abstract/3ED6FD97DD1A4672PQ/1

Kampf, R. (2011). Internet, conflict and dialogue: The Israeli case. *Israel Affairs, 17*(3), 384–400. https://doi.org/10.1080/13537121.2011.584666

Lederach, J. P. (1995). *Preparing for peace: Conflict transformation across cultures*. Syracuse University Press.

Lederach, J. P. (2005). *The Moral Imagination: The art and soul of building peace*. Oxford University Press.

Lefranc, S. (2012). A critique of "bottom-up" peacebuilding: Do peaceful individuals make peaceful societies? In B. Charbonneau & G. Parent (Eds.), *Peacebuilding, memory and reconciliation: Bridging top-down and bottom-up approaches* (pp. 34–52). Routledge.

Liambas, A., & Kaskaris, I. (2012). "Dialog" and "love" in the work of Paulo Freire. *Journal for Critical Education Policy Studies, 10*(1), 185–196.

Maoz, I., Steinberg, S., Bar-On, D., & Fakhereldeen, M. (2002). The dialogue between the "Self" and the "Other": A process analysis of Palestinian-Jewish encounters in Israel. *Human Relations, 55*(8), 931–962. https://doi.org/10.1177/0018726702055008178

McKenna, K. Y. A., Green, A. S., & Gleason, M. E. J. (2002). Relationship formation on the internet: What's the big attraction? *Journal of Social Issues*, 58(1), 9–31. https://doi.org/10.1111/1540-4560.00246

McKenna, K. Y. A., Samuel-Azran, T., & Sutton-Balaban, N. (2009). Virtual meetings in the Middle East: Implementing the contact hypothesis on the internet. *The Israel Journal of Conflict Resolution*, 1(1), 63–86.

Mollov, M. B., & Schwartz, D. G. (2010). Towards an integrated strategy for intercultural dialog: Computer-mediated communication and face to face. *Journal of Intercultural Communication Research*, 39(3), 207–224. https://doi.org/10.1080/17475759.2010.534905

Nagda, B. R. A. (2006). Breaking barriers, crossing borders, building bridges: Communication processes in intergroup dialogues. *Journal of Social Issues*, 62(3), 553–576. https://doi.org/10.1111/j.1540-4560.2006.00473.x

Nagda, B. R. A., & Gurin, P. (2007). Intergroup dialogue: A critical-dialogic approach to learning about difference, inequality, and social justice. *New Directions for Teaching and Learning*, 2007(111), 35–45. https://doi.org/10.1002/tl.284

Opotow, S. (2012). The scope of justice, intergroup conflict, and peace. In L. R. Tropp (Ed.), *The Oxford handbook of intergroup conflict* (pp. 72–86). Oxford University Press. https://doi.org/10.1093/oxfordhb/9780199747672.013.0005

Phipps, A. (2014). 'They are bombing now': 'Intercultural Dialogue' in times of conflict. *Language and Intercultural Communication*, 14(1), 108–124. https://doi.org/10.1080/14708477.2013.866127

Roberts, J. (2009, January 13). 500 citizens of Sderot contradict the Israeli government. *Palestine Chronicle*.

Saguy, T., Tausch, N., Dovidio, J. F., & Pratto, F. (2009). The irony of harmony: Intergroup contact can produce false expectations for equality. *Psychological Science*, 20(1), 114. https://doi.org/10.1111/j.1467-9280.2008.02261.x

Standish, K. (2020). *Suicide through a peacebuilding lens*. Palgrave Macmillan. https://doi.org/10.1007/978-981-13-9737-0_9

Tapper, A. J. H. (2013). A pedagogy of social justice education: Social identity theory, intersectionality, and empowerment. *Conflict Resolution Quarterly*, 30(4), 411–445. https://doi.org/10.1002/crq.21072

Walther, J. B., Hoter, E., Ganayem, A., & Shonfeld, M. (2015). Computer-mediated communication and the reduction of prejudice: A controlled longitudinal field experiment among Jews and Arabs in Israel. *Computers in Human Behavior*, 52, 550–558. https://doi.org/10.1016/j.chb.2014.08.004

Westoby, P. (2014). Theorising dialogue for community development practice – an exploration of crucial thinkers. *Journal of Dialogue Studies*, 2(1), 69–85.

White, F. A., Abu-Rayya, H. M., Bliuc, A-M., & Faulkner, N. (2015a). Emotion expression and intergroup bias reduction between Muslims and Christians: Long-term Internet contact. *Computers in Human Behavior, 53*, 435–442.

White, F. A., Harvey, L. J., & Abu-Rayya, H. M. (2015b). Improving intergroup relations in the internet age: A critical review. *Review of General Psychology, 19*(2), 129–139. https://doi.org/10.1037/gpr0000036

Witte, G., & Booth, W. (2014, July 12). Unlikely friendship blossoms across front lines in Israel and Gaza. *The Washington Post*.

Yablon, Y. B., & Katz, Y. J. (2001). Internet-based group relations: A high school peace education project in Israel. *Educational Media International, 38*(2–3), 175–182. https://doi.org/10.1080/09523980110043591

CHAPTER 9

Conclusion

In this book, I sought to explore the experiences of individuals in dialogic encounters in online environments. The research inquiry presented in these pages is situated within the broader field of peace and conflict studies, specifically within an understanding of community-based peacebuilding and dialogue practices. I began this book with the construction of a theoretical framework drawing from Galtung's theory of positive peace (Galtung, 1990) along with the dialogue theories of Martin Buber and Paulo Freire, incorporating elements such as Buber's I-Thou relation and the sphere of between (Buber, 1947), as well as Freire's theory of conscientization, including the aspects of *emergence* and *intervention* (Freire, 2000). My intent throughout the research and writing journey was to engage meaningfully, and dialogically, with whatever unfolded in the inquiry, situating myself as the researcher within my theoretical framework—through which I navigated the journey of investigation.

I then moved into a presentation of the existing literature, which revealed a gap in knowledge related to the practice of community-based dialogue for peacebuilding purposes within online environments. Acknowledging this gap, and the relevance of the inquiry to ongoing peace practice, the purpose of the remainder of this book was to explore individual experiences within an intentional and sustained online dialogue program and the relationship between these experiences and positive peace.

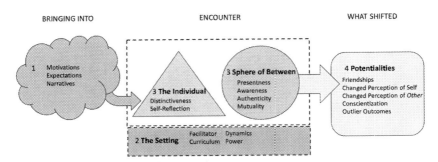

Fig. 1.1 Represents the narrative of the findings (*Note* First instance of Fig. 1.1 found in Chapter 1)

The findings of an online ethnographic research inquiry were then presented, revealing an overarching narrative of the online dialogue experience: Bringing Into, Encounter, and What Shifted. This narrative was previously illustrated in Chapter 1 and has been included again below for reference.

This narrative was presented throughout four chapters. Chapter 4 (Findings: Bringing Into) provided an introduction to the research participants, including their motivations ("Journey to Soliya"), expectations ("I Expected To..."), and pre-existing narratives ("The Source of my Knowledge"). Chapter 5 explored "The Setting," starting with a review of Soliya in relation to the characteristics of dialogue in community peacebuilding practice. The chapter then provided an overview of the program design ("Program Design: Influencing Factors"), including the facilitator role and the curriculum. The latter half of the chapter presented findings related to the intangible setting, the factors shaping the encounters and interactions, including group dynamics ("We Thought the Group is Stuck") and power dynamics ("An Expression of International Power Dynamics"). Finally, the chapter offered findings related to the perceived benefits and limitations of the online dialogue program. Chapter 6 moved into the dialogue encounter itself, beginning with what occurs for the "Individual in Encounter." The remainder of the chapter focused on what happens in the "Sphere of Between," encompassing Buber's characteristics of dialogue: presentness, awareness, authenticity, and mutuality. The final findings chapter (Chapter 7) presented the potentialities which emerged out of the dialogue encounters. These potentialities related to friendships ("New and Beautiful Friends"), changed perception of self and *other* ("To See Something Different"), conscientization ("How's the Water?"), and outlier outcomes ("I Don't Change Easily").

Following the presentation of the findings, a discussion was presented in Chapter 8 regarding the guiding question examined in this book: can engaging *other* through dialogic encounters within an online environment enable conditions for positive peace? This question was addressed through an exploration of the identified conditions of positive peace, friendship as *humanization*, and love as *transformation*. Findings related to these conditions were incorporated into the discussion of the research question. Finally, the critiques of the research were also presented.

This chapter will present final reflections on the contributions to knowledge this book offers, as well as provide recommendations for both practice and future research inquiries. In alignment with my intention to remain, as researcher, situated in the dialogical locus of this inquiry, I will conclude the chapter with a few final reflections.

9.1 Contributions to Knowledge

This research contributes knowledge to the existing body of literature regarding online dialogue for peacebuilding and positive peace theory by offering insight into the individual experiences of participants and facilitators in such a program. Specifically, this book makes the following contributions:

1. The application of dialogue theory, utilizing Buber and Freire, provided a meaningful framework for interpreting experiences, as well as contributing unique insight into the characteristics of dialogue and the presence of the sphere of between in online dialogic encounters (Chapter 6: The Encounter). The findings related to the sphere of between, including presentness, awareness, authenticity, and mutuality provide meaningful insight into the micro-level of dialogue encounters, specifically within an online context. As discussed in Chapter 6, the presence of these four characteristics contributed to feelings of safety, trust, and respect, and crafted opportunities for self-reflection and interrogation of assumptions and preconceptions amongst individuals in the dialogue program.

    The findings encompassed by the sphere of between are intimately related to the other findings from this research related to group and power dynamics, as all of these factors shape and inform

the dialogue (Chapter 5: The Setting). These dynamics inform what unfolds within the dialogue space, including which voices are heard and which remain silent. Even when the potential impact of power dynamics is considered in the design of a dialogue program, power remains pervasive—it will surface and influence the group interactions.
2. This book makes further contributions in knowledge regarding the relationship between positive peace and online dialogue practice for peacebuilding. In particular, it demonstrates the emergence of a humanized relation, understood as the 'friendship' condition of positive peace, through online dialogue encounters (Chapter 7: Potentialities). The potentialities of friendships, changed perceptions of self, and changed perceptions of *other*, as discussed in the previous chapter, signify the I-Thou relation occurring out of online dialogue. As such, this book presents an understanding that outcomes related to humanization, such as shifts in perceptions of self, *other*, and reduction in stereotypes, are possible within sustained dialogue encounters in online environments. This humanized friendship relation is presented as one of two conditions for positive peace.

The second condition for positive peace is love as action—the embodiment of conscientization. Conscientization is discussed as two elements, *emergence* and *intervention*, which both arose as important potentialities from the online dialogue program (Chapter 7: Potentialities). Participants in the dialogue began to articulate previously unseen social realities as an expression of *emergence*. Additionally, experiences in the program led to *intervention* as deliberate and intentional shifts in behaviour and actions. As a result, this book offers a unique perspective on the aspects of *emergence* and *intervention*, which can manifest from dialogue encounters online.

As the above two contributions indicate, the research presented in this book provides important implications for both the utilization of online settings for dialogue-based peacebuilding practice, as well as research into dialogue theory applied in online contexts. These findings confirm that online dialogue can provide an opportunity for authentic and meaningful dialogic encounters to occur and underscore the importance of explicitly addressing power imbalances. Further, these findings demonstrate that dialogue within online settings can enable friendship and love, facilitating the conditions for an emergent and evolving construction of positive peace.

9.2 Recommendations & Future Directions

My intention with this book is to provide a contribution to both the academic literature and to dialogue-based peacebuilding practices. As such, in the following section, I present possible future directions in terms of both practice and research inquiries.

Practice & Policy

This research has demonstrated that online dialogue for peacebuilding purposes can provide meaningful contributions in working towards positive peace. Therefore, sustained and intentional online dialogue programs should be taken seriously regarding their valuable role within peacebuilding practice. The following practice-based recommendations are offered as an outcome of the findings of this research:

1. Programs predicated on a sustained, intentional dialogue model must be cognizant that power dynamics remain present in online space, specifically concerning technology, language, and gender. These dynamics will influence the group, and therefore any program design should intentionally mitigate its effects in both platform design, program methodology, as well as facilitator training. In addition to a mitigation of the dynamics, participants must have the opportunity to critically engage with their experiences of power differentials in the group to provide an opportunity for *emergence* as the articulation of previously unseen social realities.
2. Peacebuilding organizations and practitioners should consider the implementation of their programs online when dialogue programs are occurring in contexts where face-to-face encounters are not always feasible or pose safety concerns. Additionally, dialogue-based peacebuilding organizations should include in their contingency planning the opportunities for dialogue programs to continue online, should in-person encounters not be possible. Furthermore, online programs can provide a meaningful opportunity to supplement existing initiatives through enabling ongoing connections in between the in-person meetings.
3. This research highlights the importance of a humanized and morally inclusive I-Thou relation amongst dialogue participants through changed perceptions of *other*. Programs seeking positive peace-related outcomes should incorporate an opportunity for interrogation of dominant social narratives and engagement of nuance and complex

ideas of *other* within the online dialogue. These opportunities enable a shift in perception of *other* into a humanized I-Thou relation. This I-Thou relation, in partnership with opportunities for critical engagement with social realities and dynamics of power, mitigates the risks of normalization or negative outcomes.
4. Online dialogue programs should thoughtfully consider how to incorporate opportunities for *intervention* as participants *emerge* from their previously unseen social realities. Providing these collective opportunities can prove challenging in dispersed geographic locations; however, as this research has indicated, participants do exhibit potentialities related to *intervention* individually. By making explicit within the groups these individual acts of *intervention*, it may provide a further opportunity for collective reflection and action amongst the group participants.

Finally, connecting practice with policy, a concluding recommendation:
1. Creating online dialogue platforms can be potentially cost-prohibitive, especially for small organizations. The creation of a customizable, low-cost and low-barrier platform that can be licensed by organizations would provide the necessary technology for delivering online dialogue programs across diverse contexts and demographics.

Future Research Directions

As a researcher, I engaged this topic through my own experiences, as reflected within the cogitatio passages of the book. In addition to my individual lens, I applied a specific theoretical framework and methodological design to this inquiry. There is no doubt that a different researcher would surface new interpretations and discern new understandings out of a similar inquiry. I would welcome and invite future inquiries into this field to enrich the literature and the collective knowledge regarding dialogue practices and their relationship to positive peace, both online and offline. Specifically, there may be opportunities to explore areas such as:

1. Further exploration of the friendship potentiality of the research findings. Understanding of the long-term potential and the meaningfulness of the friendships formed would provide valuable insight into the sustainability and impact of developing relationships through online dialogue.

2. An inquiry focused on the *intervention* aspect of the research findings, specifically, if there are mid-term or long-term sustained *intervention* actions which emerge for individuals out of their experiences in the dialogue program.
3. Another avenue for exploring the *intervention* component of these findings is a study based on the three elements of positive peace: direct, structural, and cultural. An inquiry into *intervention* amongst these three areas could provide further insight into the relationship between online dialogue with a holistic concept of positive peace.
4. A study situated within an ongoing or post-conflict context could provide insight into the role of online dialogue within different environments in which peacebuilding practices occur, such as protracted and/or identity-based conflicts.
5. A research study regarding online dialogue for peacebuilding employing unstructured or non-sustained program design; this could provide meaningful information regarding dialogue encounters in more 'everyday' online environments such as social media platforms.
6. I conducted this research through an 'insider' perspective as I was both facilitator and researcher. Future research could involve a collaborative research team so that the limitation experienced in a dual facilitator role could be mitigated through a team approach involving the Soliya dynamic that permits data collection from participant-only and facilitator-only perspectives. This approach would yield alternative findings and provide a more robust opportunity to explore the facilitator dynamic with participants.
7. Finally, the application of a different theoretical lens or methodological approach to this research topic may provide alternative insights not offered by this study.

References

Buber, M. (1947). *Between man and man* (R. G. Smith, Trans.). Routledge.
Freire, P. (2000). *Pedagogy of the oppressed* (30th anniversary ed.) (M. B. Ramos, Trans). Continuum.
Galtung, J. (1990). Cultural violence. *Journal of Peace Research*, *27*(3), 291–305. http://www.jstor.org/stable/423472

Index

A
Ableness, 29, 47, 56, 95
Abortion, 102
Acceptance, 19, 180
Accessibility, 5, 49, 53–56, 110–112, 116
Action, 9, 19, 24–26, 28, 31, 41, 45–48, 55, 56, 58, 93, 96, 99, 119, 165, 168–170, 173, 176, 179, 181–188, 190–198, 206, 208, 209
Activism, 49, 51, 188
Affection, 180
Age, 47, 56, 71, 108, 162
Allies, 19
Aotearoa, 2
Assumptions, 84, 85, 88, 134, 160–164, 166, 167, 170, 171, 174, 175, 184, 205
Authentic, 9, 14, 19, 20, 23, 24, 31, 55, 95, 96, 103, 139, 206
Authenticity, 7, 9, 21–23, 31, 134, 139–141, 146, 148, 204, 205
Awareness, 7, 9, 21–23, 26, 31, 52, 55, 92, 93, 102, 122, 123, 129, 130, 132, 134, 136–138, 141, 146–148, 173, 174, 180, 186, 204, 205

B
Bakhtin, Mikhail, 16
Beliefs, 23, 42–44, 50, 55, 82, 98, 114, 130, 134–136, 139, 141, 142, 145, 146, 158, 160, 165, 167, 175, 186, 190
Bias(es), 7, 53, 88, 94, 95, 97, 100, 160, 163, 164, 175
Blockades, 50
Bohm, David, 16
Bravery, 119, 139, 186
Brave space, 43, 95
Brazil, 18
 Brazilian, 18
Buber, Martin, 7, 13, 15–18, 20–24, 28, 31, 127, 133, 134, 146, 148, 179–181, 186, 203–205
Bullying, 4

© The Editor(s) (if applicable) and The Author(s), under exclusive license to Springer Nature Singapore Pte Ltd. 2022
R. Nolte-Laird, *Peacebuilding Online*,
https://doi.org/10.1007/978-981-16-6013-9

C

Camera, 99, 108, 114, 118
Camp(s), 55, 94
Catholicism, 167
Christian(s), 83, 118, 141, 143, 172
Cogitatio, 6, 7, 88
Cold War, 2
Collective action, 191
Commitment, 26, 75, 156, 186
Commonalities, 48, 82, 103, 192
Computer-Mediated Communication (CMC), 53
Confidence, 71, 157, 158
Confirmation, 23
Conscientization, 7, 9, 25, 26, 152, 165, 168, 169, 175, 176, 188–190, 194, 196, 198, 203, 205, 206
Contact Hypothesis, 3, 8, 39, 50, 52–54, 59, 123, 185
Continuum, 28, 177, 178, 196–198
Controversial, 102, 172
Courage, 115, 186
Critical consciousness, 165, 179, 190, 193–196
Critical pedagogy, 29
Critical thinking, 25, 46, 91, 102, 160, 166, 184
Cultural norms, 87, 111, 129, 160, 167, 187
Cultural peace, 14
Cultural violence, 13, 14
Culture(s), 2, 3, 15, 18, 27, 46, 48, 52, 76, 78, 87, 92, 93, 97, 100, 101, 110–112, 115, 120, 129, 131, 134, 136, 137, 140, 148, 153–155, 159, 161, 173, 174
Curiosity, 74, 76, 100, 103, 137, 139, 147
Curriculum, 91, 94, 95, 97, 100, 102, 204

D

Debate, 20, 51, 84, 135–137
Dehumanization, 14, 181, 182, 197
Dialogic moments, 7, 20, 21, 31, 104, 122, 134
Dialogic Remembering, 44
Digital divide, 56
Directness, 22
Direct peace, 14
Direct violence, 13, 14
Distinctiveness, 127, 128, 130, 133, 143, 148
Dunamis, 151

E

East-West, 94, 95
E-Contact, 53
Education, 6, 38, 51, 52, 56, 79, 91, 93, 101, 160, 162
   online education, 52, 54, 184
   peace education, 52, 123, 190
Emancipatory, 179, 184
Emergence, 3, 25, 26, 32, 42, 120, 165, 166, 168, 175, 176, 188–194, 196, 198, 203, 206, 207
Emotions, 7, 133, 140, 180, 184
Empowerment, 19, 24, 49
Energeia, 151
Equity, 14, 37, 120, 177, 187
Ethnicity, 18, 29, 88, 95
Ethnography, 6
   Online, 6
Europe, 6, 71, 72, 74, 75, 94, 111, 113, 156, 168, 184
Expectation(s), 8, 69, 81, 82, 84, 85, 88, 89, 91, 138, 161, 162, 167, 204
Extremism, 4

F

Facebook, 78, 83, 99, 153, 154
Face-to-face, 4, 40, 41, 47, 49, 50, 52–58, 110, 112, 114, 117–120, 123, 146, 155, 156, 185, 186, 190, 191, 193, 194, 207
False generosity, 19
Frankness, 22
Freedom, 14, 19, 30, 87, 142, 167, 186, 187
Freire, Paulo, 7, 13, 15, 16, 18, 19, 23–26, 28–31, 165, 169, 179, 181, 186, 188, 189, 203, 205
Friendship(s), 51–53, 152–157, 175–181, 183–186, 191, 193–195, 197, 205, 206, 208

G

Gadamer, Hans-Georg, 16
Game theory, 50
Gaza, 1
Gender, 18, 28–30, 43, 47, 56, 71, 95, 100, 101, 104, 108–112, 191, 207
Generosity, 55, 69, 180
Germany, 16, 74, 139, 140
Grassroot(s), 3–5, 38, 46, 49, 51

H

Habermas, Jurgen, 16
Hijab, 142, 143
Holistic, 7, 13–15, 31, 38, 119, 177, 178, 184, 187, 188, 196, 209
Homogenous, 29, 143, 175
Honesty, 115, 180
Hosting, 155
Humanity, 16, 17, 23, 24, 186
Humanization, 2, 7, 13–16, 23, 24, 31, 32, 146, 179–181, 183–186, 197, 205, 206
humanize, 17, 24, 179, 180, 182, 183, 195, 206–208
Humankind, 16, 26, 30, 31, 165

I

Ideal, 88, 93, 98–100, 135, 147, 178, 194, 197
Identity, 5, 7, 18, 41, 43, 44, 47, 48, 51, 58, 59, 70, 87, 88, 93–95, 98, 100, 127, 130, 141, 143, 151, 158, 159, 174, 182, 184, 187, 197, 209
  social identity, 18, 40, 47, 179
Identity group, 3, 18, 39, 42, 43, 49, 52, 56, 96, 109, 169
Ideology, 7, 14
Inclusion, 22, 183, 185
Indigenous, 2
Inequality(ies), 2, 18, 26, 27, 29, 31, 41, 42, 45, 47, 48, 53, 93, 179, 185, 192
Inequity, 13, 38, 45
In-group, 41, 43, 48, 93
Injustice, 2, 13, 26, 38
  systemic, 26, 45, 47
Instagram, 153
Integrity, 142, 180
Intentionality, 21, 27, 131–133, 136, 137, 147, 148, 169, 172, 176
Intergroup, 39, 46–48, 57, 182, 185, 192
Intergroup Dialogue (IGD), 40
Internet, 4, 5, 49, 50, 53, 54, 56, 83, 86, 105, 108, 116, 118, 119, 156
Intersectionality, 18
Intervention, 26, 32, 51, 165, 168, 175, 176, 188–194, 196, 198, 203, 206, 208, 209
Intimacy, 23, 183
Intra-regional, 95
Israel, 1, 16, 100, 137, 138

J

Judgment(s), 28, 53, 185
Justice, 19, 25, 37, 177, 180, 182, 183, 187

K

Kindness, 187
Kinēsis, 151
King Jr., Martin Luther, 19

L

Language, 2, 14, 18, 26, 29, 30, 43, 50, 52, 55–57, 71, 75, 78, 79, 104–109, 117–120, 122, 145, 160, 165, 178, 186, 191, 195, 207
LGBTQ+, 172
Liberal peacebuilding, 2
Literacy, 56, 91
  digital literacy, 56
Low-barrier, 208
Low-cost, 208

M

Manipulation, lack of, 17
Media, 14, 81, 85, 86, 91, 138
Mediation, 38, 73, 171
Micro, 9, 205
Microphone, 108
Middle East, 1, 6, 94, 102, 111, 156, 161, 163, 166, 174
Mindfulness, 20
Monological, 17
Moral, 5, 45, 182, 183, 185, 193, 207
  exclusion, 182, 190, 197
  inclusion, 45, 182, 193, 197
Moral imagination, 25, 31, 45, 197
Moral obligation, 185
Moriori, 2
Motivation(s), 8, 69, 71, 73, 75–77, 80, 81, 88, 89, 91, 121, 146, 204
Multi-Partial(ity), 95, 98, 155, 169
Muslim, 51, 73, 81–83, 86, 94, 137, 141–144, 160, 163, 167, 174, 175
Mutuality, 7, 9, 20–24, 31, 134, 136, 141–148, 180, 186, 204, 205

N

Naïve, 30
Narrative(s), 4, 7, 8, 23, 41–45, 51, 55, 58, 59, 69, 76, 80, 83, 85, 86, 88, 89, 91, 93, 96, 127, 143, 146, 152, 163, 166, 169, 170, 174–176, 184, 186, 190, 194, 195, 197, 204, 207
Nationality, 71, 94, 108, 111, 128, 130, 148
Nature, 7, 16, 17, 24, 25, 30, 31, 47, 49, 50, 52, 79, 116, 119, 120, 146, 151, 157, 175, 179
Negative contact, 46, 48, 120
Negative outcomes, 192, 208
Negative peace, 13, 19, 46, 177, 178, 187
Negotiations, 38, 121, 122
Neutral(ity), 47, 55, 95, 98, 104, 119, 154, 155, 169
New Zealand, 2
Normalization, 46–48, 104, 192, 208
Normative, 28, 169
North Africa, 6, 71, 94, 112, 159, 166
North America, 6, 94

O

Objectification, 180, 181
Observation(s), 6, 17, 104, 115, 146
Open-minded, 136, 159, 160, 163

Openness, 20, 23, 24, 102, 130, 139, 169, 190, 197
Oppressed, 14, 18, 19, 24, 25, 29, 30, 45, 119, 120, 181, 192, 193
Oppression, 18, 19, 25–27, 29–32, 47, 48, 88, 119, 165, 179, 183, 187, 188, 193
  systemic, 18, 25, 30, 32, 48, 183, 193
Oppressor, 18, 19, 25, 27, 29, 119, 181, 193
Out-group, 3, 5, 39, 41, 43, 49, 52, 54, 55, 93

P
Palestine, 100, 109, 137, 138
Peace practices, 2, 59, 203
People-to-people (P2P), 3, 38, 39, 73, 80
Perception(s), 3, 5, 8, 20, 28, 39, 41, 44, 48, 52, 53, 56, 58, 82, 84–87, 89, 95, 120, 127, 148, 152, 157, 158, 160, 162, 163, 165, 169, 170, 173–176, 183–186, 192, 194, 195, 197, 205–208
Permits, 50, 209
Personhood, 23, 182
Polarization, 4
Politically correct, 103
Politics, 95, 100, 101, 128
Populist, 87
Positionality, 7, 88, 120
Positive peace, 2, 4, 5, 7, 9, 13–15, 19, 25, 27, 28, 31, 32, 37, 40, 45, 46, 48, 49, 58, 59, 119, 120, 123, 177–180, 183, 186–188, 191, 193, 195–198, 203, 205–209
Post-conflict, 38, 48, 55, 209
Power, 7, 16–19, 23, 26, 27, 30, 31, 39, 42, 43, 46–48, 57, 58, 86, 91, 96, 98, 102, 104, 105, 107, 109, 110, 119, 120, 122, 123, 145, 151, 167, 168, 183, 188–193, 196, 204–208
  dynamics, 26, 39, 43, 46, 91, 95, 96, 102, 104, 105, 107, 109, 110, 119, 122, 123, 145, 167, 188, 190–192, 196, 204–208
  imbalances, 27, 42, 47, 48, 57, 96, 120, 192, 206
Praxis, 24, 25, 178
Preconceptions, 43, 128, 205
Prejudice, 3, 29, 39, 40, 52, 163, 185
Presentness, 7, 9, 21, 31, 134, 135, 146–148, 204, 205
Pretense, lack of, 17
Privilege, 19, 26, 27, 29, 30, 32, 43, 49, 54, 88, 104, 120, 140, 168, 190, 192
Protracted conflict, 209

Q
Qualitative, 1, 6, 69, 88, 177

R
Reciprocal, 181, 188, 197
Reciprocity, 21, 23, 193
Reflection, 5, 7, 24, 25, 57, 70, 71, 88, 89, 107, 109, 120, 130, 132, 139, 141, 143, 146, 147, 151, 170, 173–175, 179, 183, 188, 189, 195, 205, 208
Reflexivity, 7, 88
Religion, 14, 29, 82–84, 87, 88, 94, 95, 100, 101, 111, 142–144, 161, 170, 172
Religious, 38, 47, 83, 92, 95, 114, 142–144, 161, 162, 167, 172
Resistance, 183, 193
Respect, 23, 103, 135, 141–144, 146, 172, 180, 182, 205

Romantic, 186

S

Safe space, 41, 43, 58, 59, 93, 95
Safety, 42, 43, 55–57, 75, 95, 114, 146, 193, 205, 207
Saunders, Hal, 40, 42, 45
Self-examination, 130
Self-reflection, 20, 127, 130–133, 138, 148, 158, 186, 205
Self-regulate, 98
Sexual orientation, 18, 29, 47, 95, 139
Skepticism, 153, 176
Social, 2–5, 18, 23–27, 39, 41, 43, 46, 53, 55, 91, 94, 100, 102–104, 110, 119, 123, 133, 147, 153, 156, 159, 165, 176, 177, 179, 180, 182, 183, 185, 187–191, 196, 197, 206–208
  change, 25, 94, 183, 188
  discourse(s), 27, 190
  dynamics, 91, 102, 103
  identity, 18, 40, 47, 179
  justice, 187
  narratives, 170, 190
  politeness, 104
  realities, 165, 166, 168–170, 196
Social Identity Theory (SIT), 39
Social media, 4, 86, 99, 153–155, 163, 209
Social reality, 165, 166, 168–170, 196
Socio-economic, 43, 56, 108
Solidarity, 14, 18, 44, 187, 193, 197
Soliya, 6, 51, 52, 69–71, 73, 76–81, 83, 84, 91–97, 99, 101, 103, 104, 107, 113, 119, 120, 123, 130, 132, 134, 135, 146, 153–155, 157–161, 163, 169, 171, 173, 190, 191, 194, 197, 204, 209
Sphere of between, 7, 9, 20, 31, 127, 133, 134, 145, 146, 148, 151, 181, 186, 203–205
Spiritual, 16
Status quo, 19, 27, 32, 46, 47, 190, 192, 193
Stereotypes, 48, 84, 86, 111, 128, 130, 134, 160, 161, 163–165, 170, 171, 174, 182, 184, 185, 190, 206
Structural, 2, 3, 7, 13, 14, 24, 31, 32, 48, 57, 119, 120, 166, 177, 183, 187, 188, 196, 198, 209
  peace, 14, 119
  violence, 14, 119, 120
Structural peace, 14
Summit, 1, 55
Sustainability, 49, 55, 208
Systemic, 18, 19, 25, 26, 29, 30, 32, 45–49, 119, 166–168, 185, 187, 188

T

Taboo(s), 87, 95, 101, 114, 138, 171, 172
Technology, 4, 6, 49, 50, 56, 57, 93, 104, 108, 109, 115, 116, 191, 207, 208
  audio, 108, 116
  video, 108, 116
Terrorism, 4, 100, 170
Third space, 20, 31, 133, 134, 148
Tiers, 178, 196, 197
Track-one, 38
Track-two, 38
Track-three, 8, 38, 59
Transformation, 2, 3, 7, 13, 15, 16, 19, 24–27, 31, 32, 38, 46, 48, 49, 57, 93, 119, 146, 179, 183, 188–190, 205
Transparency, 7, 21, 41, 88, 103, 139, 173

Triangle, 14, 177, 178
Triggers, 98, 132, 133, 148
Tripartite, 13, 14, 177
Trust, 23, 42, 50, 55, 86, 158, 180, 205
Trustworthiness, 180
Truth, v, 17, 41, 44, 58, 93, 96

U
Uninhibited, 22
Unreservedness, 22

Utilization, 17, 206

V
Virtual exchange, 51, 52, 91
Visas, 50

W
Wallace, David Foster, 26, 102
Weak, 186
West Bank, 1

Printed in the United States
by Baker & Taylor Publisher Services